AF754221

Strategies of Sustainable Solid Waste Management

Edited by Hosam M. Saleh

Published in London, United Kingdom

IntechOpen

Supporting open minds since 2005

Strategies of Sustainable Solid Waste Management
http://dx.doi.org/10.5772/intechopen.87682
Edited by Hosam M. Saleh

Contributors
Imran Ahmad, Norhayati Abdullah, Shreeshivadasan Chelliapan, Ali Yuzur, Iwamoto Koji, Anas Al-Dailami, Thilagavathi Arumugham, Md.Azizul Moqsud, Muniyandi Balasubramanian, Kwaku Oduro-Appiah, Abraham Afful, Aziz Hasib, Abdellah Ouigmane, Otmane Boudouch, Reda Elkacmi, Mustapha Bouzaid, Mohammed Berkani, Machate Machate, Isaac Oluseun Adejumo, O.A. Adebiyi, Innocent Rangeti, Bloodless Rimuka Dzwairo, Erika Andrea Levei, Emilia Neag, Eniko Kovacs, Zamfira Dinca, Anamaria Iulia Török, Cerasel Varaticeanu, Hosam M. M. Saleh, Amal I. Hassan

© The Editor(s) and the Author(s) 2021
The rights of the editor(s) and the author(s) have been asserted in accordance with the Copyright, Designs and Patents Act 1988. All rights to the book as a whole are reserved by INTECHOPEN LIMITED. The book as a whole (compilation) cannot be reproduced, distributed or used for commercial or non-commercial purposes without INTECHOPEN LIMITED's written permission. Enquiries concerning the use of the book should be directed to INTECHOPEN LIMITED rights and permissions department (permissions@intechopen.com).
Violations are liable to prosecution under the governing Copyright Law.

CC BY

Individual chapters of this publication are distributed under the terms of the Creative Commons Attribution 3.0 Unported License which permits commercial use, distribution and reproduction of the individual chapters, provided the original author(s) and source publication are appropriately acknowledged. If so indicated, certain images may not be included under the Creative Commons license. In such cases users will need to obtain permission from the license holder to reproduce the material. More details and guidelines concerning content reuse and adaptation can be found at http://www.intechopen.com/copyright-policy.html.

Notice
Statements and opinions expressed in the chapters are these of the individual contributors and not necessarily those of the editors or publisher. No responsibility is accepted for the accuracy of information contained in the published chapters. The publisher assumes no responsibility for any damage or injury to persons or property arising out of the use of any materials, instructions, methods or ideas contained in the book.

First published in London, United Kingdom, 2021 by IntechOpen
IntechOpen is the global imprint of INTECHOPEN LIMITED, registered in England and Wales, registration number: 11086078, 5 Princes Gate Court, London, SW7 2QJ, United Kingdom
Printed in Croatia

British Library Cataloguing-in-Publication Data
A catalogue record for this book is available from the British Library

Additional hard and PDF copies can be obtained from orders@intechopen.com

Strategies of Sustainable Solid Waste Management
Edited by Hosam M. Saleh
p. cm.
Print ISBN 978-1-83962-559-6
Online ISBN 978-1-83962-560-2
eBook (PDF) ISBN 978-1-83962-561-9

For EU product safety concerns:
IN TECH d.o.o., Prolaz Marije Krucifikse Kozulić 3, 51000 Rijeka, Croatia, info@intechopen.com or visit our website at intechopen.com.

We are IntechOpen, the world's leading publisher of Open Access books

Built by scientists, for scientists

5,200+
Open access books available

129,000+
International authors and editors

155M+
Downloads

156
Countries delivered to

Our authors are among the
Top 1%
most cited scientists

12.2%
Contributors from top 500 universities

BOOK CITATION INDEX

CLARIVATE ANALYTICS

INDEXED

WEB OF SCIENCE™

Selection of our books indexed in the Book Citation Index in Web of Science™ Core Collection (BKCI)

Interested in publishing with us?
Contact book.department@intechopen.com

Numbers displayed above are based on latest data collected.
For more information visit www.intechopen.com

Meet the editor

Hosam Saleh is a Professor of Radioactive Waste Management at the Radioisotope Department, Atomic Energy Authority, Egypt. He obtained an MSc and Ph.D. in Physical Chemistry from Cairo University. Dr. Saleh has more than twenty-three years of experience in hazardous waste management with an emphasis on treatment and developing new matrixes for the immobilization of these wastes. He is also interested in studying innovative economic and environmentally friendly techniques for the management of hazardous and radioactive wastes. He has authored many peer-reviewed scientific papers and chapters and edited several books from international publishers. He was selected among the top 2% of scientists in the world according to the Stanford University report for 2020.

Contents

Preface

The world is currently experiencing increased environmental contamination with solid waste, which is one of the greatest environmental threats today. As such, this book provides guidance on treating this problem that requires the synergistic action of the scientific community.

The development and application of approaches and technologies that provide economic and safe management of such type of waste is an essential issue in the treatment and disposal of solid wastes.

In this book, the authors summarize their experience and present advances related to assessing the strategies of sustainable solid waste management. The book contains ten chapters, organized into four sections that cover important research aspects of solid waste management technologies. The first section includes the introductory chapter prepared by the editor to present a brief background on solid waste. The second section begins with the chapter "Reflections on the Influence of Family Demographics on Food Waste Generation among the City of Tshwane Households, Republic of South Africa," in which the authors investigate the influence of household demographics on food waste generation in the Republic of South Africa. The chapter "Sustainable Pathway for Closing Solid Waste Data Gaps: Implications for Modernization Strategies and Resilient Cities in Developing Countries" addresses three peculiar challenges in solid waste management systems of developing countries.

The third section contains chapters "Guide for Organising a Community Clean-up Campaign", "Economics of Solid Waste Management: A Review", "Sustainable Solid Waste Management in Morocco: Co-Incineration of RDF as an Alternative Fuel in Cement Kilns", "Effectiveness of Anaerobic Technologies in the Treatment of Landfill Leachate" and "Hydrometallurgical Recovery of Gold from Mining Wastes".

The final section of the book includes chapters "Bioelectricity from Organic Solid Waste" and "Agricultural Solid Wastes: Causes, Effects, and Effective Management".

The editor wishes to thank all the participants in this book for their valuable contributions. Thanks also go to the staff at IntechOpen, particularly Author Service Manager Ms. Dolores Kuzelj, for her continuous assistance in finalizing this work.

Hosam El-Din Mostafa Saleh
Egyptian Atomic Energy Authority,
Cairo, Egypt

Section 1

Introduction

Chapter 1

Introductory Chapter: Solid Waste

Hosam M. Saleh and Amal I. Hassan

1. Introduction

Solid wastes are solid or semi-solid materials that are produced as a result of various activities. They are discarded materials, meaning they are to be disposed of, although some of their components can be used [1]. In this case, the term "waste" is used, not waste, since the latter means that the resources left over from human activities cannot be used. Solid waste is all rotting and non-rotting waste in solid or semi-solid form, including but not limited, trash, unwanted compounds, ash or incinerator residues, street waste, dead animals, demolition and construction waste, sanitation, solid or semi-solid commercial and industrial waste [2].

2. The two major types of solid waste

2.1 Agricultural and animal waste

It includes (remaining crops after harvest - residues from processing grains such as rice. Additionally, peanuts, branches, and leaves of deciduous trees - the manure of animals raised by farmers). Animal and agricultural waste is one of humanity's most ancient forms of solid waste [3].

The first man collected these wastes and used them as fuel before he knew coal. These wastes are still used as fuel in many rural and semi-rural areas in most of the developing countries [4]. Indoor burning of these wastes, whether in open stoves or rural ovens, releases different contaminants in the indoor air, the carbon dioxide and oxides of organic compounds that have been proven to be nitrogen and nitrogen, and some of them are nitrogen compounds are the most important of these pollutants [5]. Field studies have shown high rates of chest diseases such as chronic obstructive pulmonary disease and nasopharyngeal carcinoma as detrimental consequences of these wastes. Besides, agricultural waste has been used for thousands of years as organic fertilizer after composting to improve soil condition and nourish the plants before synthetic chemicals were discovered. Organic fertilizers are still used in many countries after the composting processes have developed. It is now one of the main ingredients used in organic farming [6]. The number of residues left after harvesting the crops depends on the type of crop, the yield per feddan, and the method of harvesting. For example, the amount of waste produced from cotton cultivation ranges from 3 to 5 tons of residues per ton of cotton produced from the field [7]. The quantity of rice straw ranges from 1 to 3 tons of straw per ton of rice produced from the field, and in the case of cultivation of high-yielding rice varieties, the amount of straw ranges from 0.8–2 tons per ton of field rice [8]. The amount of animal manure also varies according to their types and weight. For example, cows produce about 1.4–5 kg of dung. Also, goats and sheep produce from 0.3–0.6 kg/day. Therefore, estimates of agricultural and animal residues differ

 IntechOpen

considerably from one region to another. In this regard, the amount of agricultural waste in the world is estimated at 2000–2500 million tons annually [8].

2.2 Municipal waste

Domestic waste - waste of organizations and agencies Public facilities - waste for hospitals and other care units - industry waste [9]. Demolition and construction - sludge - other waste such as scrap vehicles, used tires, etc., are split according to their sources. The man became familiar with the municipal waste about ten thousand years ago when he began to settle in Human settlements [10]. They started by transforming these settlements into the first cities known to humanity. The problem of municipal solid waste that was dumped in the streets appears. With the world's massive rise in population, the expansion in urban areas, the increase in per capita income, and the change in patterns of consumption, the amount of municipal solid waste has risen dramatically, and its components have changed drastically. In the face of these accelerating changes, the ability of municipalities in most countries of the world to manage waste efficiently declined [11]. The amount of waste generated varies from one country to another, according to living standards and consumption patterns. In the United States of America, the rate of waste generation per capita is estimated at 1.2 kilograms/day, it is assessed at 4.1 kilograms/day in the countries of the European Union. In high-income Arab countries such as the Gulf countries, the generation of municipal waste ranges [12].

The proper management of solid waste requires dealing with it from the perspective of an integrated multi-faceted, multi-components, and interconnected system. Each episode depends on its predecessor, and at the same time, it represents the basis on which it follows. In all cases, it is necessary at every stage to use appropriate means appropriate to the prevailing circumstances, available resources, and existing determinants. Therefore, adopting the best options that meet the technical standards, environmental safety, social compatibility, the lowest possible costs, the highest possible recovery of resources, and compliance with legislation and regulations while being flexible and able to respond to future changes. Thus, it implies a context or life cycle that involves successive stages starting with the generation or reduction from the source, storage, and collection from various sources, and transport to proper locations for interim storage or processing [13]. Then the possibility of recovery of suitable recoverable resources for a variety of uses, and then the final disposal of environmentally safe meth. It involves many other aspects and considerations related to economic, social, planning, environmental health, legislative and institutional factors in addition to technical and engineering considerations for the system. In addition to the technical and engineering concerns for the system, it includes many other aspects and considerations related to economics, social, planning, environmental, health, legislative, and institutional factors [14].

Greenhouse gases from waste are a significant factor in climate change. In 2016, 5% of global emissions were generated from solid waste management, excluding transportation. It is estimated that human activities are causing global industrial warming of approximately 1° C, with a weighted margin of 0.8 to 1.2°C [15]. Global warming is likely to reach 1.5° C between 2030 and 2052 if it continues to increase at the current rate [16]. Accordingly, the solid waste issue is one of the most critical concerns facing sustainable development. Therefore, from a resource management point of view, there is an immediate need to deal with solid waste and not waste management [17]. Waste is an essential asset for reusability and recycling and offers new opportunities for so-called green jobs. Integrated solid waste management is the selection and application of appropriate methods, technology, and management to accomplish waste management objectives, taking into account the economic, environmental, social, and legal conditions to achieve sustainability [18]. One of the basic principles in integrated waste management is the principle of using the golden quadruple rules. The reduction is part of those rules to reduce the amount of waste either at the source or at subsequent levels and implies reducing the amount of waste generated at the origin. Construction Producing longer life and reusable materials. As for reuse, it means the direct use of the waste in the form in which it was generated, and in the same process, it was generated without subjecting it to any natural, chemical, or biological treatment that may affect its shape or formation [19]. For instance, empty bottles of drinks are returned to stores in many countries, especially developing countries, which in turn take them back to the manufacturing companies to clean and ensure their protection, then fill them with their products and put them back on the market [19]. Thermal recovery and heat recovery technology are used in many countries, especially Japan, for the safe disposal of solid waste, solid and liquid hazardous waste, hospital waste, and sludge from industrial and sanitary sewage, by burning these wastes under specific operating conditions such as the temperature and duration of combustion, this is to control the emissions and their compliance with environmental laws [20]. This method is characterized by getting rid of 90% of the solid materials and converting them into thermal energy that can be used in industrial processes or generating steam or electric energy [21]. The recycling process involves treating the waste so that it can be used as a raw material in the same process that it is generated or in other processes. Recycling is considered to be one of the best alternatives for managing both municipal and agricultural waste. The recycling of waste depends on the economic viability of these processes and the demand for different products. Among the most popular waste subject to recycling are paper - glass - bone - cloth - plastic - metal waste - organic waste [22].

The manufacture of waste paper is a matter of particular environmental importance because it contributes to reducing the depletion of forests for the use of wood in the manufacture of pulp [23]. This is in addition to the fact that recycling paper waste saves a large amount of water and energy needed to manufacture it from raw materials, as recycling one ton of paper waste will save 4100 kilowatt per hour of energy and 28 cubic meters of water, according to statistics made by the Environmental Protection Agency in the states [24]. As for plastic recycling, before recycling, the plastic is washed with caustic soda with hot water added [25]. After that, the dry plastic is broken and reused in making clothespins, hangers, and plastic electrical hoses, and it is not recommended to use plastic waste in the production of products that interact with foodstuffs. The plastic bags are re-crystallized in the crystal machines. Metal scraps, which are mainly aluminum and steel; Where it can be re-melted in iron foundries and aluminum foundries, and steel is one of the waste that can be recycled by 100%, and for an infinite number of times, and the process of recycling steel requires less energy than the energy required to extract it from alloys, while aluminum recycling costs represent 20 Only 5% of its manufacturing costs, and the aluminum recycling process requires only 5% of the energy needed [26]. Recycling glass, glass from sand is a major energy-consuming industry [27]. The manufacturing process needs temperatures up to 1600° C, and recycling glass requires much less energy. Household organic waste (food residues) represents about 50% of garbage residues, and the handling of organic waste differs in cities than in villages, organic waste is used as food for birds and animals, which is the best way to use organic waste. However, organic waste in cities is a problem of serious health dimensions [28]. Therefore, care should be taken to dispose of these materials safely or make use of them urgently to avoid their spoilage, decomposition, and the toxins and pollutants that remain behind. Therefore, the focus must be placed on spreading awareness of the necessity to separate organic residues from the rest of the waste from the source, so that it can be collected and recycled to produce fertilizer materials for agricultural lands [28].

Converting waste to energy, including municipal solid waste and waste fuels, is a valuable source of renewable energy. Waste-to-energy plants have been successfully operated all over the world, and the advantages of this technology and its environmental efficiency have been confirmed and include the presence of nearly 100 waste-to-energy plants in North America, the presence of more than 500 operating stations in Europe as well as the 1600 operating stations in Asia [29]. A waste-to-energy plant converts solid waste into electrical energy and/or heat - an energy recovery method that is environmentally friendly and cost-effective. When converting waste into energy - or obtaining energy from waste - the plant converts municipal and industrial solid waste into electrical energy and/or heat for use in industrial processing and central heating systems - energy recovery means that take into account environmental safety and low cost [30]. The power plant operates by burning waste at high temperatures and using heat to generate steam. The steam then powers the turbine, which in turn generates electricity. Getting energy from waste is a way to recover valuable resources and not just a means of garbage disposal. It is a way to recover valuable resources. Converting waste to energy is a vital part of the sustainable waste management chain and perfectly complements the recycling process. Today, 90% of the minerals in bottom ash can be reused [31]. The remaining combustion residues can be reused in pavement materials. Europe is a pioneer in this field as 50 tons of waste is converted into valuable energy using waste-to-energy technology, which provides electricity to 27 million people in Europe, and yet 50 percent of municipal solid waste is still placed in landfills. It leads to the release of greenhouse gases such as methane that is 21 times stronger than carbon dioxide [31].

Author details

Hosam M. Saleh* and Amal I. Hassan
Radioisotope Department, Nuclear Research Center, Atomic Energy Authority, Giza, Egypt

*Address all correspondence to: hosam.saleh@eaea.org.eg; hosamsaleh70@yahoo.com

IntechOpen

© 2020 The Author(s). Licensee IntechOpen. This chapter is distributed under the terms of the Creative Commons Attribution License (http://creativecommons.org/licenses/by/3.0), which permits unrestricted use, distribution, and reproduction in any medium, provided the original work is properly cited.

References

[1] X. Xiong, X. Liu, K.M. Iris, L. Wang, J. Zhou, X. Sun, J. Rinklebe, S.M. Shaheen, Y.S. Ok, Z. Lin, Potentially toxic elements in solid waste streams: Fate and management approaches, Environ. Pollut. 253 (2019) 680-707.

[2] P.J. McMurdie, S. Holmes, Waste not, want not: why rarefying microbiome data is inadmissible, PLoS Comput Biol. 10 (2014) e1003531.

[3] S.D. Abou Hussein, O.M. Sawan, The utilization of agricultural waste as one of the environmental issues in Egypt (a case study), J. Appl. Sci. Res. 6 (2010) 1116-1124.

[4] M.U. Treiber, L.K. Grimsby, J.B. Aune, Reducing energy poverty through increasing choice of fuels and stoves in Kenya: Complementing the multiple fuel model, Energy Sustain. Dev. 27 (2015) 54-62.

[5] W. Du, X. Zhu, Y. Chen, W. Liu, W. Wang, G. Shen, S. Tao, J.J. Jetter, Field-based emission measurements of biomass burning in typical Chinese built-in-place stoves, Environ. Pollut. 242 (2018) 1587-1597.

[6] G. Nahar, D. Mote, V. Dupont, Hydrogen production from reforming of biogas: Review of technological advances and an Indian perspective, Renew. Sustain. Energy Rev. 76 (2017) 1032-1052.

[7] A.E. Maragkaki, T. Kotrotsios, P. Samaras, A. Manou, K. Lasaridi, T. Manios, Quantitative and qualitative analysis of biomass from agro-industrial processes in the central macedonia region, Greece, Waste and Biomass Valorization. 7 (2016) 383-395.

[8] J.E. Bradshaw, Clonal Cultivars from Multistage Multitrait Selection, in: Plant Breed. Past, Present Futur., Springer, 2016: pp. 343-386.

[9] E.S. Windfeld, M.S.-L. Brooks, Medical waste management–A review, J. Environ. Manage. 163 (2015) 98-108.

[10] Doron A. Waste of a nation: Garbage and growth in India. Harvard University Press; 2018

[11] X. Guan, H. Wei, S. Lu, Q. Dai, H. Su, Assessment on the urbanization strategy in China: Achievements, challenges and reflections, Habitat Int. 71 (2018) 97-109.

[12] P. IN-AI, D. Tungtakanpoung, Solid waste logistic system of Uthai Thani municipality, (2020).

[13] J. Pérez, J. Lumbreras, E. Rodríguez, Life cycle assessment as a decision-making tool for the design of urban solid waste pre-collection and collection/transport systems, Resour. Conserv. Recycl. 161 (2020) 104988.

[14] M. Lancaster, Green chemistry: an introductory text, Royal society of chemistry, 2020.

[15] A. Swati, S. Hait, Greenhouse gas emission during composting and vermicomposting of organic wastes–a review, CLEAN–Soil, Air, Water. 46 (2018) 1700042.

[16] O. Hoegh-Guldberg, D. Jacob, M. Taylor, T.G. Bolaños, M. Bindi, S. Brown, I.A. Camilloni, A. Diedhiou, R. Djalante, K. Ebi, The human imperative of stabilizing global climate change at 1.5 C, Science (80-.). 365 (2019).

[17] V. Venkatramanan, S. Shah, R. Prasad, Global climate change: resilient and smart agriculture, (2020).

[18] A.A. Zorpas, Strategy development in the framework of waste management, Sci. Total Environ. 716 (2020) 137088.

[19] A. Akhtar, A.K. Sarmah, Construction and demolition waste

generation and properties of recycled aggregate concrete: a global perspective, J. Clean. Prod. 186 (2018) 262-281.

[20] H.I. Abdel-Shafy, M.S.M. Mansour, Solid waste issue: Sources, composition, disposal, recycling, and valorization, Egypt. J. Pet. (2018).

[21] B. Vaish, B. Sharma, V. Srivastava, P. Singh, M.H. Ibrahim, R.P. Singh, Energy recovery potential and environmental impact of gasification for municipal solid waste, Biofuels. 10 (2019) 87-100.

[22] T. Georgi-Maschler, B. Friedrich, R. Weyhe, H. Heegn, M. Rutz, Development of a recycling process for Li-ion batteries, J. Power Sources. 207 (2012) 173-182.

[23] M. Sun, Y. Wang, L. Shi, J.J. Klemeš, Uncovering energy use, carbon emissions and environmental burdens of pulp and paper industry: A systematic review and meta-analysis, Renew. Sustain. Energy Rev. 92 (2018) 823-833.

[24] M. Abdollahbeigi, An Overview of the Paper Recycling Process in Iran, J. Chem. Rev. 3 (2020) 1-19.

[25] N. Singh, D. Hui, R. Singh, I.P.S. Ahuja, L. Feo, F. Fraternali, Recycling of plastic solid waste: A state of art review and future applications, Compos. Part B Eng. 115 (2017) 409-422.

[26] D. Brough, H. Jouhara, The aluminium industry: A review on state-of-the-art technologies, environmental impacts and possibilities for waste heat recovery, Int. J. Thermofluids. (2020) 100007.

[27] W. Khraisat, W.A. Jadayil, Strengthening aluminum scrap by alloying with iron, Jordan J. Mech. Ind. Eng. 4 (2010) 372-377.

[28] M.C. Manna, M.M. Rahman, R. Naidu, A. Sahu, S. Bhattacharjya, R.H. Wanjari, A.K. Patra, S.K. Chaudhari, K. Majumdar, S.S. Khanna, Bio-waste management in subtropical soils of India: future challenges and opportunities in agriculture, in: Adv. Agron., Elsevier, 2018: pp. 87-148.

[29] J. Malinauskaite, H. Jouhara, D. Czajczyńska, P. Stanchev, E. Katsou, P. Rostkowski, R.J. Thorne, J. Colon, S. Ponsá, F. Al-Mansour, Municipal solid waste management and waste-to-energy in the context of a circular economy and energy recycling in Europe, Energy. 141 (2017) 2013-2044.

[30] L. Makarichi, R. Kan, W. Jutidamrongphan, K. Techato, Suitability of municipal solid waste in African cities for thermochemical waste-to-energy conversion: The case of Harare Metropolitan City, Zimbabwe, Waste Manag. Res. 37 (2019) 83-94.

[31] Q. Alam, K. Schollbach, C. van Hoek, S. van der Laan, T. de Wolf, H.J.H. Brouwers, In-depth mineralogical quantification of MSWI bottom ash phases and their association with potentially toxic elements, Waste Manag. 87 (2019) 1-12.

Section 2

Estimation of Solid Waste

Chapter 2

Reflections on the Influence of Family Demographics on Food Waste Generation among the City of Tshwane Households, Republic of South Africa

Machate Machate

Abstract

This chapter presents the influence of households' demographics on food waste generation. A mixed method research approach consisting of meta-analysis, survey (structured interviews), and experimental were used to collect opinions and weigh the amount of waste generated in each household. Although not all demographic variables were investigated, the influence of: (1) family size, (2) household monthly income, (3) employment status, (4) educational level, and (5) age of respondents on food waste generation were analyzed. The results of the study confirmed that age and family size are positive factors that influence the amount of food waste generated in households of the City of Tshwane, as opposed to the level of education, employment status, and monthly income levels. It should be noted, however, that this study does not conclusively exclude the other factors as not having an influence in food waste generations. However, their influence in the current food waste generation quantities was not conclusive. Further studies with larger sample size are thus recommended.

Keywords: food waste, waste management, food losses, causes of food wastage, household demographics waste socioeconomic profile, household

1. Introduction

The complexities of food waste generation in its entirety are a subject of social and economic profile of the generator. Evidence from Gustavsson et al. [1], one of the leading global authors in food waste management, shows that food waste generation increases proportionally with the levels of development. As a result, developed countries generate more food waste than their developing counterparts. In this study, the influence of these development profiles at households' level is investigated because households are identified as the biggest food waste generators than other institutions [1]. The European Commission [2] estimates that households are responsible for 42% of the total amount of food waste generation, while the retail (including wholesale) contributes 5%, and food service and manufacturing sectors contribute 14 and 39%, respectively.

Thyberg et al. [3] points out that the amount of food waste generation increases over the years. On average, the sub-Saharan Africa and South Asia generate 145 kg of food waste per capita per year as compared to 290 kg in Europe and North America [1]. Dhia et al. [4] found a difference of 50-170 kg of food waste generated per person per year between developed and developing countries. In the sub-Saharan African countries, FAO [5] estimated that on average a person produced 145 kg of food waste generation per year in 2011. Using statistics on available food waste generation rates per person per year from 14 developed and developing countries, **Figure 1** presents the profile.

Food waste generation ranges from 0.12 to 0.4 kg per person per day, with a range of 0.28 kg as compared to 0.06–0.18 kg, with a range of 0.12 kg in developing countries. These statistics confirm the previous findings by Gustavsson et al. [1] about high food waste generation per person per day in developed than developing countries.

Available literature also shows that development levels of countries differentiate the stages at which more food wastes are generated, as evident from Abeliotis et al. [20] and Graham-Rowe et al. [21]. The former studies confirmed Gustavsson et al. [1] to the fact that developing countries generate more food waste during the early stages of the food supply chain, as compared to developed countries. The generation of food waste at early stages of food supply chain in developing countries proves to be a contributing factor of the high prevalence of hunger in these countries, as opposed to the high generation of food waste at later stages from developed countries. The former is attributed to oversupply of food and high quantity of leftover food from these socioeconomically well-off households.

Parfitt et al. [22] attributes food wastage in developing countries to the lack of advanced harvesting technologies, transport, storage, and harsh weather conditions. It can be deduced from Parfitt et al. [22] that farmers in developing countries loose more food at different agricultural stages ranging from harsh weather conditions at the farm, during harvesting, and until during storage due to partly lack of means of protecting their agricultural harvest, including preservation and processing technologies. The socioeconomic strength of these farmers and the affordability of the households who are the targeted market for these food products remain central to the challenge. This vicious poverty circle entraps both the farmer and the target end user of the food products.

Factors that differentiate households in developing countries from their developed counterparts, which are viewed as drivers of food waste generation, are the socioeconomic factors. For example, the affordability, levels of technological sophistication, levels of education, etc. Hence, Gustavsson et al. [1] concluded that

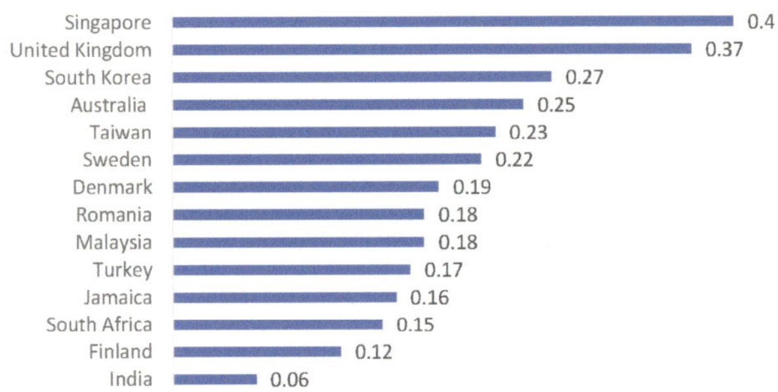

Figure 1.
Food waste generation rate per person per year from 14 countries. Source: Compiled from Liu [6], Franke [7, 8], Katajajuuri et al. [9], WRAP [10], Lisa [11], Taiwan EPA [12] and Danish Agriculture and Food Council [13], Ioannis et al. [14], Zeeda and Keng [15], Yan [16], Oelofse and Nahman [17], Meghan [18], and Manipadma [19].

households in developed and developing countries produce more food wastes at different stages of the food supply chain.

In addition to the influence of household socioeconomic factor in food waste production, Munesue et al. [23] emphasizes the fact that food production involves the use of variable input resources such as land, water, energy, etc. At a household level, the accessibility of these resources also depends on the socioeconomic capacity of each household. Similarly, food wastage is also attributable to multiple social, economic, and environmental challenges facing communities, that is, hunger, poverty, land degradation, water carbon footprint, climate change, and others. Thus food waste generation has a significant influence on major global sustainability and climate change-inducing pollutants such as carbon dioxide (CO_2), methane (CH_4), nitrous oxide (N_2O), and sulfur hexafluoride (SF_6) per fluorinated compounds (PFCs) and hydro fluorocarbons (HFCs) [24]. Hence, it became critically important for this study to investigate and report on factors that influence household generation of food waste.

The influence of five selected demographic variables (age, family size, household income, employment status, and educational levels) on food waste generation is presented in this study. The rationale beyond the selection of these variables is because a precedent on their influence on waste management in general, has been established. However, the influence of these household demographic factors on food waste has not been established. Hence the focus of this study on this specific category of waste.

1.1 Influence of age

Jörissen et al. [25]; Secondi et al. [26] and Melbye et al. [27] independently concurred that age influences the amount of food waste generation. According to these authors, older people waste less food than the younger ones. Melbye et al. [27] define old age as people at the age of 65 years or older. The reasons associated with less food waste generation are that older people are more aware of saving and recycling, because of their past and experience times of scarcity [27]. Evidence from the above studies show that households with older people as compared to young ones produce more food waste than those with older family members.

1.2 Influence of family size

According to Canali [28], the number of people in a household is associated with the amount of food wasted per person. In previous studies by Jörissen et al. [25] and Parizeau et al. [29], it was concurrently and independently concluded that bigger size households wasted less food than their smaller counterparts on a per capita basis. Based on the latter study, households with one person wasted more food per capita than the ones with bigger sizes [25]. Although affordability of bigger families and other factors could also be responsible for the food waste generation levels, they remained untested and are outside the focal point of this study.

1.3 Influence of levels of education, employment status, and household income

Inconsistencies in the findings of different studies about the influence of household income on food waste generation were observed. A study by Porpino et al. [30, 31] concluded that low-income households generate more food waste. In contrast, Hamilton et al. [32], Skourides et al. [33] and Gustavsson et al. [1] concluded that higher-income households waste more food than lower-income ones. The argument in support of high household income being proportional to high food waste generation is supported by Gustavsson et al. [1] and Pearson et al. [34], who argue that in developed countries, consumers buy more food than they need, whereas consumers in developing countries buy smaller amounts of food each time they shop. This practice is known to influence the way food is prepared or cooked and, subsequently, the amount of food discarded as waste. Quested and Johnson [35] argue that households prepare and serve more food portions than what they are able to consume, which results in more left-overs being generated. Rathje and Murphy [36], Pekcan et al. [37] and Evans [38, 39] concluded that household income does not only influence food waste generation but the generation of waste in its broad sense.

Inappropriate or lack of storage facilities for raw and cooked food in low-income households contribute to food waste at household level [40]. The household income levels are also interlinked with the levels of education and employment status of household members. Hence, these factors are compounded in their exploration in this study.

2. Materials and methods

A total of 122 females and 88 males participated in this study, representing a total of 210 households across five suburbs in the City of Tshwane (Atteridgeville, Lyttleton, Montana, Olievenhoutbosch and Silverlakes). Suburbs were purposefully selected based on their differences in income levels or status. Individual households within each suburb were selected based on convenience (accessibility of elders, wiliness of participants to be interviewed, and the availability of a competent respondent within a household). Structured interviews were used for all primary data collection, except for the physical weighing of food waste generated by each participated household, which followed experimental research design.

Meta-analysis (in-depth exploratory and explanatory analysis of authoritative secondary data sources) was used to collect and analyses secondary data. Meta-analysis studies primarily helped with the conceptualization and formulation of research variables which were investigated in this study. These secondary data sources were randomly selected through online search, using content analysis method. Subsequently, selected a range of keywords, based on their frequency appearance from the in-depth literature analysis were used to determine relevance of a secondary source for inclusion in this chapter. Following Creswell [41] and Leedy and Ormrod [42], qualitative and quantitative data (secondary and primary) data from literature sources and structured interviews were used to determine the common household demographics that influence food waste generation in general. Data analyses were descriptive and presented through qualitative figures and table in accordance with Keller [43]. Semiquantitative analysis of the factors that influence food waste generation was conducted as per Semenya and Machete [41, 44].

3. Results and discussion

These results are based on mixed methods of meta-analysis, structured interviews, and experimental research. The influence of five major household demographic factors (age, family size, household income, employment status, and educational levels) on food waste generation is presented in this study.

3.1 Influence of age on food waste generation

Figure 2 presents the relationship between age of respondents and food waste generation. (a) Age profile of respondents, (b) Correlation of age and food waste generated.

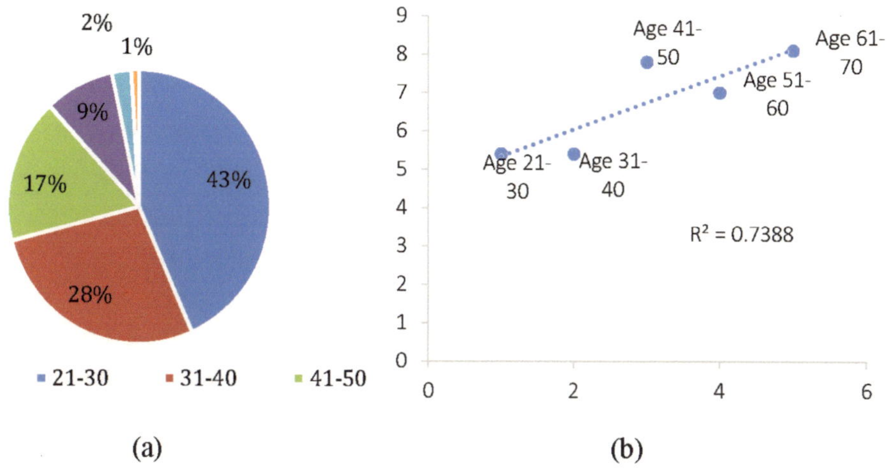

Figure 2.
Influence of age on food waste generation per kilogram per day.

The respondents' age ranged between 21 and 71 years. Majority of the respondents (43%) were between the ages of 21 and 30 years, followed by 31–40 at 28% (**Figure 2(a)**). It is evident from these results that most households were represented by the youth (age 35 and below). In line with earlier discussions of the relationship between age and food waste generation rates, these results suggest that more food waste is generated in the households with the study area. These assumptions were confirmed in **Figure 2(b)** which shows the correlational results between age and the amount of food waste generated by households. The results confirm appositive and strong correlation between age and amount of food waste generation at regression coefficient of 0.7.

3.2 Influence of family size on food waste generation

There is a correlation between family size and food waste generation rates (**Figure 3**).

According to the results in **Figure 3(a)**, households who participated in this study had between 1 and 8 2 family members at different ratios. In **Figure 3(b)**, the results show that there is a positive but weak correlation between family size and the amount of food waste generation per household. The results confirm the previous findings by Canali [28], Jörissen et al. [25], and Parizeau et al. [29].

3.3 Influence of household income on food waste generation

Figure 4 presents the influence of household income on food waste generation in the five City of Tshwane suburbs.

Three broad household income groups were categories from total household income responses of the 210 households' sampled (**Figure 4(a)**). According to the results, 55% of the households earned more than ZAR9001 per month, while the remaining 21 and 24% earned between ZAR1-5000 and ZAR5001-9000, respectively. Adopted from Semenya and Machete [45], the affordability of households was estimated by calculating:

"the 2018 minimum monthly threshold is determined using the World Bank's [46] updated global poverty line of $1.90. The following formula is used:

$$\mathbf{Y = X \times \$1.90} \tag{1}$$

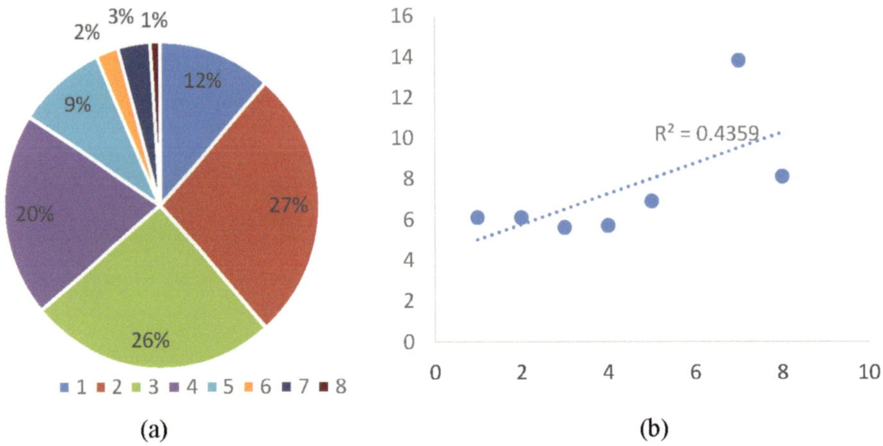

Figure 3.
Influence of family size on food waste generation. (a) Family sizes of households, (b) correlation of family size and food waste generation rate.

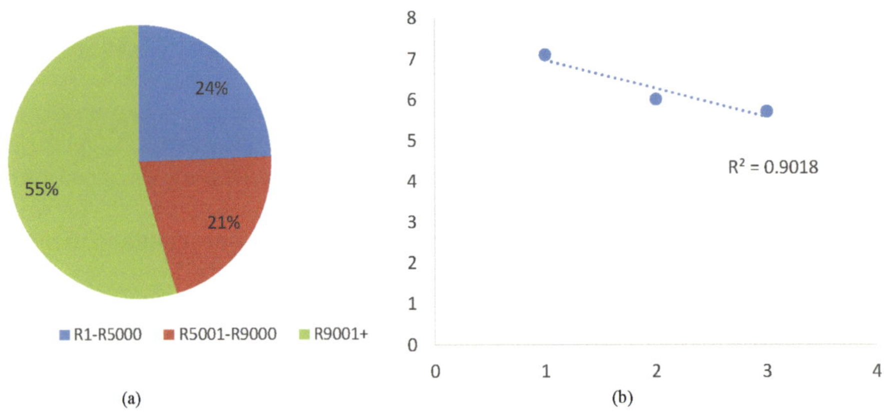

Figure 4.
Influence of household income on food waste generation. (a) Monthly households income levels, (b) correlation of household income and food waste generation.

where Y is the 2018 threshold, X is the 2001 threshold used by Schwabe [47] and $1.90 is the international poverty line set by the World Bank [46] based on purchasing power parity. According to the World Bank [46], the global poverty line is the acceptable minimum amount a person can live on per day in any country considering exchange rates."

Consequently, Semenya and Machete [45] record that the affordability of these households is as per **Table 1**.

Ultimately, in **Figure 4 (b)**, this study presents a strong, but negative correlation between household income and the amount of food waste generated by the households in the five selected suburbs in the City of Tshwane. These results imply that the higher the household's monthly income, the lesser the amount of food wastes generated. Significant number of possibilities can be attributed to these findings, that is, the educational levels, employment status, ages, and other demographic factors of individual household members. The findings of this study are contrary to most previous studies. However, these results are consistent with the findings of Koivupuro et al., (2012) who found no correlation between households' income levels and the amount of food wasted. Similarly, looking at the family sizes and income levels, this study can reveal that more than 50% of the sampled households lived below poverty line.

Family size	R (2001)	R (2013)	R (2018/9)
1	R 587 (587)	R 1174 (1174)	R 1115 (1115)
2	R 773 (387)	R 1546 (773)	R 1469 (735)
3	R 1028 (343)	R 2056 (685)	R 1953 (651)
4	R 1290 (323)	R 2589 (645)	R 2451 (613)
5	R 1541 (308)	R 3082 (616)	R 2928 (586)
6	R 1806 (301)	R 3612 (602)	R 3431 (572)
7	R 2054 (293)	R 4108 (587)	R 3903 (557)
8+	R 2503 (313)	R 5006 (626)	R 4756 (595)

Source: Adopted from Semenya and Machete [45].

Table 1.
South African minimum monthly affordability standards in 2018/9.

3.4 Influence of household employment profile on food waste generation

Figure 5 presents the relationships between employment status of households and food waste generation.

The study found that 72% of respondents were employed, 13% self-employed, and others 15%represents housewives (house executives), retired, students and other. Consequently, **Figure 5(b)** shows a weak and negative correlation between households' employment status of household members and food waste generation. Interestingly, the results suggest that employed people generate less food waste followed by self-employed. From these results, it can be noticed that house executives (housewives), students, and other categories were the ones generating higher quantities of food waste than those who were employed and self-employed. A number of scenarios may be responsible for the above, namely: (1) the main food waste generators may be the people who prepare food in the households, (2) the main waste generators may be those who spend most of their time within the household than those who leave home in the morning and only come back late after work, and (3) the main waste generators may be those who are not responsible for making food available in the households.

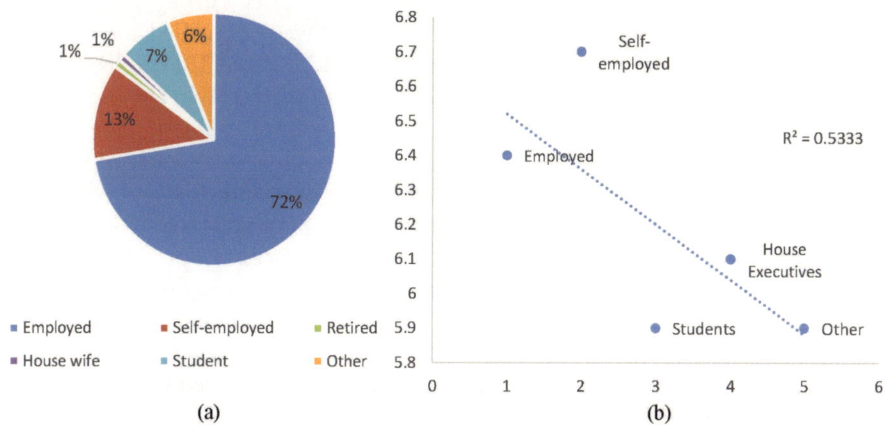

Figure 5.
Influence of employment status on food waste generation. (a) Households' employment profiles, (b) correlation of household employment status and food waste generation rate.

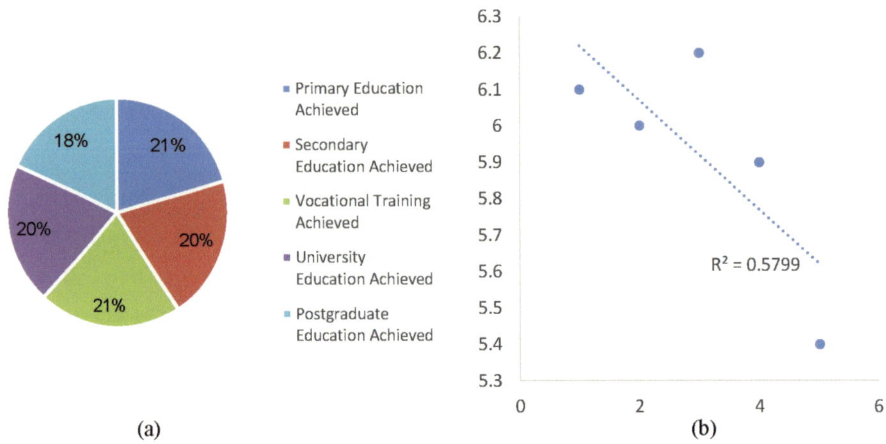

Figure 6.
Influence of household educational levels on food waste generation. (a) Educational levels of despondence, (b) correlation of households' educational levels on food waste generation.

3.5 Influence of household educational level on food waste generation

The last demographic variable investigated in this study was the influence of educational level of respondents (households) on food waste generation (**Figure 6**).

These results show only 21 and 20% of the population achieved primary (grades 1–7) and secondary (grades 9–12) as their highest level of education. The remaining 59% of the population achieved vocational training and university undergraduate and postgraduate levels. No correlation was proven between educational levels of respondents and the amount of food waste generated. More than 90% of the respondents had some form of education (e.g., matric, diploma, and degree), while only 1% was unschooled (no form of education and no certificates).

4. Conclusion

This chapter presented the influence of households' demographics on the amount of food waste generated by five suburbs in the City of Tshwane. In-depth analysis (meta-analysis) of secondary data sources, structured interviews, and experiments were the mixed methods used for data collection and analysis. Through meta-analysis, five major household variables (potential factors) were identified and investigated, namely, (1) family size, (2) monthly household income, (3) employment status, (4) educational level, and (5) age. The results confirmed that age and family size are positive factors that influence the amount of food waste generated in households in contrast to households' levels of education, employment status, and monthly income levels. However, this study does not conclusively exclude levels of education, employment status, and monthly income levels as non-potential factors that may influence food waste generation. Instead, these factors may not be primary drivers of food waste generation. They may be secondary factors, meaning they are triggers of other factors that influence food waste generation. For example, educational levels may influence household income and household head's decision about family size. Similarly, the employment status of individual household members influences the household monthly income, which ultimately has proven to directly influence food waste generation. Given the sample size of the current study and mixed results thereof, it is recommended that further studies with bigger sample size and multi-variable households be investigated to validate the outcomes of the current study.

DOI: http://dx.doi.org/10.5772/intechopen.93755

Acknowledgements

The authors would like to gratefully thank Mr. Philix Mnisi, the Environmental Specialist at the Transnet Freight Rail, Ms. Fhumulani Ramukhwatho and Mr. Tumisang Polasi, Researchers at the Council of Scientific and Industrial Research (CSIR), for their invaluable support through reviews and inputs, including data collection. Many thanks to the unabated support from the Ph.D. candidate at the Kent Law School, University of Kent, Ms. Allison Lindner, who contributed a great deal to review and make literature inputs to the study.

Author details

Machate Machate
College of Agriculture and Environmental Sciences, University of South Africa, Republic of South Africa

*Address all correspondence to: 4machate@gmail.com; machef@unisa.ac.za

IntechOpen

© 2020 The Author(s). Licensee IntechOpen. This chapter is distributed under the terms of the Creative Commons Attribution License (http://creativecommons.org/licenses/by/3.0), which permits unrestricted use, distribution, and reproduction in any medium, provided the original work is properly cited.

References

[1] Gustavsson J, Cederberg C, Sonesson U, Otterdijk R, Meybeck A. Global Food Losses and Food Waste: Extent, Causes and Prevention. Rome: Food and Agriculture Organization of the United Nations; 2011

[2] European Commission. Technical Report for End of Waste Criteria on Biodegradable Waste Subject to Biological Treatment. Seville, Spain: Institute for Prospective Technological Studies; 2011

[3] Thyberg KL, Tonjes DJ, Gurevitch J. Quantification of Food Waste Disposal in the United States: A Meta-Analysis. Environmental Science Technology; 2015

[4] Dhia BH, Alyce B, Alexander O, George S. Managing Costa Rica's Waste e Recommendations for a Municipal Solid Waste Management Plan. Costa Rica: Worcester Polytechnic Institute; 2010-2011

[5] FAO. Food Wastage Footprint: Impact on Natural Resources, Rome: Food and Agriculture Organization of the United Nations. 2013. Available: http://www.fao.org/docrep/018/i3347e/i3347e.pdf [Accessed: 11 July 2014]

[6] Liu G. Food Losses and Food Waste in China: A First Estimate. OECD Food, Agriculture and Fisheries Papers. 2013. 30 p

[7] Franke U. Food Waste in Sweden. 2013. Available from: http://www.oecd.org/site/agrfcn/Session_5_Ulrika%20Franke.pdf [Accessed: 19 October 2016]

[8] National Environment Agency (NEA). Food Wastage in Singapore over the Years. 2013 Singapore Government Agency. Available from: https://www.nea.gov.sg/our-services/waste-management/3r-programmes-and-resources/food-waste-management

[9] Katajajuuri JM, Silvennoinen K, Hartikainen H, Heikkilä L, Reinikainen A. Food waste in the Finnish food chain. Journal of Cleaner Production. 2014;**73**:322-329. DOI: 10.1016/j.jclepro.2013.12.057 [Accessed: 12 November 2016]

[10] WRAP. Household food and drink waste in the United Kingdom 2012. Final Report. 2013. Available from: http://www.wrap.org.uk/sites/files/wrap/hhfdw-2012-main.pdf.pdf [Accessed: 08 January 2015]

[11] Lisa H. South Korea's Food Waste Solution: You Waste, You Pay. Common Wealth Mag. 2013. Available from: http://english.cw.com.tw/article.do?action¼show&id¼14067&offset¼0 [Accessed: 02 December 2016]

[12] Taiwan EPA. The Current Status for Kitchen Waste Recycling and Reuse. 2013. Available from: http://www.epa.gov.tw/en/epashow.aspx [Accessed: 23 September 2014]

[13] Danish Agriculture and Food Council. Food Waste: A Global Tragedy. Aarhus University, CONCITO, the Institute of Food and Resource Economics; 2011. p. 31

[14] Ioannis B, Leonidas M, Almut R. Municipal Waste Management in Turkey. European Environment Agency (EEA); 2013

[15] Zeeda FM, Keng J. Opportunities and Challenges in Sustainable Waste Management Transition in Malaysia: A Multi-level Socio-technical Perspective. 2014. Kuala Lumpur, Malaysia. Available from: http://www.globelics.org/wp-content/uploads/2013/ 03/Zeeda-and-Keng-2013-Malaysia.pdf [Accessed: 06 December 2016]

[16] Yan. Romania to Develop National Strategy to Reduce Food Waste: Minister. 2014. http://news.xinhuanet.com/english/world/2014-04/01/c_133230744.htm [Accessed: 08 December 2016]

[17] Oelofse S, Nahman A. Estimating the magnitude of food waste generated in South Africa. Waste Management & Research: The Journal of the International Solid Wastes and Public Cleansing Association, ISWA. 2013;**31**(1):80-86

[18] Meghan S. Caribbean Biogas Company to Provide Energy from Waste to Housing Development in Jamaica. 2014. GVEP International. Available from: http://www.gvepinternational.org/en/business/news/caribbean-biogascompany- provide-energy waste-housing-development-Jamaica [Accessed: December 6, 2016]

[19] Manipadma J. India's Food Security Rots in Storage. 2013. Available from: http://www.ipsnews.net/2013/06/indias-food-security-rots-in-storage [Accessed: 05 December 2016]

[20] Abeliotis K, Lasaridi K, Chroni C. Attitudes and behavior of Greek households regarding food waste prevention. Waste Management & Research: The Journal of the International Solid Wastes and Public Cleansing Association, ISWA. 2014;**32**:237-240

[21] Graham-Rowe E, Jessop D, Sparks P. Identifying motivations and barriers to minimising household food waste. Resources, Conservation and Recycling. 2014;**84**:15-23

[22] Parfitt J, Barthel M, Macnaughton S. Food waste within food supply chains: Quantification and potential for change to 2050. Philosophical Transactions of the Royal Society Biological Sciences. 2010;**365**(1554):3065-3081

[23] Munesue Y, Masui T, Fushima T. The effects of reducing food losses and food waste on global food security, natural resources and greenhouse gas emissions. Environmental Economics and Policy Studies. 2015;**17**:43-77

[24] Burrit RI, Saka C. Quality of physical environmental management accounting-developing linkages in implementing environmental management accounting: Status and challenges. Eco-Efficiency in Industry and Science. 2006;**18**:123-140

[25] Jörissen J, Priefer C, Bräutigam K-R. Food waste generation at household level: Results of a survey among employees of two European research centers in Italy and Germany. Sustainability. 2015;7:2695-2715. DOI: 10.3390/su7032695

[26] Secondi L, Principato L, Laureti T. Household food waste behavior in EU-27 countries: A multilevel analysis. Food Policy. 2015;**56**:25-40. DOI: 10.1016/j.foodpol.2015.07.007

[27] Melbye EL, Onozaka Y, Hansen H. Throwing it all away: Exploring affluent consumers' attitudes toward wasting edible food. Journal of Food Products Marketing. 2017;**23**(4):416-429. DOI: 10.1080/10454446.2015.1048017

[28] Canali M, Östergren K, Amani P, Aramyan L, Sijtsema S, Korhonen O, et al. Drivers of current food waste generation, threats of future increase and opportunities for reduction. In: FUSIONS Reducing Food Waste through Social Innovation. Bologna: Università di Bologna; 2014

[29] Parizeau K, von Massow M, Martin R. Household-level dynamics of food waste production and related beliefs, attitudes, and behaviors in Guelph. Ontario. Waste Management. 2015;**35**:207-217. DOI: 10.1016/j.wasman.2014.09.019

[30] Porpino G, Parente J, Wansink B. Food waste paradox: Antecedents of

food disposal in low-income households. International Journal of Consumer Studies. 2015a;**39**(6):619-629

[31] Porpino G, Parente J, Wansink B. Food waste paradox: Antecedents of food disposal in low income households. International Journal of Consumer Studies. 2015b;**39**:619-629. DOI: 10.1111/ijcs.12207

[32] Hamilton C, Denniss R, Baker D. Wasteful Consumption in Australia. Discussion Paper Number 77, March. 2005. Manuka, Australia: The Australia Institute. Available from: http://www.tai.org.au/documents/dpfull text/DP77.pdf [Accessed: 11 October 2012]

[33] Skourides I, Smith SR, Loizides M. Sources and factors controlling the disposal of biodegradable municipal solid waste in urban and rural areas of Cyprus. Waste Management & Research. 2008;**26**:188-195

[34] Pearson D, Minehan M, Wakefield-Rann R. Food waste in Australian households: Why does it occur? Australian Pacific Journal or Regional Food Studies. 2013;**3**:118-132

[35] Quested T, Johnson H. Household Food and Drink Waste in the UK: WRAP, Banbury, UK. 2009

[36] Rathje W, Murphy C. Rubbish: The Archaeology of Garbage. Phoenix, AZ, USA: University of Arizona Press; 2001

[37] Pekcan G, Köksal E, Kücükerdönmez Ö, Özel H. Household food wastage in Turkey. Working Paper Series, No: ESS/ESSA/006e. 2005 Food and Agriculture Organization of the United Nations. Available from: http://www.fao.org/docrep/013/am063e/am063e00.pdf [Accessed: 02 January 2015]

[38] Evans D. Blaming the consumer-once again: The social and material contexts of everyday food waste practices in some English households. Critical Public Health. 2011;**21**(4):429-440

[39] Evans D. Binning, gifting and recovery: The conduits of disposal in household food consumption. Environment and Planning D: Society and Space. 2012;**30**:1123-1137

[40] WRAP. Food Behavior Consumer Research: Quantitative Phase. 2007. Available from: http://www.wrap.org.uk/sites/files/wrap/Food%20behaviour%20consumer%20research%20quantitative%20jun%202007.pdf [Accessed: 13 April 2014]

[41] Creswell J. Qualitative Research Introduction. Educational Research: Planning, Conducting and Evaluating Quantitative and Qualitative Research. 3rd ed. Upper Saddle River, N. J: Pearson, Education; 2009

[42] Leedy PD, Ormrod JE. Practical Research Planning and Design. 9th ed. United States of America: Pearson Education; 2010

[43] Keller G. Statistics for Management and Economics. 10th ed. Canada: Cengage Learning; 2014

[44] Creswell J. Educational Research: Planning, Conducting and Evaluating Quantitative and Qualitative Research. 4th ed. Upper Saddle River, N. J: Pearson, Education; 2012

[45] Semenya K, Machete F. Factors that influence firewood use among electrified Bapedi households of Senwabarwana villages, South Africa. African Journal of Science, Technology, Innovation and Development. 2019. DOI: 10.1080/20421338.2019.1572336

[46] World Bank. World Bank Forecasts Global Poverty to fall below 10% for first Time: Major Hurdles Remain in Goal to End Poverty by 2030. Available

from: http://www.worldbank.org [Accessed: 12 June 2018]

[47] Schwabe C. Fact Sheet: Poverty in South Africa. Pretoria: Human Sciences Research Council (HSRC); 2004. Available from: https://www.sarpn.org/documents/d0000990/ [Accessed: 12 June 2018]

Chapter 3

Sustainable Pathway for Closing Solid Waste Data Gaps: Implications for Modernization Strategies and Resilient Cities in Developing Countries

Kwaku Oduro-Appiah and Abraham Afful

Abstract

This chapter addresses three peculiar challenges in the solid waste management system of developing countries, namely: the chronic lack of reliable data for planning purposes, the absence of participatory engagement strategies in data gathering for wider ownership and usage, and the lack of monitoring of the climate change burden of existing waste disposal practices. A team of researchers has collaborated with system managers and a responsible philanthropic organization to engage key stakeholders to address these gaps in a sustainable manner. The strategy deployed has been to work in a participatory and evidenced-based frame to solicit support, enhance capacities, empower each other to understand the problems and find for ourselves the practical routes by which solid waste data gaps can be closed in the greater Accra region of Ghana. Stakeholders have participated in a comprehensive waste audit and landfill emission monitoring exercise to develop a baseline, and have used local resources and ideas to recommend steps to sustain reliable data flows and the development of a climate action plan for purposes of modernization. The methodological processes and research outcomes suggest that structural collaboration between researchers and system stakeholders is necessary to break the vicious circle of chronic data gaps and substitute virtuous circles of reliable data for planning purposes.

Keywords: reliable data, participatory processes, municipal solid waste, waste composition, calorific value, greenhouse gases, Ghana, developing countries

1. Introduction

Reliable solid waste (SW) data and information are essential to sustainable waste management systems [1]. It supports decision-makers and professional solid waste management (SWM) staff to build their knowledge-base to effectively plan and develop strategies for modernization [2, 3]. Its usefulness has been recognized in the developed and industrialized worlds, making it a prerequisite and a routine to almost all planning processes [4]. Of the many data sets required in SWM, baseline data on generation rates, composition analysis, and other chemical and mechanical

IntechOpen

properties are considered vital to the planning of collection and transportation systems, to the choice of treatment and disposal technologies, and the design of municipal solid waste (MSW) recycling and valorization pathways [5, 6].

But despite their significance and usefulness, there exist a chronic lack (or absence) of waste characteristics data in most lower-middle income cities of developing countries, depriving managing authorities the basis to assess their systems and further develop interventions and action plans for modernization [7].

Where some form of MSW data exist, their reliability is affected by many factors such as the collection methodology, the baseline from which they were extrapolated, the number of years since they were collected, and the purpose and circumstances to which they were collected. More often than not, the limited available MSW data has been the product of external consultants (working under time pressure for donors) who have extrapolated from non-validated global or regional data sets. Such data sets are mostly gathered in relation to planning a facility, and are likely to be overestimated to capture the maximum amount of donor funding for the project. Despite the fact that such data are not always readily accessible within the SWM system, stakeholders rarely embrace its usage.

Conventional top-down ways of creating baseline information have also not helped to address this issue, in part because they are most often derived from a paradigm for engineering-based SWM, in which assuring that most waste reaches engineered disposal is most often the main goal of waste system upgrading in many a developing country city. For planning for disposal, generally the gross capacity of the sink (landfill) is important, and so the tendency in most solid waste (SW) plans is to take any available data and update it to make sure that the facility that is built has more than sufficient capacity [3].

Such a strategy has not always been successful even in its own right, and when it comes to planning integrated and sustainable waste management (ISWM), it provides too little basis for assessing the performance of the system, to allow for the participatory formulation of interventions to fix what is failing, and strengthen what is working.

Whilst disposal on land is the most inevitable MSW treatment option after collection in most developing countries, its burden to climate change is seldom assessed, preventing system handlers the opportunity of developing climate change mitigation policies, such as the separation of waste at source and the diversion of recyclables from disposal [8].

The contribution of this chapter is to address these data challenges by engaging academic researchers, solid waste managers, the informal waste sector, and other relevant stakeholders in a participatory process to comprehensively quantify and characterize the solid waste of households, institutions and markets in the greater Accra region of Ghana, and monitor the Greenhouse gas (GHG) emissions from existing SW disposal landfills. Being the first of its kind, the objective has been to strengthen local capacities in data collection and promote participatory research-based decision-making towards SWM system modernization in Ghana. Ideally the result of participatory engagement will work to create knowledge, awareness, transparency, self- and collective-correction, and ownership of results in addition to empowering stakeholders to use same to develop locally responsive interventions and action plans for system improvement.

2. Overview of the solid waste data challenge in developing countries

The publications "What a Waste 2.0, Africa Waste Management Outlook (AWMO) and Solid Waste Management in the World's Cities," encapsulate the MSW data challenge of Sub-Saharan African countries and the developing world [7, 9, 10]. The challenge is exacerbated by the absence of a common framework for comprehensive data capture in especially Sub-Saharan Africa. The AWMO identifies the gravity of this data challenge and articulates it in the statement: One of the limitations of the AWMO is the lack of reliable, comprehensive and up-to-date data for Africa, which is a constraint to effective waste management on the continent. This lack of comprehensive data is further compounded by the different approaches to data collection [7].

This concern is followed by a question to which this chapter seeks to associate with and attempts to find a solution to, namely: "If this issue (lack of data) has been recognized for the past two decades, why have adequate measures not been put in place to ensure the generation and reporting of reliable, comprehensive waste data for Africa?"

Experience from the community of practice and the scholarly literature shows that the generation of reliable data is dependent on a mixture of factors, namely:

- stakeholders realization that reliable data is vital to the planning and development of a well-functioning and sustainable municipal solid waste management (MSWM) system

- availability of the human resource capacity required to generate the data

- commitment of system managers and decision-makers to source the necessary funds for generation of the data

But almost by design, most waste management departments in developing countries are constrained with the required human resource capacity and technical knowledge to support the collection of reliable data [11]. Whilst there may be a growing awareness of the importance of reliable data to planning and system sustainability, the competing need and high cost of waste collection and disposal prevents system handlers from allocating already limited funds for capacity building and data collection [12]. Failure in MSWM governance, characterized by the lack of monitoring stakeholder performance and the continuous refusal to recognize the contribution of informal sector actors, especially in most Sub-Saharan African cities further denies the system of any operational-related MSW data.

The reality on the ground has been the use of consultants working on donor financed projects to collect data, which most often are undertaken without the participation of the local system handlers. Where they are involved in the process, their roles are limited to objects of investigation and validation of information, affecting ownership and eventual usage of such data for planning purposes.

If developing countries would be able to formulate sustainable MSWM plans to modernize their systems, a new approach that create the enabling environment to allow local authorities and system handlers to participate in the planning, collection, analysis and validation of all waste-related data needs to be adopted [13]. The new normal will have to equip those in charge with the necessary know-how and hands on practices to support them generate, replicate and update their own data, and use same for system assessment, intervention development, implementation and the formulation of action plans for system modernization [14].

Interestingly, all the three publications that comprehensively discuss the data challenge in developing country cities embrace participatory engagement strategies as vital to the closing of such data gaps. Participatory action research processes offer researchers and stakeholders the opportunity to build alliances with the commitment and desire to understand, investigate and design solutions to the very problems that affect their systems [13, 15].

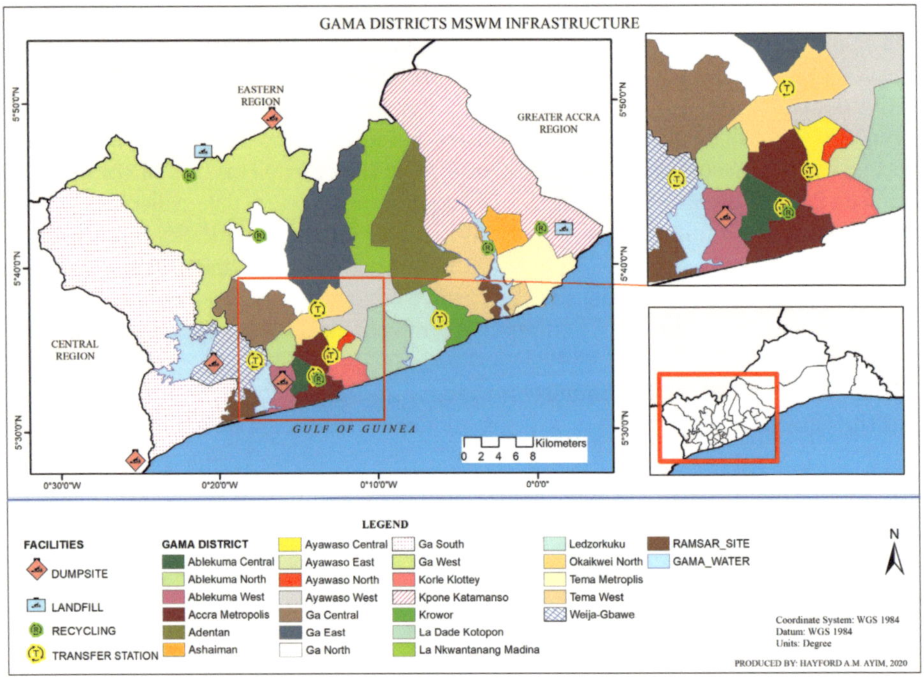

Figure 1.
The greater Accra metropolitan area showing the 25 municipalities, MSWM facilities and the sampled area for analysis. Source: The authors, 2020, Accra, Ghana.

3. The Greater Accra Metropolitan Area

The Greater Accra Metropolitan Area ("the GAMA") comprises 25 municipalities along the South-Eastern Coast of Ghana and covers an area of 1453.53 km^2 (**Figure 1**). The region harbors the capital city, Accra, and the industrial hub, Tema, of the country. The estimated population is 4.63 million with a daily MSW generation rate of 3293 tons [3]. Formal private companies have the concession to collect waste, but poor performance have resulted in the growth of an informal waste collection sector who are significantly filling gaps especially in low-income areas of the region [16]. More than 90% of collected MSW ends up on a system of controlled and uncontrolled landfills, with the informal waste pickers and recyclers contributing to 84% of the reported 8.4% recycling rate [3]. The level of user and provider inclusivity in decision-making, the financial sustainability of the MSWM system, the cohesiveness of the institutions managing the system, and the proactiveness of the legislative and regulatory framework has been reported to be inadequate [17]. Although initially planned for the capital city, Accra, the working group to the research in this chapter selected the GAMA to increase the scope of the assignment and make the outcome more representative of the region.

4. Materials and methods

The research to this chapter has made use of a team of researchers, municipal officials (planners, public health engineers), the informal waste sector (both service- and value-chain actors) and policy institutions to use participatory research action processes to plan and generate comprehensive MSW characterization and landfill emission data for the GAMA. The goal has been to engage public-sector stakeholders as team members to seek their support and build their capacities as part of efforts towards the closing of reliable MSW data gaps within the municipalities. The main activities include the:

- training of stakeholders in MSW data collection processes and GHG monitoring
- determination of the physical (generation rate, composition analysis and bulk density) and selected chemical properties (moisture content, calorific value nutrient analysis and ash content) of the MSW of the region
- monitoring of the GHG (Carbon IV Oxide, Methane and volatile Organic Compounds) directly, and through estimations from the city's final disposal sites to help measure the contribution of the existing MSWM practices to climate change

4.1 Stakeholder mobilization, training and preliminary planning processes

The planning processes to the collection of data began with the mobilization of eight relevant stakeholders to support the characterization exercise (**Table 1**). The objective was to stimulate the potential for wider contribution, ownership, acceptance and eventual usage of the data and the outcomes of the processes. A second objective was to equip the staff within the municipalities with the technical and non-technical know-how to enable them replicate the processes and use same for further planning of their MSWM system [14]. The authors, themselves stakeholder's and researchers worked with managers from the Waste Management Department (WMD) of the Accra Metropolitan Assembly (AMA) as a focal planning and coordinating team. The following activities were agreed upon for implementation as part of the initial meetings between the stakeholders, namely the:

- development of a training manual on MSW characterization and landfill gas monitoring for use in the training of municipal staff
- selection of the municipalities and determination of the scope of analysis
- consultation of private MSW service companies for support on venue and personnel for the solid waste analysis
- scope of the quantification and characterization analysis
- development of the various forms for data capture
- identification of laboratories for chemical analysis of MSW samples
- agreement to outsource the GHG monitoring to a willing and capable consultant
- consideration of the available budget, its sufficiency and the development of a plan to solicit further support from local stakeholders where necessary

4.2 Sample size, scope, distribution of receptacles and collection of demographic data

The MSW for the exercise was collected randomly from households within 10 (out of 25) municipalities, traders within the three largest markets in the GAMA,

No.	Stakeholder (no. of representatives)	Role
1	Accra Metropolitan Assembly (13)	Coordination, support, field work and data collection
2	Ga North Municipality (3)	Mapping, field work participation and observation
3	Ablekuma North Municipality (2)	Field work participation, observation & distribution of receptacles
4	Okaikwei North Municipality (2)	Field work participation and observation
5	Ayawaso West Municipality (2)	
6	Ayawaso East Municipality (2)	
7	Ayawaso Central Municipality (2)	
8	Ashiedu Keteke Municipality (1)	
9	Ablekuma West (1)	
10	Ministry of Sanitation and Water Resources (3)	Field work observation
11	Environmental Protection Agency (1)	
12	Regional Coordinating Council (2)	Field work observation and sampling for laboratory analysis
13	Jekora Ventures Limited (14)*	Coordination, support, field work and data collection
14	Informal MSW collectors (10)	
15	Informal MSW pickers (5)	
16	Nation Builders Corps (NABCO) (10)	
17	National Service Persons (4)	
18	Foreign Intern, Netherlands (1)	
19	University of Cape Coast (3)	
20	Nemas Consult Limited (2)**	Landfill Gas Monitoring
21	Kwame Nkrumah University of Science and Technology (3)**	Laboratory Analysis, Wet and Dry Season
22	University of Ghana (2)**	Laboratory Analysis, Wet Season
23	C40 Cities	Funding

**A private waste management company that provided venue and personnel.*
***These stakeholders did not partake in the day to day activities. We sought their services for landfill gas monitoring and laboratory analysis.*

Table 1.
Stakeholders and their roles within the MSW characterization exercise in the GAMA.

and workers within 15 institutions (**Figure 2**). Twenty households were randomly selected in each of the 10 municipalities (grouped into three income divides) for the analysis (**Figure 2**). A total of 3150 samples of different weights and sizes (2000 samples from households, 700 from markets and 450 from institutions) were analyzed for 10 days during the wet season (August 2019). The process was repeated for the dry season (December 2019). The minimum computed household sample size of approximately 400 [18] was increased almost fivefold to 2000 to allow for a large margin of representation. This decision was taken with the knowledge of having stakeholder's support and the financial resilience to contain the increase.

A 45 member team of service persons, Nation Builders Corps (NABCO) representatives, informal solid waste collectors, municipal officers and the coordinating team sought the consent of the various households, institutions and markets and

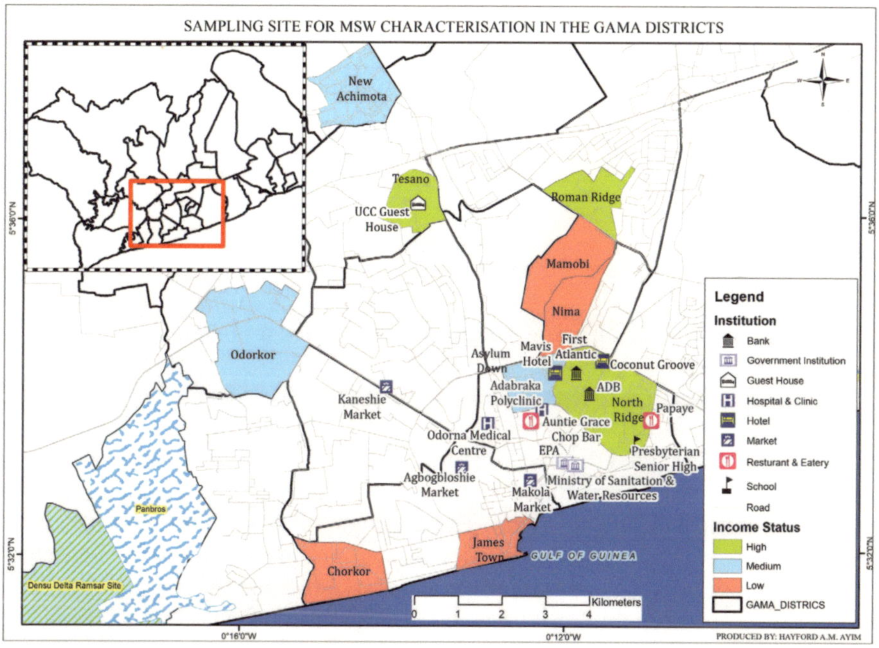

Figure 2.
The 10 municipalities, 3 main markets and the 15 institutions sampled for the MSW characterization exercise within the GAMA of Ghana. Source: The authors, 2020, Accra, Ghana.

Figure 3.
The receptacles used for the collection of MSW from households, markets and institutions respectively. Source: The authors, 2020, Accra, Ghana. Legend: AMA: Accra metropolitan assembly.

distributed labeled and AMA embossed polyethylene bags of volumes 30 ml, 240 ml and sacks (150 ml) respectively for the daily storage of their waste. The printing of the AMA's logo on the receptacles (**Figure 3**) was to promote trust and also to add value and a high level of importance to the exercise.

The demographic data (name, house number, household size etc.) of the various participants were taken in the process of distribution of the receptacles and each participant was introduced to the informal solid waste collector tasked to collect the stored MSW every morning from the participants. Each participant was expected to use one receptacle per day but records were taken each day to justify the provision of more receptacles to participants/institutions/traders who needed more than one a day. A total of 6316 (30 ml) polyethylene bags, 3000 sacks and 400 (240 ml) polyethylene receptacles were distributed for sample collection during the wet and dry seasons.

Participants were provided with telephone numbers and were encouraged to ask questions about the process when the need arose. They were advised to opt out of the process if they felt to do so.

A period of four days was left between the end of distribution of the receptacles and the collection of the first set of samples for analysis in both seasons. In between the four days:

- the site for analysis was prepared
- tarpaulin on which the sorting of MSW was to be undertaken was procured and laid
- canopies, tables and chairs to provide shade and convenience to the workers were installed
- manual and digital scales for weights measurement were installed and calibrated
- plastic containers of different volumes were labeled and weighed
- special sampling bags for the laboratory aspect of the analysis were procured

The same period served the purpose for rehearsals to the characterization team on the expected daily routines including the distribution of procured coveralls and other personal protective equipment (PPEs). The demographic data collected from the households were also analyzed and verified through telephone calls to the households during the period. Selected representatives were tasked within the last two days before collection of samples to remind all participants of the date of collection of samples.

4.3 Collection of MSW from participants for analysis

Tricycle operators from the informal waste sector collected the MSW from the various households, markets and institutions across the 10 municipalities. Collected samples were sent each day to the site for the various characterization analysis. Samples of MSW received on the field were taken on the 6th, 7th, 9th and 10th days in both seasons to the laboratory for various nutrient and heat value analysis.

4.3.1 Determination of generation rate

Samples received were weighed on an OHAUS Defender 3000 Digital Bench Scale (model D31P150BX) of maximum capacity 150 kg and readability of 0.02 kg and recorded against the identities of the various households, market participants and institutions. The various quantities were divided by the corresponding household sizes and the weighted average daily quantities per capita per day was computed.

4.3.2 Determination of MSW composition

A total of 35 participants, informal waste pickers and collectors were divided into four teams for the segregation of the weighed MSW samples into various fractions. Segregated fractions were placed into labeled containers, weighed and recorded. The coordination team supervised and also recorded all daily measurements/weights, initially on paper and later onto the field laptop. Each day's measurements were recorded unto the laptop to prevent backlog of entries and also to identify and address any possible challenges in the daily data recording process. Recorded data was later analyzed using Microsoft Excel. All samples for the composition analysis were based on the recommendation of ASTM D5231-92 [19].

4.3.3 Determination of bulk density

The bulk densities of both comingled and biodegradable MSW within the samples from the various economic divides were determined by filling a plastic bucket container of known volume with waste and then weighing the loaded container. The bulk density was then computed by dividing the net weight of waste by the volume and expressing the unit in kg/m^3. Three bulk density measurements were carried out each and every other day on samples from each municipality to allow for the computation of means.

4.3.4 Determination of moisture content

The moisture content was determined by bulk drying the laboratory samples in an oven at 105°C ± 5°C for a 24-hour period until a constant weight was achieved. The ratio of the weight loss of the sample to the initial weight of the sample was computed and multiplied by 100% as depicted in Eq. (1).

$$M = \frac{M_w - M_d}{M_w} \times 100\% \tag{1}$$

where M = Moisture Content, M_w = Weight of wet sample received and M_d = Net weight of waste sample after oven drying.

4.3.5 Determination of calorific value

The gross calorific value was determined using the PARR 6400 Bomb Calorimeter. A known weight (0.5 g) of the representative samples (prepared after pulverizing the combustible portions of the dried sample) was picked and combusted in the bomb calorimeter. The equipment provides the user the opportunity to input the weight to be combusted. The equipment calculates the calorific value by an internal program and displays the dry-based higher calorific value (HCV). A reference material (Benzoic Acid) whose calorific value is known was used to ascertain the proper functioning of the bomb calorimeter before the samples were analyzed. The calorific value of the benzoic acid was within the recommended range (26.454 MJ/Kg ± 0.50 MJ/Kg). The lower heating value (LHV) was then computed from the HCV.

4.3.6 Nutrient analysis

The following methods were used in the determination of the various nutrients within the samples

- Walkley-Black wet oxidation method for the determination of Carbon (C)
- Kjeldahl method for Nitrogen (N)
- Titrimetric method for Hydrogen (H)
- Spectrophotometric method for Sulfur (S)
- Flame Photometery for Potassium

Phosphorus was determined using methods recommended by Motsara and Roy [20].

4.3.7 Determination of ash content

5 g ± 0.1 g of dried waste was accurately weighed with a precision of 0.0001 g and placed into a crucible that had been dried to a constant weight at 815 ± 5°C.

The crucible and its content was then placed into a muffle furnace. The furnace was heated slowly to 300°C within 30 mins. Heating was continued until 815 ± 5°C. The crucible was scorched for 3 hours at this temperature. The scorching was stopped and the crucible taken out of the furnace after the temperature had dropped to about 300°C. The crucible was then placed on asbestos wire gauze, covered and cooled for 5 minutes in a drier and weighed at room temperature after cooling. The crucible was scorched again for 20 mins and weighed at room temperature after cooling until the difference in value of the two measurements was less than 0.0005 g. The Ash content was computed using Eq. (2).

$$Ash\ Content = \frac{Weight\ of\ Ash}{Mass\ of\ Sample} \times 100\% \tag{2}$$

5. Results and discussion of the MSW characterization exercise

5.1 Generation rate

The analysis in the GAMA points to an average MSW generation rate of 0.70 kg per capita per day and 0.83 kg capita per day for households and institutions respectively. Markets recorded an average of 1.32 kg per shop per day. The result for households is closer to the averages (0.72 kg) and (0.71 kg) respectively in earlier solid waste characterization studies for metropolitan cities of Ghana [17, 21], but above the average 0.54 kg estimate for developing countries [9]. Whilst average per capita generation rates within low-income areas is 0.51 kg, that of their high-income counterparts is 0.91 kg; confirming already known trends in which the affluent in society is reported to generate more MSW than their urban poor counterparts [5].

The waste generation trend within each income divide is provided in (**Figure 4**). There are reasonable deviations about the MSW generation means in low- and middle-income areas but not in high-income areas. The significantly high generation rates for the first and sixth days in high-income areas are possible contributory

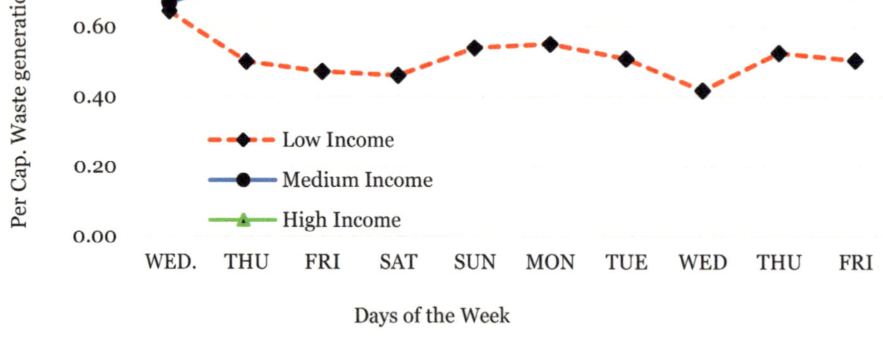

Figure 4.
Household MSW generation trends within three income divides in the GAMA.

factors. Whilst the generation rate per capita per day for the first-day is considered an outlier (likely due to the suspicion that the first day MSW received for analysis might not be a true reflection of the previous day's waste). The relatively high generation rate per capita on the sixth day (Monday) is likely a result of real generation rates from the weekend. Most middle- and high-income dwellers generate more waste during the weekends than the other days since they might mostly be at work; away from home during the weekdays.

There is a negative correlation between generation rate and household size (**Figure 5**) which is also indicative of earlier research findings in which smaller household sizes, mostly in single family dwellings within sparsely dense and affluent areas generate more MSW per capita per day than their poor urban counterparts in multifamily dwellings (locally known as compound houses) within densely populated areas [5].

5.2 Composition analysis

The three most significant components within households MSW are organics, a combination of food waste and garden waste (53.84%), plastics (16.05%) and inorganics (12.89%). Inorganics referred to here are virtually silts and ash swept from dirt floors and fetched from coal pots respectively in low income areas of the region [17]. The seasonal variation in composition is shown in (**Figure 6**). The high organic component is indicative of similar reports in developing countries that points to a large percentage of biodegradables in the household MSW [7].

System managers and other stakeholders will need to look for a locally responsive intervention to not only reduce the biodegradable content of the MSW of the municipalities, but also to find sustainable handling and treatment options to reduce its climate change burden on the environment. There is however significant variation in the MSW composition of institutions. Whilst there is relatively higher percentage of plastics within the MSW of government agencies, hospitals and schools, the MSW of restaurants/eateries, hotels and banks are rather dominated by organic wastes. Expectedly, schools generate the highest of paper waste followed by government institutions and banks. The MSW from markets is highly composed of organics (56.27%) followed by plastics (13.59%), textiles (13.17%) and paper (8.75%).

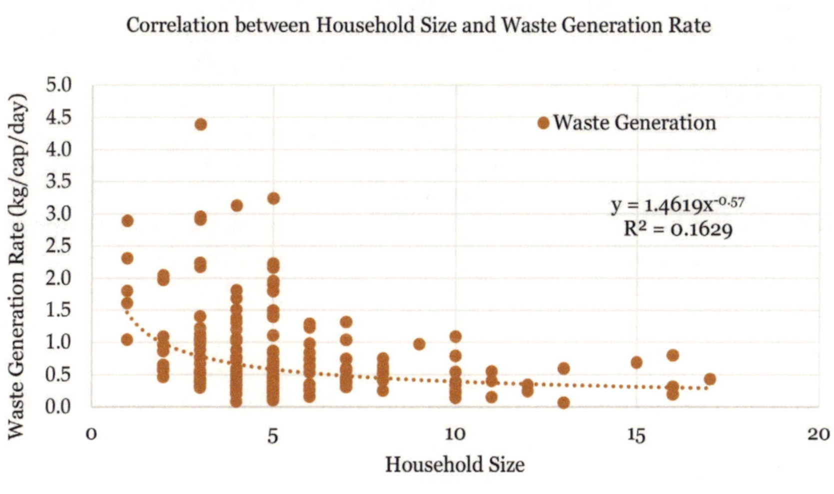

Figure 5.
MSW generation rates as a function of household size within the GAMA.

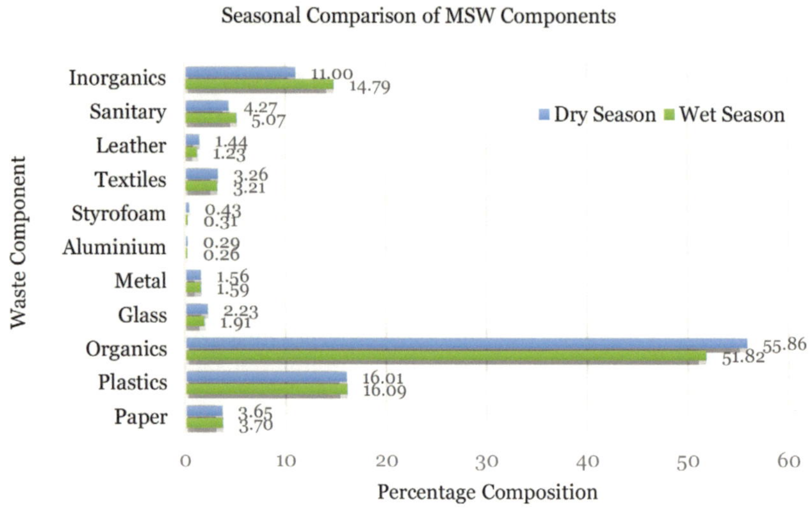

Figure 6.
Seasonal comparison of household MSW composition within the GAMA.

5.3 Bulk density and moisture content

The bulk density of MSW plays a major role in the determination of the lifespan of landfills, an inevitable disposal option for most developing countries. The average bulk densities for food waste (517. 73 kg/m^3) and mixed waste (331.39 kg/m^3) are typical of the MSW of developing countries. These relatively high densities are mostly due to the high moisture content of the MSW, which more often than not is open to precipitation before collection [10]. The average moisture content is 50%, which is highly unlikely to support the adoption of waste to energy (e.g. incineration) as a treatment option within the municipalities.

5.4 Calorific value of the MSW of the GAMA

The calorific value of the MSW was determined by two approaches: through model prediction based on the composition and water content of the MSW [22] and also by the bomb calorimetric method. The model prediction provides information on the net calorific value is also known as the lower calorific value (LCV); while the bomb calorimetric method provides the gross calorific value (higher calorific value, HCV), which is then converted to LCV for informed decision-making. The LCV is a technical criterion for the incineration of solid wastes. The LCV must on average be at least 7 MJ/kg and must not fall below 6 MJ/kg in any season if a particular waste stream is to be considered for incineration [22].

The estimated LCV of the MSW of the GAMA, based on the waste composition computation and water content of Eq. (3) is 6.74 MJ/kg (**Table 2**). The estimated LCV for the wet and dry season analysis are 6.47 MJ/kg and 7.01 MJ/Kg respectively.

$$LCV = 40\,(A + B + C + D) + 90E - 46W \qquad (3)$$

Where A, B, C, D, E and W represents the wet weight composition (%) of the MSW of the GAMA as shown in (**Table 2**).

The results of the Bomb calorimetric method (**Table 3**) has been converted to the net calorific value using Eq. (4) [23, 24].

Variable	Parameters	Wet season	Dry season	Ave. GAMA
A	Paper	3.74	3.65	3.70
B	Textile	3.21	3.26	3.24
C	Wood and Leaves	16.44	15.42	15.93
D	Food waste	36.11	41.07	38.59
E	Plastic and Rubber	16.29	16.01	16.15
W	Water	49.97	50.03	50.00
LCV (kcal/kg)	4.18E-03	1547.48	1675.52	1611.90
LCV (MJ/kg)		**6.47**	**7.01**	**6.74**

Table 2.
Estimated lower calorific value based on the wet MSW composition values of the GAMA.

	Community	Mean HCV, (MJ/Kg)	Water (%)	Hydrogen (%)	Wet base HCV, (KJ/Kg)	Mean calorific value LCV, (MJ/Kg)	
Wet Season	Jamestown	19.15	48.20	8.74	9919.70	7.75	**7.71**
	Odorkor	20.58	41.90	7.35	11,956.98	10.00	
	Tesano	21.25	51.70	6.90	10,263.75	8.27	
	New Achimota	20.90	50.00	8.70	10,450.00	8.27	
	Roman Ridge	17.96	60.00	8.18	7184.00	5.00	
	Nima/Mamobi	17.64	48.50	8.29	9084.60	6.96	
Dry Season	New Achimota	16.25	45.70	8.80	8823.75	6.66	**6.71**
	Odorkor	19.08	52.80	9.80	9005.76	6.70	
	North Ridge	16.61	56.80	8.68	7175.52	4.97	
	Tesano	19.04	45.20	6.96	10,433.92	8.49	
Average calorific value (MJ/Kg)					**7.31**		

Table 3.
Bomb calorimetry heating values for the MSW of the GAMA.

$$LCV = \frac{HCV * 1000 * (100 - M)}{100} - 24(\mathrm{M} + 9 * \mathrm{H} * \frac{(100 - M)}{100} \tag{4}$$

Where LCV, HCV, H and M represents net calorific value, gross calorific value, hydrogen (%) and moisture content (%) respectively of the MSW of the city.

The average net calorific value (LCV) of the city's MSW is 7.31 MJ/Kg. The LCV for the wet and dry season analysis are 7.71 MJ/kg and 6.71 MJ/Kg respectively (**Table 3**). The results from both methods present LCVs which are close to 7 MJ/Kg, required in literature for probable consideration of incineration as a treatment choice for the MSW towards the recovery of energy.

5.5 Ultimate analysis of the MSW of the GAMA

The ultimate analysis of MSW involves the breakdown of the MSW into its elemental components. It plays an important role in the determination of the energy recovery potential of the waste as well as its application to support agricultural

SN		Community	% C	% H	% S	% N	% P	% K	% Ash	C:P	C: N
1	**Wet Season**	New Achimota	24.9	8.7	0.7	1.4	0.4	0.7	18.1	58.9	18.1
2		Roman Ridge	22.6	8.2	0.7	1.3	0.2	2.1	25.0	120.1	17.4
3		Nima/Mamobi	18.9	8.3	0.6	1.1	0.2	1.5	28.0	112.1	17.0
4		Odorkor	27.0	7.4	0.5	1.2	0.2	1.0	17.6	121.1	22.4
5		Jamestown	29.1	8.7	0.6	1.2	0.2	0.7	8.8	169.6	24.6
6		Tesano	26.6	6.9	0.6	1.8	0.2	2.5	20.8	154.9	14.6
7	**Dry Season**	New Achimota	27.9	8.8	0.7	1.4	0.2	1.0	19.6	144.1	20.7
8		Odorkor	27.5	9.8	0.6	1.4	0.1	1.3	21.2	194.2	20.4
9		Kaneshie Market 1	28.9	10.1	0.7	1.7	0.2	1.3	15.7	165.7	17.4
10		Kaneshie Market 2	28.3	7.4	0.4	1.4	0.2	0.6	7.6	145.9	21.0
11		North Ridge	28.1	8.7	0.4	2.2	0.7	1.3	15.2	42.7	12.8
12		Tesano	32.1	7.0	0.6	1.5	0.2	2.1	12.7	162.2	21.5

Table 4.
Ultimate nutrient analysis of the MSW of the GAMA.

needs. Composting is increasingly being considered as a favorable SWM strategy in most developing countries where larger portions of the waste are biodegradable. The Carbon to Nitrogen (C: N) and Carbon to Phosphorus (C: P) ratios are essential parameters for the sustainable valorization of MSW. Carbon to Nitrogen ratios of 25:1 and 30:1 of raw MSW is recommended by literature [6] for achieving maximum efficiency in composting and anaerobic digestion processes. Carbon to Phosphorus (C: P) ratio, on the other hand, has received little attention in literature even though it can be a limiting factor. A C: P ratio of 120:1 to 240:1 is necessary when the C: N ratio is 30:1.

The C: N ratio of the MSW of the GAMA ranges from 12.8:1 (North Ridge) to 24.6:1 (Jamestown) as shown in **Table 4**. The low C: N ratio means that material with high Carbon content such as wood and saw dust must be added to the waste to support composting and anaerobic digestion treatment technologies as part of the city's MSWM strategy. With the exception of the results from New Achimota and Nima/Mamobi in the wet season and North Ridge in the dry season (**Table 4**), the C:P ratio for the city's waste falls within the recommended range in literature.

6. Greenhouse gas monitoring and estimations within the GAMA

This section presents the methods and results of the GHG emissions from the waste sector (specifically, the MSW disposal practices) within the GAMA. Two methods were used: field measurement using the Aeroqual series 500 (A-S500) portable gas sensor method and indirect estimation using the auto-populated Microsoft Excel tool of the City Inventory Reporting Information System (CIRIS).

6.1 Field monitoring of the greenhouse gases

The concentration levels of the gases Methane (CH_4), Carbon IV Oxide (CO_2) and volatile organic compounds (VOCs) were monitored directly for four continuous days each during the wet and dry seasons, using an A-S500 potable gas meter instrument. The A-S500 portable gas sensor meter is a highly-rated device that enables accurate real time monitoring of common indoor and outdoor air pollutants

Figure 7.
The A-S500 portable gas instrument with sensors being mounted on the Nsumia landfill and a control site for GHG measurements.

and gas emissions, all in an ultra-portable air quality monitor [25]. The Instrument (**Figure 7**) consists of a monitor base and a gas sensor head of the respective gas under investigation. A particular gas was measured, when the sensor head of the gas was connected to the monitor base. The Nsumia landfill and one control site located about 500 meters away from the landfill was selected to monitor the various gases. The Global Positioning System (GPS) locations were, 5° 46′ 59.1″ N, 0° 21′ 14.1″W for the landfill site and 5° 46′ 53.5″N, 0° 21′ 03.1″W for the control site.

The instrument once fitted with a particular sensor head is also activated to measure ambient temperature (T) and relative humidity (RH) by inserting the TRH sensor into the PS/2 connector at the base of the monitor. Connection of the required sensor head to the monitor was done prior to the turning on of the equipment before measurement. The monitor was switched on and allowed to warm up for 3 minutes to "burn off" any contaminants trapped in the sensor prior to monitoring. The gas concentrations logged by the instrument were automatically saved in high capacity internal flash memory built within the instrument. The results of the measurement were then transferred to a laptop for analysis and reports were created using the A-S500 V6.5 Software.

The following sensor heads were used for the determination of the various gases

- Gas Sensitive Semiconductor (GSS) for CH_4 gas
- Non-Dispersive Infrared (NDIR) for CO_2 gas
- Photoionization Detector for VOCs

For the sake of brevity, the time series of the measured CH_4 and CO_2 gases, for both the wet and the dry seasons are displayed in (**Figure 8**).

6.2 Greenhouse gas computation using the city inventory reporting information system

Methane (CH_4) and biogenic Carbon IV Oxide ($CO_{2(b)}$) are the two GHGs considered in this section since they predominate the GHG from solid waste degradation and decomposition. The landfill data used in the estimation of GHGs was sourced from a recent research output in Ghana [26].

6.2.1 Method of estimation

The Methane Commitment Method within the CIRIS Excel tool was used to calculate the GHGs originating from solid waste disposed of in the GAMA.

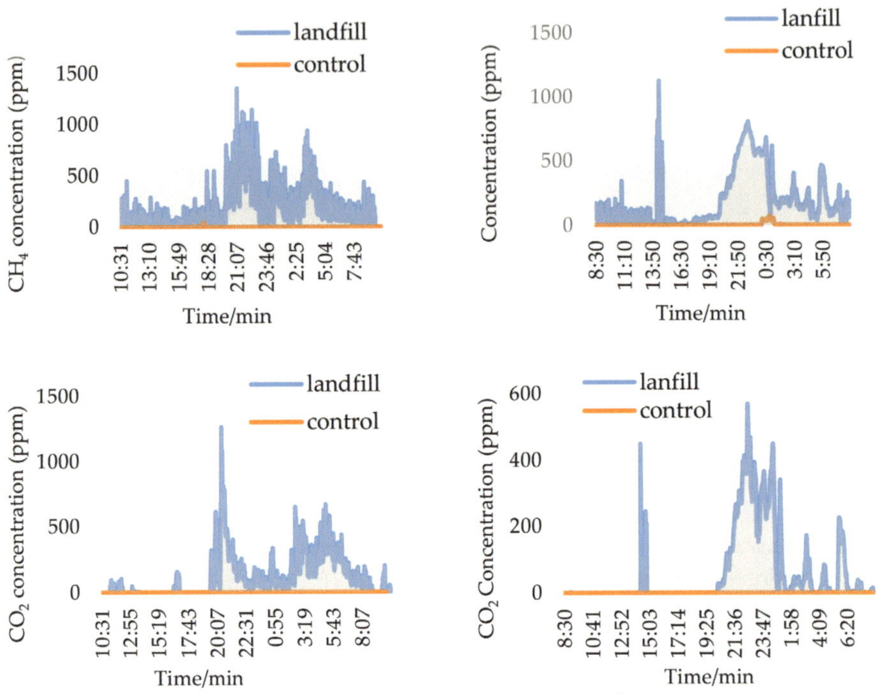

Figure 8.
Time series of hourly averaged CH_4 and CO_2 from measurements made by the Aeroqual CH_4 and CO_2 gas monitors during the wet and dry seasons.

The CIRIS make use of landfill disposal data of the year of inventory, the city's background information, the city's global warming assessment report, the city's waste composition data, and the city's landfill depth and management criteria as inputs for GHG estimation.

The GHG emissions computations are based on the total emissions from the two main repositories for the MSW of the GAMA (**Figure 1**). Both landfills are considered unmanaged and have depths more than 5 metres. The consideration of the landfills as unmanaged stems from the fact that daily covering is absent and highly inconsistent, and gases are not collected for controlled release. Although the Kpone landfill, which falls within the boundaries of the GAMA has a network of gas seams for the collection of gases, these seams have virtually been covered in the process of waste deposition into the fill, preventing the smooth release of gases, a situation which led to fire outbreak on the landfill in the second half of 2019. The other landfill (Nsumia) outside the boundaries of the GAMA, however, has no gas collection system.

There is, however, daily records and control of waste tipping on both landfills. The total MSW disposed on these two landfills in the year 2019 was 688,482.65 metric tons; 346,633.17 and 341,849.50 metric tons at Kpone and Nsumia respectively. The composition data (**Table 5**) was used for the computations. The locations of the two landfills (within and outside the city's boundaries) respectively required the use of Scope 1 and Scope 3 of the Excel tool of the CIRIS.

6.2.2 Results of estimation

The total emissions of the various GHGs are presented in tonnage of Carbon IV Oxide equivalence, tCO_2-eq in (**Table 6**). The Methane Commitment Method supports the computation of the total quantity (metric tons) of Methane (CH_4) and biogenic Carbon IV Oxide $CO_{2(b)}$ produced from the disposed waste. These values

Component	Composition (%)
Food waste	36
Paper/cardboard	4
Wood	1
Textile	3
Garden & park waste	16
Nappies	5
Rubber/leather	1
Plastics	16
Metal	2
Glass	2
Other, inert	14
Total	100

Table 5.
MSW composition averages of the GAMA.

Scope	Disposal site	Waste quantity disposed (tons)	Methane, CH_4 (tons)	Carbon IV oxide, CO_2(b) (tons)	Methane, CH_4 CO_{2-}eq	Carbon dioxide, tCO_{2-}eq
1	Kpone landfill	346,633	14,250	39,187	356,247	39,187
3	Nsumia landfill	341,849	14,053	38,646	351,331	38,646
	Total	688,482	28,303	77,833	707,578	77,833
Total emission in carbon dioxide equivalence, tCO_{2-}eq (Tons)					785,411	

Table 6.
GHG computations from the two main landfills using the CIRIS method.

are then converted to Carbon IV Oxide equivalence, tCO_{2-e} (**Table 6**). The regions two main landfills produced 28,303 tons of CH_4 and 77,833 tons of $CO_{2(b)}$ in 2019. The total emissions for CH_4 have been converted to $tCO_{2\text{-eq}}$.

The total GHGs emissions from Scope 1 compares approximately to the emissions from scope 3 (**Table 6**). The management criteria, the MSW quantities and composition disposed of at the two main landfills remain almost equal. A total 395,434 $tCO_{2\text{-eq}}$ of GHGs are emitted from the solid waste generated and disposed on the Kpone landfill in 2019. The corresponding emission realized on the Nsumia landfill site was 389,977 $tCO_{2\text{-eq}}$. These together put the total GHG emissions arising from the MSW of the GAMA in 2019 to 785,411 tCO_2e. Methane (CH_4) accounts for 90% of the GHGs emissions with $CO_{2(b)}$ contribution as 10%. The quantity of GHGs emissions from solid waste disposal is highly influenced by the depth and the management of the landfill. A limitation of this approach at estimating GHG emissions is the possible likelihood of overestimation resulting from the assumption that all the computed methane was generated in the year of computation.

7. Implications and recommendations for system modernization

Characterizing MSW of households, markets and institutions in addition to monitoring and estimating greenhouse gas emissions from solid waste disposal practices in a lower-middle-income city of 4.63 million people is both an elaborate and quite expensive venture. It starts well when solid waste managers and local government decision-makers realize and accept that, they lack the requisite baseline data for planning purposes and are committed to bridge such data gaps. These two factors initiate the thought processes of looking for the requisite funding and the relevant stakeholders to support the participatory gathering of relevant data.

Although funding might be obtained (as the city of Accra received some funding from C40 Cities), it might not be enough to conduct a comprehensive exercise. There is therefore the need for collaboration with researchers and other local stakeholders for technical assistance and logistical support towards participatory and inclusive planning processes. In Accra, the WMD of the city had since 2015 shown commitment to work together with researchers in a locally conceived project to develop interventions to modernize the MSWM system [17].

This structural cooperation was essential to the conception, implementation and delivery of the study to this chapter. The coordinating team was able to secure some logistical support (in terms of sorting grounds and human resources to add to the numbers planned and budgeted for) from a local solid waste management company. There is no doubt, the municipalities of developing countries and economies in transition need technical assistance towards capacity building and research to sustain SWM at the local level [27].

The lead researchers and their counterparts from the municipalities of the GAMA made a firm but difficult decision during budget preparation to refuse remuneration commensurate with international best practices for such an assignment. This was necessary to ensure that the available funds could procure the necessary items for the work and pay for field staff.

Participatory action research processes that strengthens the capacity of MSWM system handlers and relevant stakeholders presents a unique opportunity and a greater potential to support cities of developing countries, to not only close their reliable MSWM data gaps, but also use such data to further assess their systems to assist them to strengthen what works and fix what is failing.

The ISWM Wasteaware framework methodology for assessing the performance of MSWM systems of cities presents an open and free-to-use shareware [28] which can be adopted for use across cites of developing countries as a starting point towards the closing of chronic MSWM data gaps [7]. The framework allows for the collection of background information of a city and baseline waste related data similar to what has been presented in this chapter. It further supports the use of a comprehensive set of indicators to measure and benchmark the performance of all cities, irrespective of their Gross National Income (GNI) levels, in both the physical components (collection, treatment and disposal, recycling) and the governance aspects (user and provider inclusivity, financial sustainability, sound institutions and proactive policies) of the MSWM systems.

The team of stakeholders has evaluated the methodological processes and the results of the characterization and GHGs monitoring exercises in the GAMA and has made the following recommendations towards further research and system improvement.

1. The training programme and the participatory action research approach (PAR) has contributed to strengthening capacities of municipal staffs towards data collection and inclusive decision-making which is essential for continuous development of locally responsive interventions based on the baseline data collected. Municipal authorities and system handlers are encouraged to continue in such participatory processes to stabilize gains, sustain data flows and possibly improve the dynamics of good MSW governance within the GAMA.

2. The use of relevant stakeholders (formal and informal service providers), researchers, municipal officials, policy makers, etc. for the MSW characterization exercise and the validation of the data provide a greater potential for data ownership and usage. We recommend the establishment of a working group of relevant stakeholders to continue with the development of interventions and action plans based on the data obtained.

3. The average daily household solid waste generation rate per capita of 0.7 kg, though lower than that of other similar cities in the developing world is of great concern; partly due to the fact that SW generation rates in lower-middle income cities like Accra is projected to increase by more than threefold by 2050 [9], against the background of population growth, urbanization, improved living standards and inadequacies in system service delivery. Decoupling generation rates from economic growth is the way to go, but that is no easy task [29]. A holistic mix of policies that addresses citizen education and awareness, responsible production and consumption, and extended producer responsibility may provide a pathway. We do not have direct answers to the problem of increasing generation rates, but a possible charging of service user fees based on tonnages generated and collected (different from what is currently practiced) can prove to be a successful intervention towards MSW minimisation in the GAMA.

4. The composition data shows that a significant amount of the city's MSW stream is putrescible organics (within household, market and institutional solid waste streams) in addition to increasing plastics. A planned diversion of these components from disposal has the potential to reduce the GHG emission burden of the current MSW handling practices.

5. We recommend further deliberations among the proposed working group towards the development of locally appropriate interventions for organic waste valorization and plastic recycling purposes. This would require an urgent development of an action plan towards diversion from disposal. The action plan may include among others:

    - introduction and piloting of a three-stream separation of biodegradable waste, plastics and all others at source (the point of generation)

    - investments into infrastructure for locally appropriate and low cost composting and anaerobic digestion [30]

    - establishment of bring-back (buy-back) centres to encourage recycling behavior

    - recognition and integration of the informal waste sector (both in the service- and value-chains to play an integral role in the collection and recycling of segregated materials

    - training of municipal staff and system handlers in the processes of recycling, composting and anaerobic digestion

    Introducing a MSW segregation process must precede with a behavioral study of the latent variables (attitudes, personal norms, subjective norms, and perceived behavioral control) and the dynamics that has the greatest potential to influence waste generators intentions towards MSW separation at source. This also means that plans geared towards the use of results based financing mechanisms as an incentive towards an efficient source separation process needs to be explored further for consideration as part of the action plan.

6. The average calorific value (7.31 MJ/kg) of the MSW of the GAMA is in conformity with the recommended threshold for consideration of the use of Waste-to-Energy (WtE) plants for the treatment of the MSW of the GAMA. But we do not recommend the adoption of such treatment (WtE) technologies, since there are many other factors which need to be addressed if WtE treatment technologies are to be adopted by cities of developing countries [31]. Some of the factors worth addressing include but not limited to:

    - the high moisture content (50%) and high biodegradable fraction (54%) of the MSW of the GAMA;

    - the relatively significant amounts of silts and fines (13%) within the waste;

    - existing inefficiencies in service delivery and the absence of an integrated and sustainable MSWM strategy

    - limited financing in the SWM sector of the GAMA

7. The average carbon to nitrogen ratio of the MSW of the GAMA is below recommended averages to support efficient aerobic and anaerobic valorization processes (composting and aerobic digestion). This can be improved upon by the addition of carbon related materials such as saw dust if valorization processes are to be considered as part of the treatment options in the action plan.

8. Soliciting for support from local stakeholders is a necessary undertaking to support the efforts of external funding organizations in such research studies. When planned well, local stakeholders can provide support in many aspects to reduce the budgetary constraints which often prevents system handlers in generating such relevant baseline data.

8. Conclusion

The Chinese Confucian philosopher Xun Kuang is credited to have written the statement paraphrased as: "Tell me and I forget, teach me and I may remember, involve me and I learn." The work in this chapter has demonstrated how participatory engagement strategies can support the planning and closing of reliable data gaps in MSW quantities, composition, chemical proprieties and GHG emission burdens of the municipalities of the GAMA; a recurring challenge for most developing countries. The average household MSW generation rate per capita for the municipalities of the GAMA is 0.7 kg per day. That for institutions is 0.83 kg per day and markets are recorded to generate 1.32 kg per stall per day. The composition of the waste has significant percentage of biodegradable (54%), plastics (16%), silts and fines (13%). Bulk density is 518 kg per cubic metre and the moisture content of the waste is 50%. The average C: N ratio is 19:1 well below the recommended 30:1 for efficient waste valorization processes. The laboratory measured calorific value of 6.74 MJ/kg is comparable to the computed value of 7.31 MJ/kg. The methodological process of gathering the data in addition to the monitored and estimated concentrations of MSWM-related GHG will support system handlers to not only replicate and update data flows but most importantly develop locally responsive interventions to address the mirage of SWM challenges confronting the GAMA and other developing countries.

Acknowledgements

We are grateful for the support of the Municipal Chief Executive of the AMA, Mohammed Adjei Sowah, the C40 Cities representative of the city of Accra, Desmond C. Appiah, the director and deputy director of the WMD of the AMA, Solomon Noi and Victor N. Kotey for their support for the research to this chapter. We thank the municipalities of the GAMA and especially the AMA for their collaborative support. We appreciate the support and diverse roles of the following institutions towards the research to this chapter namely: the Directorate of Research, Innovation and Consultancy of the University of Cape Coast, Nemas Consult Ghana Limited and Africa Environmental Sanitation Consult, Jekora Ventures Ghana Limited and Waste Landfills Ghana Limited.

The research to this chapter was funded by the C40 Cities Climate Leadership Group Incorporated under the Empowering Cities with Data Project grant [R-1609-01540].

Conflict of interest

No potential conflict of interest was reported by the authors.

Author details

Kwaku Oduro-Appiah[1]* and Abraham Afful[2]

1 University of Cape Coast, Cape Coast, Ghana

2 Waste Management Consultant, Accra, Ghana

*Address all correspondence to: koduro-appiah@ucc.edu.gh

IntechOpen

© 2020 The Author(s). Licensee IntechOpen. This chapter is distributed under the terms of the Creative Commons Attribution License (http://creativecommons.org/licenses/by/3.0), which permits unrestricted use, distribution, and reproduction in any medium, provided the original work is properly cited. (cc) BY

References

[1] Guerrero LA, Maas G, Hogland W. Solid waste management challenges for cities in developing countries. Waste Management. 2013;33(1):220–32.

[2] Godfrey L, Scott D. Improving waste management through a process of learning: the South African waste information system. Waste Management & Research. 2011;29(5):501–11.

[3] Oduro-Appiah K, Scheinberg A, Afful A, de Vries N. The contribution of participatory engagement strategies to reliable data gathering and inclusive policies in developing countries: Municipal solid waste management data in the Greater Accra Metropolitan Area of Ghana. African Journal of Science, Technology, Innovation and Development. 2020:1–12.

[4] Mohee R, Bundhoo MAZ. A comparative analysis of solid waste management in developed and developing countries. In: Mohee R, Simelane T, editors. Future Directions of Municipal Solid Waste Management in Africa. 6. Pretoria, South Africa: The Africa Institute of South Africa; 2015

[5] Worrell WA, Vesilind PA. Solid Waste Engineering. Stamford, Connecticut: Cengage Learning; 2011. 427 p.

[6] Diaz LF, Savage GM, Eggerth LL. Solid Waste Management. California, USA: CalRecovery Inc.; 2005. 558 p.

[7] UNEP. Africa Waste Management Outlook. Nairobi, Kenya: United Nations Environment Programme; 2018 [Available from: http://hdl.handle.net/20.500.11822/25514.

[8] Oteng-Ababio M, Annepu R, Bourtsalas A, Intharathirat R, Charoenkit S. Urban Solid Waste Management. In: Rosenzweig C, Solecki WD, Romero-Lankao P, Mehrotra S, Dhakal S, Ibrahim SA, editors. Climate Change and Cities: Second Assessment Report of the Urban Climate Change Research Network. New York: Cambridge University Press; 2018. p. 553–82.

[9] Kaza S, Yao LC, Bhada-Tata P, Van Woerden F. What a Waste 2.0: A Global Snapshot of Solid Waste Management to 2050. Urban Development Series. Washington, DC: World Bank. The World Bank; 2018.

[10] Scheinberg A, Wilson DC, Rodić L. Solid Waste Management in the World's Cities. In: Scheinberg A, Wilson DC, Rodic-Wiersma L, editors. UN-Habitat's State of Water and Sanitation in the World's Cities Series. Newcastle-onTyne, UK: Earthscan; 2010.

[11] Rodić L, Wilson DC. Resolving governance issues to achieve priority sustainable development goals related to solid waste management in developing countries. Sustainability. 2017;9(3):404.

[12] Coffey M, Coad A. Collection of municipal solid waste in developing countries: UN-Habitat, United Nations Human Settlements Programme: Nairobi, Kenya; 2010.

[13] Serge Kubanza N, Simatele MD. Sustainable solid waste management in developing countries: a study of institutional strengthening for solid waste management in Johannesburg, South Africa. Journal of Environmental Planning and Management. 2020;63(2):175–88.

[14] Herat S. Waste management training and capacity building for local authorities in developing countries. Waste Management and Research. 2015; 33(1):1–2.

[15] McIntyre A. Participatory Action Research. Los Angeles, USA: Sage Publications; 2007.

[16] Oduro-Appiah K, Afful A, Kotey V, de Vries N. Working with the Informal

Service Chain as a Locally Appropriate Strategy for Sustainable Modernization of Municipal Solid Waste Management Systems in Lower-Middle Income Cities: Lessons from Accra, Ghana. Resources. 2019;8(1):12.

[17] Oduro-Appiah K, Scheinberg A, Mensah A, Afful A, Boadu HK, de Vries N. Assessment of the municipal solid waste management system in Accra, Ghana: A" Wasteaware' benchmark indicator approach. Waste Management and Research. 2017;35(11):1149–58.

[18] Cochran WG. Sampling Techniques. New York, USA: John Wiley & Sons; 1977.

[19] ASTM. D5231–92, Standard Test Method for Determination of the Composition of Unprocessed Municipal Solid Waste. West Conshohocken, PA, USA: ASTM International; 2008.

[20] Motsara M, Roy RN. Guide to laboratory establishment for plant nutrient analysis: Food and Agriculture Organization of the United Nations Rome; 2008.

[21] Miezah K, Obiri-Danso K, Kádár Z, Fei-Baffoe B, Mensah MY. Municipal solid waste characterization and quantification as a measure towards effective waste management in Ghana. Waste Management. 2015;46:15–27.

[22] Wilson DC, Whiteman AD, Tormin A. Strategic Planning Guide for Municipal Solid Waste Management. Washington: World Bank; 2001.

[23] Lin X, Wang F, Chi Y, Huang Q, Yan J. A simple method for predicting the lower heating value of municipal solid waste in China based on wet physical composition. Waste Management. 2015;36:24–32.

[24] Zhou H, Meng A, Long Y, Li Q, Zhang Y. An overview of characteristics of municipal solid waste fuel in China: physical, chemical composition and heating value. Renewable and Sustainable Energy Reviews. 2014;36:107–22.

[25] Lin C, Gillespie J, Schuder M, Duberstein W, Beverland I, Heal M. Evaluation and calibration of Aeroqual series 500 portable gas sensors for accurate measurement of ambient ozone and nitrogen dioxide. Atmospheric Environment. 2015;100:111–6.

[26] Oduro-Appiah K, Scheinberg A, Miezah K, Mensah A, de Vries NK. Existing Realities and Sustainable Pathways for Solid Waste Management in Ghana. In: Pariatamby A, Hamid FS, Bhatti MS, editors. Sustainable Waste Management Challenges in Developing Countries. Pennsylvania, USA: IGI Global; 2020. p. 115–43.

[27] Marino AL, Chaves GdLD, dos Santos Junior JL. Do Brazilian municipalities have the technical capacity to implement solid waste management at the local level? Journal of Cleaner Production. 2018;188:378–86.

[28] Wilson DC, Rodić L, Cowing MJ, Velis CA, Whiteman AD, Scheinberg A, et al. 'Wasteaware' benchmark indicators for integrated sustainable waste management in cities. Waste Management. 2015;35:329–42.

[29] Fell D, Cox J, Wilson DC. Future waste growth, modelling and decoupling. Waste Management & Research. 2010;28(3):281–6.

[30] Rousta K, Ordoñez I, Bolton K, Dahlén L. Support for designing waste sorting systems: A mini review. Waste Management and Research. 2017;35(11): 1099–111.

[31] Mutz D, Hengevoss D, Hugi C, Gross T. Waste-to-Energy Options in Municipal Solid Waste Management A Guide for Decision Makers in Developing and Emerging Countries. Deutsche Gesellschaft für Internationale Zusammenarbeit (GIZ) GmbH. 2017.

Section 3

Economic Techniques for Solid Waste Management

Chapter 4

Guide for Organising a Community Clean-up Campaign

Innocent Rangeti and Bloodless Dzwairo

Abstract

While it is the government's and municipality's mandate to ensure that its citizens stay in a clean and safe environment, it is of concern that waste management remains a big challenge in urban areas especially in developing countries. Increased economic development, rapid population growth and improvement of living standards are among the factors attributed to increased quantity and complexity of solid waste being generated. On the other hand, while people generate wastes, they continue to be looked at as passive recipients of municipality services. Ultimately, citizens fail to recognise their role in waste management and become unwilling to either pay for service delivery or participate in clean-up campaigns. Waste dumps are prime breeding sites for communicable disease vectors such as rodents, mosquitoes and houseflies, which can exacerbate the prevalence of water, food and waterborne diseases such as cholera and typhoid. This chapter thus describes the methodology of successfully conducting a community-led cleanup campaign. It is based on experience gained during implementation of an urban water, sanitation and hygiene (WASH) project. Ward level clean-up campaigns were organised and conducted by community members and local leaders. Besides clearing illegal dumpsites, the activity was also used to raise awareness on the consequence of waste dumping. The experience showed that organising a clean-up campaign only requires careful timeous planning. Overall, it was concluded that not only does the activity serve the practical purpose of cleaning, but it also creates a greater sense of unity and friendship among community members. Additionally, the power of beautification in a clean-up campaign wold naturally motivate residents to believe that their problems could be solved, resulting in a shared responsibility for sustainable management of waste and commons at local level.

Keywords: clean-up campaign, solid waste manage, community participation, illegal waste dumping, waste dumps, community volunteers

1. Introduction

Solid waste is any material that is primarily not a liquid or gas and is unwanted and/or unvalued, discarded by its owner, and can be from domestic, commercial or industrial operations [1]. Globally, there are ongoing campaigns to promote sustainable use of the environment while considering the negative effects of waste in general as well as climate change, which have become evident in a number of regions [2–5]. In particular, the primary aim of sustainable solid waste management is to address concerns related to environmental pollution, public health, land use, resource management and socio-economic impacts associated with improper disposal of waste. However, as urbanisation continues, the management of solid waste in particular, remains a major public health and environmental concern. Specifically in Zimbabwe's urban areas, more than 2.5 million tonnes of industrial and household waste is produced per annum [6]. The bulk of this waste has been noted to end up in open, illegal dump sites, urban streams and wetlands, resulting in blocked drainage systems, contaminated surface and groundwater, which causes several environmental, health and economical challenges.

Even though several studies have been conducted globally on waste management and the effects of pollution [7–11] this unfortunately, has not translated into an improvement in solid waste management especially in developing countries such as Zimbabwe. Various factors, for example, rapid urbanisation, population and economic growth as well as elevated human standard way of living have also been cited as key determinants enhancing waste generation in developing countries [12]. Zimbabwe, despite having some well crafted legislations on waste management (Environmental Management Act (EMA), Chapter 20: 27, Urban Councils Act, Chapter 29:15), has not been spared from solid waste management challenges. These include low collection coverage, irregular collection services, crude open dumping and burning. Section 70 (1) of the country's EMA Act stipulates that 'No person shall discharge or dispose any waste in a manner that causes environmental pollution or ill health to any person'. Additionally, Section 83 (1) of the same Act prohibits littering by stating that: No person shall discard, dump or leave any litter on any land or water surface, street, road or site in or at any place except in a container provided for that purpose or at a place which has been specially designated, indicated, provided or set apart for such purpose [13].

Solid Waste management entails the collection, transportation and disposal services. While it is a mandate of governments and local authorities to ensure that their citizens stay in clean and safe environments, it is of concern that solid waste management still remains a big challenge in urban areas, especially of developing countries. Various studies have highlighted that active community participation is essential for improved service delivery including solid waste management [14–16]. Community participation can comprise varying degrees of involvement of the local community ranging from contribution of cash, labour, consultation, adaptation of behaviour, involvement in administration, management and decision-making. Countries continue to be expected to progress in improved waste management by 2020; through the sharing of knowledge, experience and best practices [17]. The benefits of this integrated sustainable solid waste management approach includes natural resource conservation, reduction of the amount of waste to be recycled or transported for land filling, decrease in air pollution and greenhouse production, reduction in production of toxic waste and ultimately reduction in cost related to the collection and disposal of waste [18]. Countries thus need to take all possible measures to prevent unsound management or illegal dumping of waste particularly hazardous waste especially given the negative effects of waste.

2. Effects of illegal waste dumping

Poorly managed wastes have several effects and impact on human and animal health, economic development and social impact [19–21]. Waste dumps are prime breeding sites for communicable disease vectors such as rodents, mosquitoes and houseflies [22]. These vectors tend to exacerbate the prevalence of food, water and waterborne diseases such as cholera, typhoid and malaria, among other. For example, Zimbabwe experienced a huge cholera outbreak between from 2008 to 2009, recording 98,952 cases and cases and a mobidity of 4288. Key drivers cited for this huge outbreak was inadequate supply of good quality water as well as poor solid waste management [23]. On the other hand, waste incineration, which had and continue as common practise in urban areas, releases fumes that naturally cause acute respiratory infections as well as odours that make the environment uninhabitable. It is reported that less than 30% of urban waste in developing countries is collected and disposed appropriately.

Leachate from dumpsite pollutes underground water, which has emerged as an alternative water source in most urban areas such as Harare in Zimbabwe, as the city continues to experience serious municipal water supply challenges. Besides the public health concern, illegal waste dumps tend to reduce the aesthetic status of a neighbourhood, thus reducing the economic value of properties within the vicinity [24]. Solid waste tends to clog drains thus causing flooding. Additionally, solid waste may also harm animals that consume it unknowingly, as well as affect economic development through diminished environmental value and tourism, which are generally viewed as externalities as they are negative costs [25], which need to be incorporated into sustainable development models.

The proliferation of rubbish is attributed to many factors, key among them being, population increase, rapid urban growth, lack of environmental education, inadequate bins and irregularities in waste collection by the responsible authority [12]. While efforts are being made by some local authorities to secure modern state of art waste management equipment such as compactors, this development has not yielded the desired results as communities still continue to dump waste. Insufficient technical services, lack of spare parts and low maintenance budgets are among the factors attributed to the poor performance of advanced waste management technologies currently being adopted by some local authorities in low developed countries. When such sophisticated equipment breaks down the entire waste management system fails. On the other hand, generally people litter because for lack of ownership for the public facilities and areas, because they believe someone else will do it, eg the municipality, or that they find the litter tolerable or even that they would have given up since the litter had already accumulated anyway. Hence the challenge where common resources are subject to neglect and the widely used phrase "tragedy of the commons" [26–29].

Rangeti, Tendere [16] highlighted that the failure of the top-down approaches towards waste management especially in developing countries, cannot only been attributed to technical and financial challenges, but also to the low involvement of communities in service delivery. Whereas every person generates waste, they continue to be looked at as passive recipients of municipality services. Ultimately, citizens fail to recognise their role in waste management and become unwilling to either pay for service delivery or participate in clean-up campaigns. Dillon and Steifel [30] further elaborated that people's engagement involves the deliberate and systematic mobilisation of local communities around issues and problems of common concern. Even LeBan, Perry [31] attested to the understanding that people gain information, skills, and experience in community involvement that helps them take control of their own lives and challenge social systems. Thus the success of any programme of action depends on the response by citizens, particularly the targeted beneficiaries [32, 33]. With that background, this paper is based on experiences by the author during implementation of a water, sanitation and hygiene project in Bindura, Zimbabwe, where the community was engaged to voluntarily clean up there neighbourhoods. The paper provides lessons on how to organise an effective community ward based clean-up campaign [34].

3. Study area

Bindura (**Figure 1**) is the administrative capital of Mashonaland Central Province, Zimbabwe. It is located in the Mazowe Valley, about 88 km north-east of Harare. It is made up of 12 wards. According to the 2012 census, Bindura had a population of has 46,275.

During implementation of a water, sanitation and hygiene project, the project team successfully mobilised communities to conduct 27 ward based clean-up campaigns over a period of eight months (February – September 2015). This was done following some ward-based sensitisation on the importance of improved waste management and hygiene issues. The Citizen Supporting Service Delivery (CSSD) concept was used to sensitise the community on the need for participation in waste management efforts. In addition, five waste management groups undertaking various waste recoveries and recycling projects as shown in **Figure 2**, were established.

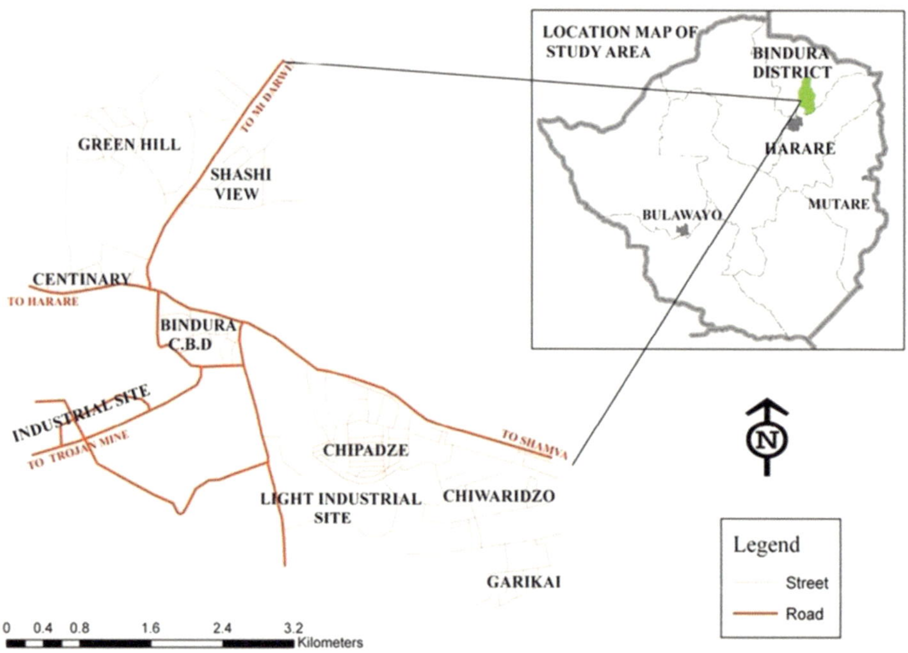

Figure 1.
Bindura town map.

Figure 2.
Illegal waste dumping at Chipadze shopping Centre (left) and waste recycling through making of bins (right).

4. Methodology

While considering that a collaborative effort to clean the local environment can send a clear message to community members on the need for them to be good stewards of their environment, sensitisation meetings were conducted in the 12 residential wards of the study area to educate communities on the consequences of waste dumping. Communities were encouraged to take action and be responsible to the environment. The result was a series of community-led ward based clean-ups to clear illegal dumpsites at street corners, shopping centres and open spaces. The clean-ups were initiated and coordinated at ward level by community health facilitators and councillors who were local leaders at ward level. **Figure 3** summaries the methodology developed from the experience.

4.1 STAGE 1: Planning

4.1.1 Organising a committee and supervisors

Organising a working committee is one of the crucial initial steps when planning to conduct a clean-up campaign. The committee should be led by a coordinator who oversees the activity and is the primary contact person during the event. Committee size depends on various determinants such as tasks to be performed and number of volunteers expected to participate. In general, committee members should be energetic, responsible and able to enforce the schedule while motivating participants to complete their assigned tasks. Choosing a community member with an interest in hygiene and environmental protection issues such as community health facilitator makes sense given their dedication. However, it is critical that each member is comfortable with his/her tasks.

Among the responsibilities of a committee is to (1) set the agenda, (2) secure tools and ensuring their return, (3) mobilise volunteers and (4) solicit contributions and donations. Where a large number of volunteers are expected, consider forming some sub groups and selecting group coordinators. A group coordinator should be a good communicator and able to handle arising situations. To avoid confusion, the committee and coordinators should visit the proposed site for action for

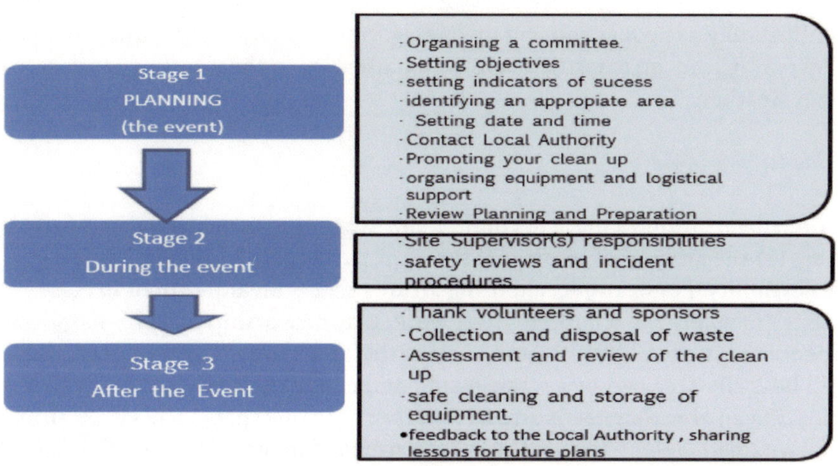

Figure 3.
Methodology for organising a clean-up.

familiarisation prior to the clean-up day. On the day of the clean-up, group coordinators must arrive earlier than the rest of the community, at the event meeting point and when possible, identifiable by reflectors.

4.1.2 Setting objectives of a clean-up campaign

To ensure that participants work towards the same outcome, the committee needs to set specific goals and define the scope of the campaign. The scope should clearly detail what is to be done, when, how and by whom. The objectives must be clear, achievable and measurable, with common goals for a clean-up campaign being to remove waste, environmental protection awareness and fundraising.

4.1.3 Setting indicators for success

It is important for the committee to clearly define how success will be evaluated. The working committee will define and list measurable indicators of success. Examples of such indicators are; (1) number and types of participants (e.g., community members), (2) amount/weight of refuse collected (3) approximate area cleaned, (4) time spent and (5) the impact of clean-up activity on the targeted area. It is also important to remember collecting that information on the day of activity. Taking photos before and after the event will assist in measuring the impact of the event.

4.1.4 Setting up the campaign date

Advance planning is crucial for the smooth conducting of a clean-up campaign. Because good planning takes time, it is reasonable to set a date about one or two months in advance. When deciding the date, consider several factors such as; weather, availability of volunteers and availability of waste haulage truck. In most cases, Saturdays are ideal for a community clean-up since most people do not go to work. Beside the availability of participants, 16 clean-up campaigns conducted in Bindura were conducted on Saturdays given the availability of waste haulage trucks from the municipality. Considering a day that coincides with the municipality refuse collection routine in that given area also makes sense. It is reasonable to avoid a day that conflicts with a local event such as a major sporting game, church event or political rally as people will end up having to choose to attend to the more prioritised events. Clean-up campaigns are better attended in the morning especially in warmer weather.

4.1.5 Identifying a place

When determining a place to conduct the campaign, consider various factors such as; (1) the amount of waste, (2) safety of participants (3) location and (4) accessibility. For example, choosing an area that is meaningful or in close proximity to where the volunteers live, work, play or worship makes sense given that people are normally motivated to clean their own area. The proposed area should be easily accessed by a waste hauler and emergency services. It is worthwhile considering an area that needs attention rather than one that is already clean and well maintained. Where the goal of the clean-up campaign is to raise awareness, public places such as the recreational park and shopping centres will have a huge impact. In some instances, the local authority may recommend an area that needs to be cleaned. Visiting the proposed area during the planning stage would assist in refining the project goals and logistical arrangements. For example, where a school

DOI: http://dx.doi.org/10.5772/intechopen.94515

health club or youth are volunteers, consider an area that is safe. Creating a site map showing 'hotspots', dumpsite would assist in evaluating the results. Once the area has been chosen, decide on a convenient meeting point for participants.

4.1.6 Coordinate the activity with the local authority

Since a clean-up campaign significantly contributes towards the delivery of the local authority's environmental sustainability commitment, it is important to register your event with them. Beside, local authorities can provide support logistically and financially, and thus it is always worth discussing the proposal with relevant personnel. Assistance may be in form of; (1) recommendations for a clean-up area, (2) permission to access public area, (3) promotion of the event, (4) free waste haulage service and (5) free disposal of collected waste at designated dumpsite. Once permission has been granted and date confirmed by the local authority, the committee can start mobilising volunteers.

4.1.7 Mobilisation of volunteers

While a clean-up campaign can be conducted using any population size, finding volunteers can be the hardest part of this activity. However, it is still the key for conducting a successful event. One of the best practises of a community based clean-up is the participation by all ages despite cultural background and abilities. Involving children would assist in efforts to foster them into adult that are responsible to the environment and who are able to work harmoniously with others (**Figure 4**). It is important to quantitatively determine the number of volunteers needed and be prepared to accommodate others who might hear about the activity and also want to participate.

Depending on the targeted volunteers, various methods can be used to invite volunteers. Newsletters, notice boards, email, flyers etc. are effective in low density community. Community organisations such churches, community health clubs, school health clubs etc., are also effective ways of inviting volunteers. In Bindura, community health clubs and the local leaders played an important role in mobilising the volunteers. Inviting representatives of relevant stakeholders such government

Figure 4.
Community briefing and organising before the start of a clean-up.

ministries, religious and traditional bodies would be influential in the program and in mobilising volunteers.

Volunteers should be reminded on relevant information such as: location, date and time of the clean-up and clothing (e.g. enclosed footwear, gloves, hat, etc.), a week or two before the event.

4.1.8 Soliciting funding

Where possible, consider mobilising donations in the form of refreshments or financial assistance for the event. Local businesses are normally willing to sponsor clean-ups to demonstrate their commitment to the protection of the environment. In some cases, the organiser might encourage the business community to advertise their business by printing t-shirts for volunteers, which also bears an environmental protection message. In Bindura, the councillors which are local leaders were more involved in soliciting for donations.

4.1.9 Promotion and media coverage

It is important for the community to know what the facilitators are doing. Publicity and promotion of an event depend on various factors such as budget and time. When possible, consider inviting the local media such as local newspaper to ensure that inspiring success stories are published. Environmental protection organisations also normally have interest in such event and would be delighted to promote. In Bindura, a government parastatal, the Environmental Management Agency (EMA) supported the clean-ups with awareness raising vehicles as shown in **Figure 5**. It is important to recognise that publicity includes promoting the clean-up before, sharing the results and thanking volunteers and sponsors afterwards.

4.1.10 Organising equipment and logistical support

The number and type of tools required vary depending on the area to be cleaned, number of participants and type of waste. Ensuring that there are enough tools for

Figure 5.
Awareness raising during community-led clean-up campaign using a vehicle provided by the environmental management agency in ward 7.

the clean-up is critical to a successful event. It is important to also ensure that all equipment is checked during and after the event. In some cases, volunteers might be required to bring their own equipment for the event. Prior arrangement should be made with the local authority department responsible for solid waste management to determine if a waste haulage truck can be arranged for this day. Where the municipality is not able to collect the garbage, consider alternatives such as a private waste haulage company.

4.2 STAGE 2: Day of the event

Group coordinators should arrive first and register all participants. Thereafter, the project coordinator should (**Figure 4**);

1. thank volunteers for coming

2. highlight the goals and importance of the campaign

3. highlight the roles and responsibility of the participant

4. review of safety and emergency procedures

5. schedule for the event

6. site plan review, and

7. distribution of the equipment.

Group coordinators should be reminded of their roles in assisting their respective working groups. They should encourage their teams to accomplish their assigned tasks and coordinate the removal of the collected litter.

4.2.1 Safety review and compliance

Ensure that all participants have gloves and dust mask. Protective gloves prevent cuts associated with the handling of sharp objects with bare hands. Be clear with your volunteers about how to handle hazardous waste such as pesticide containers, cleaning chemicals containers and sharp objects such broken glass. Closed feet shoes are safer than sandals or flip-flops. Where children will be participating, plan for adequate adult supervision (**Figure 6**).

4.3 STAGE 3: After the clean-up

After, the clean-up, the project coordinator should thank everyone who volunteered their time and effort. A follow up thank you letters should be written to all stakeholders including sponsors who would have assisted. Remind participants to wash their hands especially when refreshments are to be served. Where a hand-washing facility is not available, arrangements must be in place for an alternative facility such as a portable water dispenser and soap.

4.3.1 Disposing of garbage

One of the most important aspects, when organising a community clean-up, is organising for removal of trash. Waste should be removed as soon as possible after

Figure 6.
Chipadze primary school health Club cleaning up Chipadze shopping Centre.

Figure 7.
Community members clearing a dumpsite during a clean-up campaign.

the event to prevent the creation of unhygienic conditions and to avoid it becoming an eyesore and an environmental externality (**Figure 7**). It is the responsibility of the project coordinator to make arrangements with the local authority for the collection of garbage collected. Where the local authority is not able to provide haulage service, prior arrangements should be done for alternative methods such as private companies.

4.3.2 Assessment of the results

It is important to assess the event as soon as possible after it occurs. Success is measured using the indicator listed during the planning stage. A report detailing the number of volunteers (aggregated by sex and age group), hours worked, area covered, illegal dumpsite cleared, weight of waste removed among other indicators should be produced. Including lesson learnt and suggestions should help in improving the next clean-up. It should be remembered to share the results and photographs, where possible, with all stakeholders.

5. Lessons Learnt

1. Community participation is indispensable to the success of solid waste management at the local level.

2. Clean-up campaigns offer the residents an opportunity to demonstrate their willingness to do community development work and show that they are good citizens.

3. Community participation is key to the successful implementation of any initiative towards solid waste management in urban areas.

4. A clean-up campaign is an effective platform to show communities that waste management is important.

5. If educated, a community has the power to police each other on littering and waste dumping

6. Urban communities, are more "reactive" than "proactive".

7. The demand for improved solid waste management needs to be facilitated by community groups such as health clubs.

8. Residents are willing to look after their environment, if educated

6. Conclusion

Lack of awareness and low participation of communities tend to exacerbate solid waste management challenges that are being experienced by the urban population especially the poor communities. People's attitudes towards waste and understanding of the consequences of poor waste management play a significant role in encouraging their participation in improved solid waste management. By participating in clean-ups, citizens can contribute in creating immediate and long-term solutions for their neighbourhoods. Clean-ups can serve as catalysts for permanent changes in behaviour and attitude as well as encouraging communities to adopt good practices such as reuse and recycling, which have a profound effect on waste management in a community. The experience also showed that organising a clean-up campaign requires careful timeous planning. Overall, it was concluded that not only did the activity serve the practical purpose of cleaning up, but it also created a greater sense of unity and friendship among community members. A clean-up provides community members an opportunity to bond with one another. It also assists to cross or dissolve racial, cultural, ethnic and other established neighbourhood divides. Further, the power of beautification in a clean-up campaign would naturally motivate residents to believe that their problems could be solved. This would then result in a shared responsibility for sustainable management of waste and commons at local level. This activity assisted the community to measure (hypothetical) how much control they had over their lives if they worked together for a common goal. Therefore, communities need to consider clean-up campaigns as ongoing activities that they could turn into neighbourhood tradition.

Author details

Innocent Rangeti[1]* and Bloodless Dzwairo[2]

1 Faculty of Health Sciences, Department of Community Health Studies, Durban University of Technology, Durban, South Africa

2 Durban University of Technology, Civil Engineering Midlands, Imbali, South Africa

*Address all correspondence to: innoranger@gmail.com

IntechOpen

© 2021 The Author(s). Licensee IntechOpen. This chapter is distributed under the terms of the Creative Commons Attribution License (http://creativecommons.org/licenses/by/3.0), which permits unrestricted use, distribution, and reproduction in any medium, provided the original work is properly cited.

References

[1] Oyedele O, editor Municipal Solid Waste Management as Panacea for Economic Development and Wealth Creation: The Roles of the Private Sector. Being text of Paper presented at the International Conference on Solid Waste Management (ICSW) on April; 2014.

[2] Koop S, Koetsier L, Doornhof A, Reinstra O, Van Leeuwen C, Brouwer S, et al. Assessing the governance capacity of cities to address challenges of water, waste, and climate change. Water Resources Management. 2017;31(11):3427-43.

[3] Koop SH, van Leeuwen CJ. The challenges of water, waste and climate change in cities. Environment, development and sustainability. 2017;19(2):385-418.

[4] Rahmasary AN, Robert S, Chang I-S, Jing W, Park J, Bluemling B, et al. Overcoming the challenges of water, waste and climate change in Asian cities. Environmental management. 2019;63(4):520-35.

[5] Rahmasary AN, Koop Steven H, van Leeuwen Cornelis J. Assessing Bandung's governance challenges of water, waste and climate change. Lessons from urban Indonesia. Integrated Environmental Assessment and Management. 2020.

[6] Practical_Action. Emerging Issues in Urban Waste Management Workshop Report (Unpublished). 2006.

[7] Yukalang N, Clarke B, Ross K. Solid waste management solutions for a rapidly urbanizing area in Thailand: Recommendations based on stakeholder input. International journal of environmental research and public health. 2018;15(7):1302.

[8] Nyarai MP, Willard Z, Moses M, Ngenzile M. Challenges of solid waste management in Zimbabwe: a case study of Sakubva high density suburb. Journal of Environment and Waste Management. 2016;3(2):142-55.

[9] Paya C. An integrated system of waste management in a developing country case study: Santiago de Cali, Colombia: University of Waterloo; 2016.

[10] Jerie S. Analysis of institutional solid waste management in Gweru, Zimbabwe. Eastern Africa Social Science Research Review. 2006;22(1):103-25.

[11] Nyanzou P. Analysis of solid waste management practices in high density suburbs: A case of Budiriro 3, Harare. Unpublished dissertation, Midlands State University. 2014.

[12] Minghua Z, Xiumin F, Rovetta A, Qichang H, Vicentini F, Bingkai L, et al. Municipal solid waste management in Pudong new area, China. Waste management. 2009;29(3):1227-33.

[13] Environmental Management Act: Chapter 20:27, (2004).

[14] Ekere W, Mugisha J, Drake L. Factors influencing waste separation and utilization among households in the Lake Victoria crescent, Uganda. Waste management. 2009;29(12):3047-51.

[15] Kalwani JDS. Community participation in municipal solid waste management in informal settlements: morogoro municipality, Tanzania: The Open University of Tanzania; 2010.

[16] Rangeti I, Tendere T, Guzha E, Gwisai R. Community Participation, the Missing Link towards Sustainable Solid Waste Management: Lessons from Bindura Town, Zimbabwe. Greener Journal of Social Sciences. 2018;8(2):018-28.

[17] UNCSD. Report of the United Nations Conference on sustainable development, Rio de Janeiro, Brazil 20-22 June, 2012. 2012.

[18] Khatib IA. Municipal solid waste management in developing countries: Future challenges and possible opportunities. Integrated waste management. 2011;2:35-48.

[19] Cabral JP. Water microbiology. Bacterial pathogens and water. International journal of environmental research and public health. 2010;7(10):3657-703.

[20] Achudume A, Olawale J. Microbial pathogens of public health significance in waste dumps and common sites. Journal of Environmental Biology. 2007;28(1):151.

[21] Ziraba AK, Haregu TN, Mberu B. A review and framework for understanding the potential impact of poor solid waste management on health in developing countries. Archives of Public Health. 2016;74(1):1-11.

[22] Ekram W, Wahab E, Safaa M. Adverse health problems among municipality workers in Alexandria. International Journal of Preventive Medicine. 2013;5:545-56.

[23] Chimusoro A, Maphosa S, Manangazira P, Phiri I, Nhende T, Danda S, et al. Responding to cholera outbreaks in Zimbabwe: Building resilience over time. Current Issues in global health. 2018.

[24] Onifade O, Nwabotu F. Implications and causes of illegal refuse dumps in Ilorin South local government area, Kwara State. Oman Chapter of Arabian Journal of Business and Management Review. 2014;34(2597):1-8.

[25] Dzwairo B. Modelling raw water quality variability in order to predict cost of water treatment [DTech thesis]. Pretoria: Tshwane University of Technology; 2011.

[26] Freije AM, Naser HA, Abdulla KH. Attitudes and opinions towards public littering in the Kingdom of Bahrain. Arab Journal of Basic and Applied Sciences. 2019;26(1):354-61.

[27] Ostrom E. Tragedy of the commons. The new palgrave dictionary of economics. 2008;2.

[28] Schultz PW, Bator RJ, Large LB, Bruni CM, Tabanico JJ. Littering in context: Personal and environmental predictors of littering behavior. Environment and Behavior. 2013;45(1):35-59.

[29] Khawaja FS, Shah A. Determinants of littering: An experimental analysis. The Pakistan Development Review. 2013:157-68.

[30] Dillon B, Steifel M. Making the concept concrete: The UNRISD participation programme. Bulletin. 1987;21.

[31] LeBan K, Perry H, Crigler L, Colvin C. Community participation in large-scale community health worker programs. Developing and strengthening community health worker programs at scale: a reference guide and case studies for program managers and policy makers Washington, DC: USAID Maternal and Child Health Integrated Project (MCHIP). 2014.

[32] Mubita A, Libati M, Mulonda M. The importance and limitations of participation in development projects and programmes. European Scientific Journal. 2017;13(5):238-51.

[33] Cornwall A. Unpacking 'Participation': models, meanings and

practices. Community development journal. 2008;43(3):269-83.

[34] Martin M. Clean City Community Clean-up Guide. 2005. In: Clean City COMMUNITY CLEAN-UP: Guide 2005 [Internet]. Toronto: TDSB Printing Services.

Chapter 5

Economics of Solid Waste Management: A Review

Muniyandi Balasubramanian

Abstract

Solid Waste Management is one of the importance environmental issues at many developing countries. There is a lack of studies on economic analysis of solid waste management in the many cities at the national and international level. Most of the Municipal Corporation or city management is the major responsibility for better waste management. However, the local governments has been allocated budget for solid waste management without analysing cost and benefit of solid waste. Although, waste management budget is focusing on collected waste but, uncollected waste has been creating a number of socio, economic and health issues. Therefore, this chapter has presents a details review on economics of solid waste management at the various developing and developed countries. The main policy implication of the paper is to emphasis on better understanding of economic importance of solid waste management to the local policy makers.

Keywords: economics, solid waste, cost, recycling

1. Introduction

Solid waste is the byproducts of human activities such as production, consumption and distribution of various goods in the society. There are a number research has been investigated in the various aspects such as technology, innovation, recycling of solid waste management in the developing and developed countries. There are a lack of studies on economic analysis of solid waste management particularly in the developing countries, for example cost and revenue aspects [1, 2]. Most of the municipal corporation has not been maintained proper data on solid waste generation, collection, transportation and final disposal. Therefore economists are confused economic estimation of solid waste management [3]. Moreover, economic analysis of solid waste management is the most helpful to local policy makers on various aspects for instance, designing waste management tax/charges or subsidies at the municipal level [4]; cost and benefits of waste to energy [5] and determining of urban property through the better environmental amenities [6, 7]. There are various economics estimation of per ton of solid waste management in India, For example, National Institute of Urban Affairs [8] had estimated at Rs 135 for per ton of solid waste collection and disposal and another study by National Solid Waste Association [9] had calculated at Rs 417 per ton of solid waste management [3, 10]. Therefore, this chapter has discussed the economics of solid waste management and public policy at the municipal level in various developing and developed countries.

IntechOpen

2. Economics of solid waste management

Harisch [11] was the first author who had made an important methodology contribution to study the methods of Solid Waste Management. Attention had then been shifted to the second generation of research, particularly to the work of Stevens [12] who had made substantial improvements in the Model of Hirsch [11] and those of Dubin and Navarro [13] whose papers had included some methodological innovations also. Don Fullerton and Thomas Kinnaman [14] and Beede and Bloom [15] had made generation reforms and had introduced new methods of making an econometric analysis of Solid Waste Management. Finally, a few Indian studies had made use of new methodological approaches and innovations which had used more of the statistical methods. So, more recent studies had been considered in greater detail in this section.

The First empirical study to use econometric analysis for determining, among other things, as to which form of service delivery (public or private) had an effect on the municipal cost, was that of Hirsch [11], who had studied a sample of 24 Municipalities in St. Louis country (Missouri). However, this study had used econometric model in terms of the explanatory variables were limited to the data that was an available in 1960s, the year for which he had collected the information. Therefore, the variables that were finally used to explain cost (the average costs per service) were the number of waste collection locations, the weekly collection frequency, whether the collection point was an alone or a collective agencies, the residential area, sources of finance and the form of service management, and the distinction between the municipal and the private delivery. The Article had concluded that there were significant differences in the service cost between the municipal and the private delivery. This study did not find any economies of scale with respect to the output in the service. Hardy and Greission [16] had analysed the possibility of saving costs through cooperative efforts in the collection and the disposal of the solid waste material. Heuristic algorithms had been used to determine the best locations for landfills and the best routes for the collection trucks to follow in the study area in five countries. They had discussed about the rural public service delivery problems, and had designed a method to determine the least cost solid waste management system for the selected areas. According to them the economies of scale to be realised in the disposal phase of a solid waste management system and the costs of collection were dependent on the population density and the size of the service area. The combined collection and disposal costs had indicated that the regional system could be justified for the selected study areas. The least cost system for the five countries have two regional landfills. The annual costs associated with this system of $ 447.275, was found to be substantially lesser than the amount of $ 519,815 estimated for the system with each county operating the system independently. The results of the economic analysis had indicated that a regional system for the solid waste collection and disposal could be justified from the standpoint of view of costs.

Kumar et al. [17] had applied the fuzzy regression approached of forecasting for the years 2007 to 2024. The Study had emphasised the importance of forecasting the waste composition and the significance of the waste segregation for the efficient operation of the various reuse-recycle treatment and for producing efficient disposal facilities. The fuzzy regression coefficient was estimated based on the historical data of socioeconomic conditions (in this study, per capita income, GDP, persons per household, Total Population and Density) and the respective solid waste compositions (in this study; paper waste, plastics, food items, metals, glass pieces and other wastes). The fuzzy regression analysis had estimated the variations in the composition of the wastes: the percentages of wastes paper and food wastes were expected to decrease from 29.50 to 24.58 per cent and from 36.37 to 27.55 per cent, respectively, between the years 2007 and 2024. On the other hand, the waste of plastic contents was expected to increase from 2.74 to 3.55 per cent. The most significant changes were expected in respect of the percentage changes in the case of metals and glass, which had been estimated to increase by three times and two times, respectively, as compared to the present percentage levels. Maria Eugenia Ibarraran Viniegra [18] had attempted to examine the people's willingness to pay for making improvements in the quality of the environment that could be brought about by a proper garbage collection system. The Study had carried out an econometric estimation of the determinants of Willingness to pay for environmental quality in San Pedro Cholula and was focused on the Municipality of San Pedro Cholula, located to the North of the city of Atlixco and to the West of the city of Pueble. Its area was 712 square kilometres and its population was approximately 150,000 inhabitants. The majority (36.5 per cent) of them was agricultural engaged in activities, and next in important were people engaged in arts and crafts and workers (14.5 per cent); and businessmen (8.3 per cent). An average Willingness to pay for the Project was $ 1.85 dollar her month per household. Age was a factor of significance and it was having an inverse relationship with to Willingness to Pay. The relationship between environmental ethics and that of Willingness to pay had shown a contradiction between people's willingness to pay and their interest for environmental quality. This might be due to the fact that they did not express their true Willingness to pay because they feared that the garbage collection fees might increase. Finally, they had suggested a step towards valuation of the environmental quality and had allowed for making investment decisions with more and better information in Developing Countries.

Sarkhel and Banerjee [19] had calculated the economic value of municipal solid waste management in West Bengal. This study had interviewed 570 individual households and the mean Willingness to pay from the responses to the open-ended questions was calculated to be Rs. 12. with a median at Rs. 5.00 and a 75 per cent of the respondents expressing their willingness to pay at less than Rs.10.00, the distribution appeared to be skewed to the left with a very few extreme observations in the right-tail, pulling the mean substantially to a higher had level than that of the median. The Authors had also estimated the benefits that could derive by adopting the improved system of municipal waste management in Bally the Municipality in West Bengal. Altaf and Deshazp [20] had studied about the problem of the "Household Demand for Improved Solid Waste Management in: Pakistan" and the objectives of the study focused on integrating the demand side information into the planning process. Most of the attempts at improving the performance had been focused on the supply-side issues such as the collection, disposal and the capacity but had not yielded significant results. The sampling frame was provided by the Federal Bureau of Statistics (FBS). This census sampling frame work divided Gujranwala into 436 enumeration Blocks which represented the neighbor hoods containing 200 to 250 households. The Blocks were stratified according to income by the FBS. This stratification was retained for the study as the municipal solid waste services were provided at the block level and not at the household level. This study had followed stratified random sampling method for 1000 households. The distribution of the wastes from both the houses and the streets were tabulated at the disposal sites. About 20 per cent of the households had reported that their wastes were collected directly by the municipal disposal collectors using handcarts. The remaining households had disposed of the wastes outside their in houses with only 2 per cent of them doing so in bins provided by the municipal corporation. The most common disposal site, reported by 30 per cent of households, was an empty plot in the neighbourhood.

3. Economic instruments for solid waste management

Economic instruments are the major role in the effective solid waste management sectors of many developed and developing countries. There are a number of instruments available in the literature. The economic instruments have been used for the different aspects, for instance, reducing waste generation, improving environmental quality and human well-being [21]. Economic instruments are listed revenue generating instruments, revenue providing instruments and non-revenue instruments. First, Revenue generating instruments such as Charges taxes and subsides. Second, revenue providing instruments are includes charges and tax reductions, fiscal incentives, development rights, funds. Finally, non-revenue instruments are trade off arrangements, deposit refund system, and take back systems. **Table 1** highlights various type of economic instruments of solid waste management have adapted many developing and developed countries. Economic instruments have also help for cost-effectiveness, economic efficiency of solid waste management sector Nahman and Godfry [22]. However, the implementations of the economic instruments are especially in the developing countries very difficult due to involvement of institution and governance. For instance, in India has been generated more tones of solid waste from several years, therefore, economists they want to estimate cost of waste disposal, but there is lack of economic analysis of solid waste management [3].

Revenue generation	Revenue provide	Non-revenue
Disposal Taxes	Tax credits	Deposit refund system
Pollution Taxes	Environmental improvement fund	Tradable permit
Eco-taxes	Development rights	Eco-labeling
Pollution charges	Research grants	Product stewardship
Waste generation taxes	Host community compensation	Liability insurance
Producer charges	Tax rebates	Take-back system
Waste tipping charges	Charge reduction	Disclosure requirements
Product charges	Carbon sequestration fund	Bonds and sureties

Source: Adapted from [21]

Table 1.
Types of major economic instruments.

4. Policy issues in the solid waste management

Callan and Thomas [23] in their study on "Adopting a Unit Pricing System for Municipal Solid Waste: Policy and Socio-Economic Determinants" had carried out a detailed analysis by adopting a unit pricing system for municipal solid waste in USA. 351 Towns are included in the estimation, with 79 of these communities employing the MSW unit pricing approach and they had used the logistic regression equation for their estimation. The estimated parameters and their asymptotic standard error and each parameter gave the estimated change in the log of the odds of adopting unit pricing associated with a unit change in the corresponding independent variable. This study had empirically estimated the influence of the various theorised determinants of unit pricing adoption. From a broad perspective, this study had found that certain socio-economic and demographic characteristics appeared to have influenced the adoption decision. Although such factors were not controllable by the policy makers, an awareness of these determinants could correct false expectations and hence diminish the risk of costly failure. This Study had suggested that a community's decision to adopt unit pricing was explainable and therefore predictable to some extent. In certain instances, the decision may be directly or indirectly controllable through policy initiatives. The relevance of these findings to MSW policy initiatives development should motivate further empirical investigations of unit pricing adaptation and the associated implications for policy makers and for the society at large.

Kinnaman [24] had used a skeletal model to develop and to frame a discussion of optimal policy design. This Model employed the virgin and the recycled materials so that the ratio of input prices was equal to that the ratio of marginal products. The Households might choose between the garbage and the recycling in a similar manner. Since agents in this simple model internalized all of the costs and benefits of their choices, resources were allocated efficiently and the optimal quantities of garbage and recycling were produced. The household utility would have an impact due to by these effects. So assume now that $u = u\ (c,g)$, where $u_g < 0$. Under this assumption, households failed to internalise the fuel social costs of their disposal decisions. Too much garbage and too little recycling could be adopted by a decentralized economy. The majority of the households are paid traditional ways such as garbage removal fee or local property tax to the municipalities. Miranda [25] in the study on "Unit based Pricing in The United States: A Tally of Communities" had highlighted 21 communities with unit-pricing programmes and had compared the quantity of garbage and that of recycling over the year preceding the implementation of the unit-pricing system with the year following it. Results had indicated that these towns had reduced garbage by 17 per cent and had increased recycling by 128 per cent. These large estimates could not be attributed directly to pricing garbage, since in every programme curbside recycling programsme were implemented during the same year as that of the adoption of the unit-pricing programme. Callan and Thomas [26] had predicted that the implementation of a user fee had increased the portion of the wastes recycled by 6.6 percentage points. This impact increased to the level of percentage 12.1 points when the user fee was accompanied by a curbside recycling program.

Kinnaman and Fullerton [27] had demonstrated that the disposals of household wastes were constrained by two disposals an option that is garbage disposal at landfill and recycling, and then marginal cost pricing which would tend to substitute recycling for garbage disposal. But if illegal disposal or burning features was a third alternative in the household disposal choice set, then unit pricing would encourage illicit dumping. If marginal cost pricing resulted in an increase in illegal dumping, and if the externality costs are high, the efficiency losses from under- pricing services might be smaller to bear with. In fact, the initial introduction of the unit pricing system resulted only in a modest reduction in waste disposal through dumping [28]. Fullerton and Kinnaman [29] had estimated that 28 per cent of the reduction in garbage resulting from pricing garbage disposal at the curb might be due to of illegal dumping. Jenkins [30], Blume [31] and Miranda and Aldy [32] had also come out with similar findings. The unit pricing model was used in a household production framework Morris and Holthausen [33] had shown that a price increase on the conventional disposal method did not affect recycling. In the system of unit pricing, the households found it more convenient to increase the total waste reduction efforts. The resources like Time and the prices of the purchased inputs devoted to the recycling process were high but they became less effective because of the reduction of wastes. Maraco Runkel [34] had attempted to develop a partial equilibrium vintage model of a durable good in which the producers determined the output and the product durability either under perfect or under imperfect competition.

The Model differed from the previous durable goods Models in explicitly accounting for the consumption waste and for the disposal costs. This Paper had investigated as to how the Extended Producer Responsibility (EPR) in waste management had influenced the product durability and welfare. At the end of the products' life the households had to pay a unit-based waste tax that coved the marginal disposal costs also. When purchasing consumption goods, rational households anticipate the tax, adjust their demand such that less waste was generated and rendered the resource allocation very efficient. The analysis derived the first-best and the second-best regulatory schemes and, on the basis of these schemes and had, investigated as to how EPR had influenced durability and welfare. All considered EPR instruments had exerted a positive effect on durability. Under perfect competition, the first-best outcome was attained provided the EPR had assigned a few marginal disposal costs to producers at the end of the products' life; for example, through a take-back requirement combined with a regulated private disposal by the firms.

Marcello Basili et al. [35] had analysed and evaluated the costs and benefits of the New Garbage Plan (NGP), and had used hypothesis that Willingness To Pay (WTP) should reflect the value of the community of having a better environmental quality according to the contingent valuation literature. The study sample was divided into two subsets: firms and households, through the information gathered with the help of a detailed questionnaire and the, parametric and the non-parametric estimates were elaborated to analyse the willingness to pay of the population for the benefits flowing from increased SWC, increased incineration and through the cutting down of the landfills. The non-parametric from (using the double-bounded format) had produced an estimation of the minimum willingness to pay for the households and the firms, without the need to make any assumption about the true probability distribution of the values in the population. The mean willingness to pay for an increasing SWC was € 15.89 for households and € 20.89 for firms. The mean willingness to pay was easy to calculate but did not convey enough information for the policy makers. This was because of the fact that it was not possible to know the possibility of the willingness to pay to the socio-economic characteristics which could be obtained through parametric estimation producers. The Non – parametric estimates were robust, whereas the parametric estimates gave more information, and the authors had combined the non-parametric with the parametric estimates.

There are some recent literature have focused on economics of solid waste management at the national level. For example, cost and revenue aspects of municipal solid waste management, Al-Salem et al. (2014) had estimated the cost and revenue aspects of municipal solid waste management in the Great London. This study had found material resource recovery is more favorable in the context of economic in the city. Another study, Nahman [4] estimated the external cost of solid waste landfill in Cape Town, South Africa. The external costs are includes environmental as well as social cost in the estimation methodology. This study had estimated at the US$ 16 per tons of waste which has energy generation process from the municipal solid waste in the Cape Town. Aleluia and Ferrão [1] calculated the costs of solid waste management in the Asian Countries. The cost have included such as capital and operational expenditure for the municipal solid waste management. This study had estimated the average capital expenditure cost per ton US$ 21,493 for the Asian cities. Casado et al. [6] had calculated that the cost of municipal waste incineration through the Hedonic Pricing Method in England. This study had found that the impact of effective incineration the house prices range between 0.4 % to 1.3% in the study area. Sun et al. [7] had estimated the value of real estate price due to municipal solid waste landfill in Shenzhen, China through the hedonic price method. This study has found that the property value has been increased by 1.30% if the landfill away from houses.

5. Conclusion

There is lack of primary investigation on economics of solid waste management at the various municipalities in the many developing countries. The present chapter has discussed the various aspects on economics of solid waste management such as economic instrument, policy issues etc. However, the implementations of economic instruments are the major problems. Therefore, need to strengthen local institution and governance. In many developing countries like India, economists are facing many difficulties for estimating economics of solid waste management due to lack of data on waste generation, disposal and recycling [3, 36–38]. Economic estimate of solid waste is better understanding for local policy makers for designing healthy urban planning towards achieving sustainable cities. Most of the developing countries are in lack of finance and technology for effective solid waste management. Economics of solid waste management could provide a good framework for solid waste management especially cost and benefit aspects at the local and regional level [39]. Further, economics estimation of solid waste is more helpful to decision makers for designing tax/charges or other economic instrument for efficient allocation of financial and technological resources at the city level [24]. A number of Asian countries are difficult to design better solid waste management due to lack of studies on economic estimation in terms of cost of collection, transportation, segregation and final disposal [1]. Although, there are other economic problems raised due to lack of economic estimation of solid waste, for example negative externality [2]. Therefore, need to support economics of solid waste related studies at the regional, local and national level through the grants, support and guidance for better solid waste management for achieving environmental sustainability.

Author details

Muniyandi Balasubramanian
Centre for Ecological Economics and Natural Resources, Institute for Social and Economic Change, Bangalore, Karnataka, India

*Address all correspondence to: balasubramanian@isec.ac.in

IntechOpen

© 2020 The Author(s). Licensee IntechOpen. This chapter is distributed under the terms of the Creative Commons Attribution License (http://creativecommons.org/licenses/by/3.0), which permits unrestricted use, distribution, and reproduction in any medium, provided the original work is properly cited.

References

[1] Aleluia, J. and Ferrão, P., 2017. Assessing the costs of municipal solid waste treatment technologies in developing Asian countries. *Waste Management*, *69*, pp.592-608.

[2] Atkinson, G., Mourato, S., 2016. Cost-Benefit Analysis and the Environment. OECD Working Papers, No. 97, OECD Publishing, Paris.

[3] Balasubramanian, M., 2015. Economics of solid waste in India. *Economic and political Weekly*, *50*(25), pp.17-20.

[4] Nahman, A., 2011. Pricing landfill externalities: Emissions and disamenity costs in Cape Town, South Africa. Waste Management, 31(9-10), pp.2046-2056.

[5] Panepinto, D., Senor, A. and Genon, G., 2016. Energy recovery from waste incineration: economic aspects. Clean Technologies and Environmental Policy, 18(2), pp.517-527.

[6] Casado, M.R., Serafini, J., Glen, J. and Angus, A., 2017. Monetising the impacts of waste incinerators sited on brownfield land using the hedonic pricing method. Waste Management, 61, pp.608-616.

[7] Sun, C., Meng, X. and Peng, S., 2017. Effects of waste-to-energy plants on China's urbanization: Evidence from a hedonic price analysis in Shenzhen. Sustainability, 9(3), p.475.

[8] National Institute of Urban Affairs (2005): "Status of Water Supply, Sanitation and Solid Waste Management in Urban Areas," Research Study Series No 88, National Institute of Urban Affairs, New Delhi.

[9] National Solid Waste Association of India (2010): "Economics of Solid Waste Management," E NVIS, March.

[10] Appasamy, Paul P (2004): "Economic Benefi t–Cost Analysis of a Proposed Solid Waste Resource Recovery Plant," Kopal Kadaikodi (ed), Environmental Economics in Practice, Oxford University Press, pp 268-291.

[11] Hirsch Werner Z (1965) "Cost Functions of an Urban Government Service: Refuse Collection", The Review of Economics and Statistics, No 47.

[12] Stevens, B.J., 1978. Scale, market structure, and the cost of refuse collection. The review of economics and statistics, pp.438-448.

[13] Dublin Jeffrey A and Peter Navarro (1998) How Markets for Impure Public Goods are Organized: The Case of Household Refuses Collection," Journal of Law Economics and Organization 4 (2).

[14] Fullerton Don and Thomas C Kinnaman (1995): "Garbage, Recycling and Illicit Burning Dumping, Journal of Environmental Economics and Management 29 (1).

[15] David N Beede and David E Bloom (1995) " The Economics of Municipal Solid Waste", The World Bank Research Observer, Vol 10, No 2.

[16] William E Hardy and Curtis L Greission (1976) "An Economic Analysis of a Regionalised Rural Solid Waste Management System", American Journal of Agricultural Economics

[17] Kumar Amitabh Srivastava and Arvind K Nema (2008) Forecasting of Solid Waste Composition Using Fuzzy Regression Approach: A Case of Delhi, International Journal of Environment and Waste Management, Vol. 2 No 1/2.

[18] Maria Eugenia Ibarraran Viniegra (2001) "Economic Valuation of the Environmental Impact of Solid Waste

Management: A case Study", Working Paper , University of De las America

[19] Prasenjit Sarkhel and Sarmila Banerjee (2009) "Municipal Solid Waste Management, Source- Separated Waste and Stakeholder's Attitude: a Contingent Valuation Study", Journal of Environment and Development.

[20] Miranjum Altaf and J.R Deshazp (1996) Household Demand for Improved Solid Waste Management: Pakistan", World Development Vol. 24 No 5.

[21] Inter-American Development Bank (2003) Economic Instruments for Solid Waste Management. Global Review and Applications for Latin America and Caribbean. Washington DC.

[22] Nahman, A. and Godfrey, L., 2010. Economic instruments for solid waste management in South Africa: Opportunities and constraints. Resources, Conservation and Recycling, 54(8), pp.521-531.

[23] Scott Callan and Janet M Thomas (1999) "Adopting a Unit Pricing System for Municipal Solid Waste: Policy and Socio-Economic Determinants", Environmental and Resource Economics, No 14.

[24] Kinnaman, T.C. and Fullterton, D., 1999. The economics of residential solid waste management (No. w7326). National Bureau of Economic Research.

[25] Miranda M L Hale B (1999): Re-Covering All the Bases: A Comparison of Landfills and Resource Recovery Facilities in Puerto Rico. Duck University, Nicholas School of the Environment, Working Paper

[26] Callan S J Thomas J M (1997) The Impact of State and Total Policies on the Recycling Effort: Eastern Economic Journal 23 (4).

[27] Kinnaman, T.C. and Fullerton, D., 2000. Garbage and recycling with endogenous local policy. Journal of Urban Economics, 48(3), pp.419-442.

[28] Ackerman, Frank (1997) Why Do We Recycle?, Washington, DC: Island Press.

[29] Fullerton D. and Kinnaman T C (1996) Household response to pricing garbage by the bag. The American Economic Review 86, 971-984

[30] Jenkins Robin R. (1993); The Economics of Solid Waste Reduction," Hans, England Edward Elgar Publishing Limited.

[31] Blume Daniel R (1991) "Under What Conditions Should Cities Adopt Volume Based Pricing for Residential Solid Waste Collection", Unpublished Manuscript, the Office of Management and Budget of Information and Regulating Affairs, National Resources Branch

[32] Miranda M L and J E Aldy (1998) Unit Pricing of Residential Municipal Solid Waste: Lessons From Nine Case Study, Journal of Environmental Economics and Management, 52 (1).

[33] Morris Glenn E and Duncan M Holthausen Jr (1994) The Economics of Household Solid Waste Generation and Disposal', Journal of Environmental Economics and Management, 26.

[34] Maraco Runkel (2003) "Product durability and extended producer responsibility in solid waste management", Environmental and Resource Economics No 24.

[35] Marcello Basili Massimo Di Matteo and Silvia Ferrini (2006) "Analysis demand for environment quality: A willingness to pay/accept study in the province of siena Italy", Journal of Waste Management, No 26

[36] Balasubramanian, M. and Birundha, V.D., 2012. An economic analysis of solid waste management in Madurai District, Tamil Nadu. *Applied Journal of Hygiene*, *1*(1), pp.1-7.

[37] Balasubramanian, M., 2018. Municipal solid waste management in India: status, problems and challenges. *International Journal of Environment and waste management*, *21*(4), pp.253-268.

[38] Balasubramanian, M., 2019. Household Willingness to Pay for Improved Solid Waste Management Services: Using Contingent Valuation Analysis in India. In *Municipal Solid Waste Management*. IntechOpen.

[39] Defra (2011) The Economics of Waste and Waste Policy, Department for Environment, Food and Rural Affairs, London.

Chapter 6

Sustainable Solid Waste Management in Morocco: Co-Incineration of RDF as an Alternative Fuel in Cement Kilns

Aziz Hasib, Abdellah Ouigmane, Otmane Boudouch, Reda Elkacmi, Mustapha Bouzaid and Mohamed Berkani

Abstract

The management of municipal solid waste (MSW) is a major obstacle for the majority of municipalities in developing countries because of the impacts related to the landfilling of waste. Garbage is an energy-rich material. As a result, energy recovery is considered to be a sustainable waste management method. In Morocco, 7.4 million tons are produced annually; most of the waste is landfilled without any recovery despite the impacts related to this method of disposal. The objective of this chapter is to characterize combustible fractions (RDF) from household waste in Morocco and to study the economic and environmental benefits of their use as alternative fuels in cement kilns. The results of this research show that the combustible fractions contained in household waste in Morocco constitute a potential sustainable energy source with a high lower calorific value (4454 kcal/kg). The study of the advantages of co-incineration shows that the substitution of pet coke by 15% RDF reduces the pollution linked to gaseous emissions. In addition, the cement plant can make financial savings 389 USD/h by minimizing the use of fossil fuels.

Keywords: municipal solid waste, energy recovery, RDF, cement plant, Morocco

1. Introduction

With population growth and improved living standards, the generation of household waste continues to increase throughout the world [1, 2]. Despite its health and environmental impacts, landfilling remains the most common method of waste disposal in developing countries [3, 4]. Several treatments can be used to recover the material and energy contained in the waste. The main energy recovery methods that can be used are incineration, pyrolysis, gasification, bio-methanation and RDF production [5]. The choice of treatment method depends on the qualitative and quantitative characteristics of the waste. A study conducted by Ouigmane et al. [6], showed that household waste in Morocco is a potential source of combustible fractions [6]. These fractions are the basic element of RDF production. Indeed, studies have been carried out in developed countries related to the use of RDF in cement kilns as an alternative fuel for petroleum coke have shown several economic and environmental advantages of this line of recovery [7–18].

IntechOpen

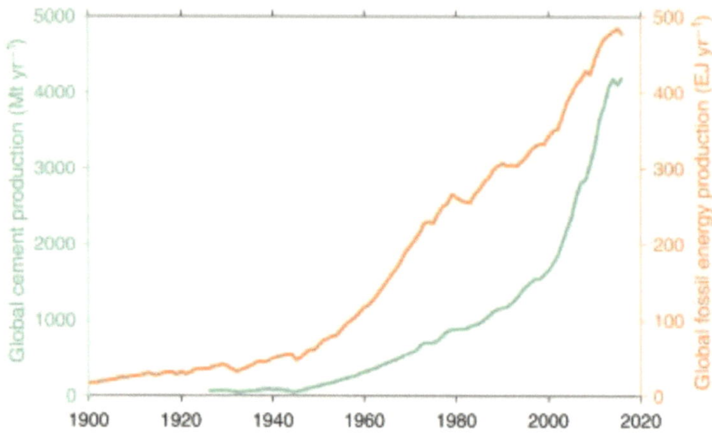

Figure 1.
World cement and fossil energy production until 2016 [21, 22].

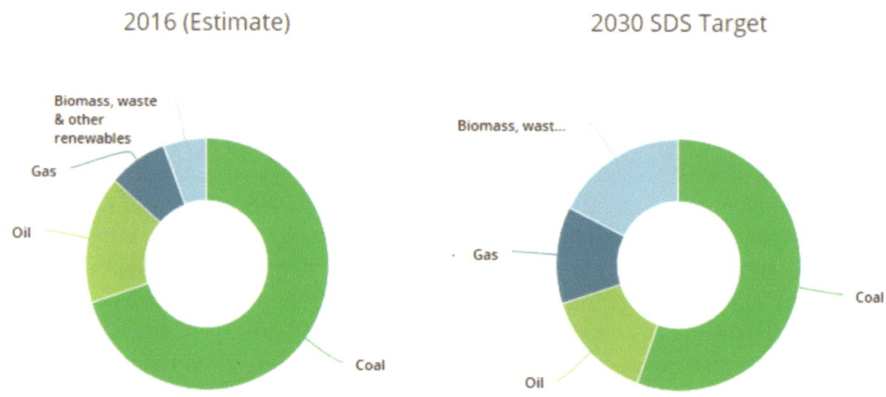

Figure 2.
Overall thermal energy consumption for cement production by fuel [25].

The cement sector is a major energy consumer [19], a simple change in the management of energy consuming sources can have a positive effect on the plant's energy consumption [20]. Indeed, the cement sector is largely linked to the consumption of fossil fuels (**Figure 1**) [21, 22].

Improving the energy efficiency of energy-intensive industries (e.g. cement plants) will contribute significantly to improving their economic competitiveness in the global market [23, 24]. In order to improve their image, cement plants are trying to replace petroleum coke, which is a polluting fossil fuel, with less polluting alternatives such as RDF or renewable energies. To achieve the 2030 sustainable development goals, the share of fossil fuels must decrease as shown in **Figure 2** [25].

The objective of this chapter is to assess the economic and environmental benefits of using RDF as a substitute for fossil fuels in a cement plant for a region in Morocco.

2. Waste management in Morocco

2.1 Legislative framework for waste management in Morocco

The management of municipal solid waste (MSW) requires knowledge of the legal and institutional contexts that concern this sector. In Morocco, the main problem of the MSW management sector is manifested in the legal and institutional context, in particular the weakness of the means available to the competent local authorities in terms of solid sanitation and the inadequacy of legal and regulatory texts. Despite all these problems, Morocco has made several efforts and launched Law 28-00 on waste management in 2006 and the national plan for household waste management. Thus, the new Organic Law of Territorial Communes 113-14 relating to communal organization, specifies in its Article 83 that solid sanitation, household waste collection and waste treatment fall within the competence of the communities [26].

2.2 The production of household waste in Morocco

The production of waste in Morocco, as in the rest of the world, does not stop increasing due to the intervention of several factors (population, standard of living, urbanism etc.). The waste production rate in urban areas is 0.76 kg per capita per day and 0.28–0.3 kg per capita per day in rural areas [6–28]. Waste production varies from one region to another, in the region of Rabat the production ratio is 0.96 kg per capita per day [29] and in the city of Beni Mellal the rate is 0.89 kg per capita per day [30].

2.3 The composition of household waste in Morocco

The qualitative aspect of waste is a key parameter in the choice of treatment method. The general composition of waste in Morocco is characterized by a high content of biodegradable material with a percentage that varies according to urban and rural areas and decreases over time as a result of the improvement in living standards. The average composition of MSW in Morocco is shown in **Figure 3** [28].

2.4 Waste disposal in Morocco

Prior to the implementation of the National Plan for Household Waste, almost all of the waste generated in Morocco is disposed of in uncontrolled landfills without any control. The country has become increasingly sensitive to the impacts of uncontrolled dumping and the costs of environmental degradation that can result. As a result, the Ministry of the Environment has launched the National Plan for Household Waste to rehabilitate all uncontrolled landfills and replace them with controlled landfills or landfill and recovery centers (LRC) with a 20% recovery by 2022.

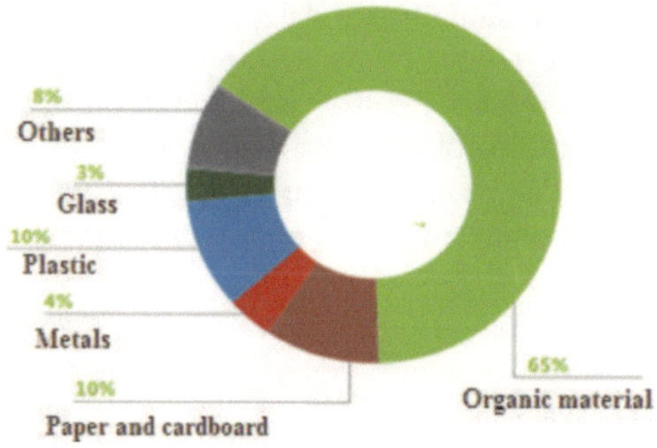

Figure 3.
Average composition of household waste in Morocco [28].

Municipal solid waste	Average cost (Million MAD)
Dommage	
Cost of non-coverage of the population by collection	1118
Cost of groundwater pollution	195
Depreciation of land in the vicinity of landfills/disposal sites	19
Loss of opportunity	
Lost electricity potential	848
Lost recycling potential	204
Total in Million MAD	**2384**
% GDP	**0.26**

Table 1.
Costs related to environmental degradation by the waste sector [31].

2.5 The cost of environmental degradation through waste management in Morocco

Environmental deterioration is not limited to damage to health and ecosystems, but can affect a country's economy. Morocco's efforts in recent years have led to an improvement in the situation of the environmental sector, which is proven by the results of the studies of the cost of environmental degradation in Morocco in 2000 and 2014. These studies are carried out by the World Bank and have shown a 20% reduction in this cost in 14 years. Indeed, the cost of environmental degradation has gone from 590 MAD per inhabitant in 2000 to 450 MAD per inhabitant in 2014 [31]. The costs of environmental degradation related to waste management are presented in **Table 1** [31].

3. Cement sector in Morocco

3.1 Data on the cement sector in Morocco

Cement is one of the oldest industries developed in Morocco, with a first plant in Casablanca at the beginning of the 20th century. Today, the activity is structured and covers the whole territory. The Moroccan cement sector is made up of four companies that operate a total of 12 production plants distributed throughout the country (**Figure 4**) with an annual production capacity of almost 21 million tons [32]. All the plants benefit from modern technologies and an efficient management system. In addition, the professionalism and expertise of the staff and the support of three of the world's largest cement groups guarantee product quality.

The development of the cement industry is linked to the economic development of the country and the upgrading of the construction and housing sectors. In 2011, cement consumption peaked at 16 million tons. Since 2012, the construction materials market has been in decline, mainly due to the drop in construction activity [32].

4. Case study

The objective of this part is to make a case study on a region in Morocco in order to assess the economic and environmental benefits of the co-incineration of RDF in a cement kiln.

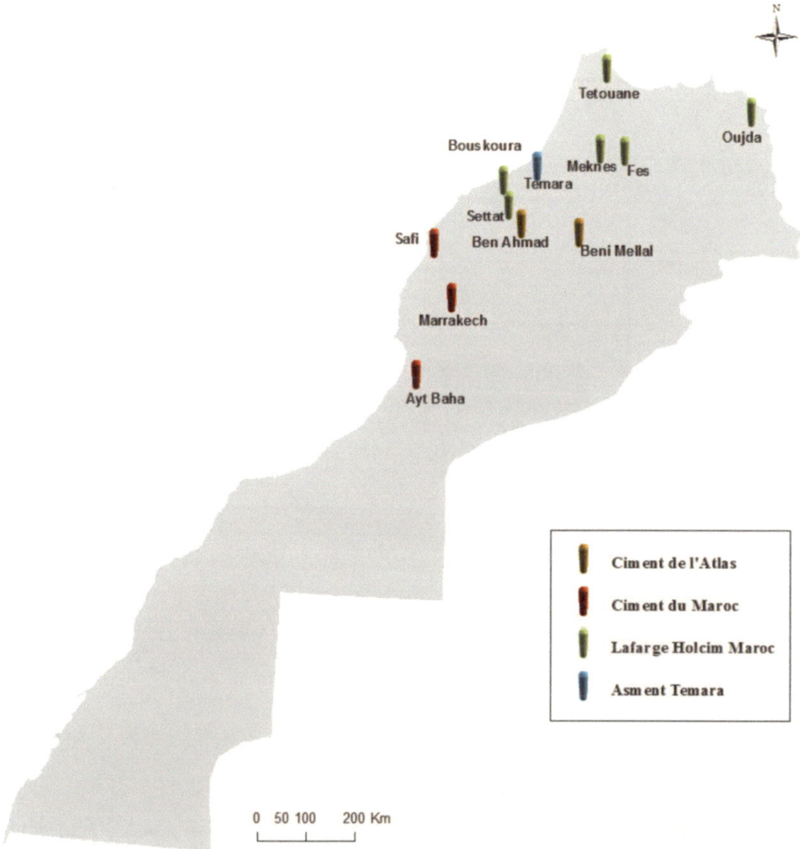

Figure 4.
Distribution of cement production plants in Morocco.

4.1 Materials and method

4.1.1 Waste management in the study area

The province of Khenifra is located in the center of Morocco and is made up of 22 communities (**Figure 5**) with an estimated population of 379,639 inhabitants in 2019 [33]. The management of household waste is a major obstacle for the territorial communes, especially in the disposal phase. Since 2017, an evolution in the mode of waste management in the province of Khenifra has been noticed, with the organization of burial by changing the mode of uncontrolled dumping to a mode of controlled landfill. Despite the efforts made by the communities and the Ministry of the Environment, current waste management is encountering problems and does not meet expectations, since the energy and matter contained in the waste is lost underground. In addition, the controlled landfill is poorly located, as its geographical location can cause several impacts on health and the environment (**Figure 5**). Therefore, it is necessary to look for sustainable and cost-effective solutions to take advantage of the material and energy without causing any impact on the environment.

4.1.2 Presentation of the cement plant in the study area

The closest cement plant to the Study Area is located in the province of Beni Mellal and is 81 km from the Study Area landfill (**Figure 5**). The potential for

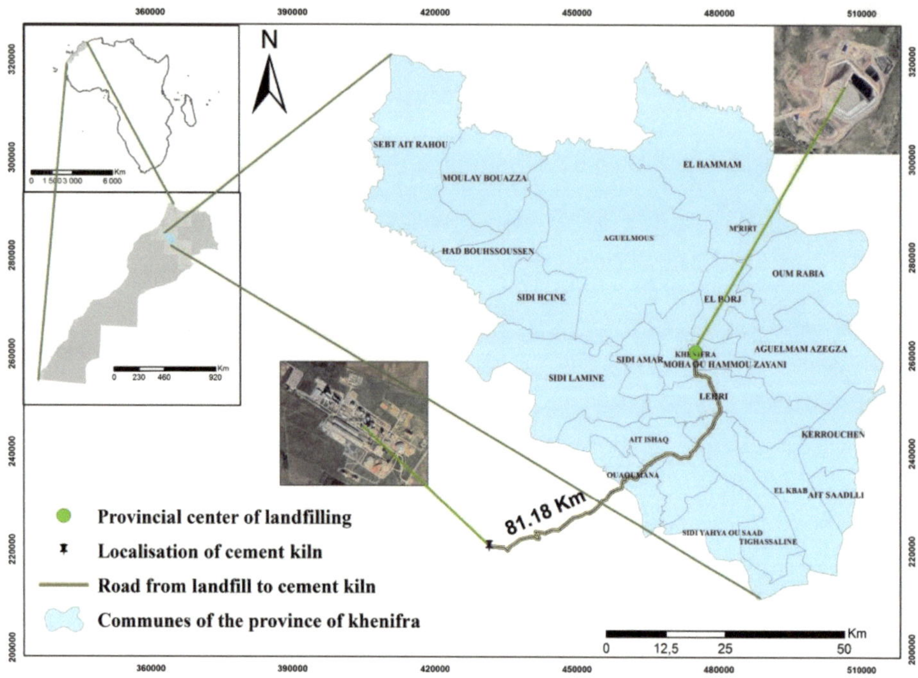

Figure 5.
Location of the study area and cement plant.

cement production at the plant is 1,600,000 million tonnes per year. The dry process is used to produce clinker. Calcination is done in a rotary kiln using fossil fuels (petroleum coke) (**Figure 6**).

4.1.3 Dry fractions potential in the study area

The scenario taken for this work is the recovery of all dry fractions that can be extracted from household waste following a sorting into two fractions (**Figure 7**). The percentage of dry fractions in household waste in Morocco is 30% of the total flow of household waste [30]. The lower caloric value (LCV) of these fractions has been determined in the laboratory according to the EN 15400 standard [34] the value found is 4454 kcal/kg.

The annual RDF potential in the study area is estimated based on the population of the municipalities in the province and the national average waste generation in urban and rural areas. The results of the RDF production estimated are presented in **Table 2**.

4.1.4 Calculation method

In order to demonstrate the economic and environmental benefits of co-incineration of RDF in cement kilns, several aspects will be evaluated in this case study. The economic gain of the cement plant and the carbon dioxide reduction will be determined. Several data have been collected in order to complete this study, including information on the cement plant in the study area (petroleum coke consumption, LCV of petroleum coke, clinker production, etc.), data on waste management in Khenifra province (potential in combustible fraction, PCI of RDF waste, etc.).

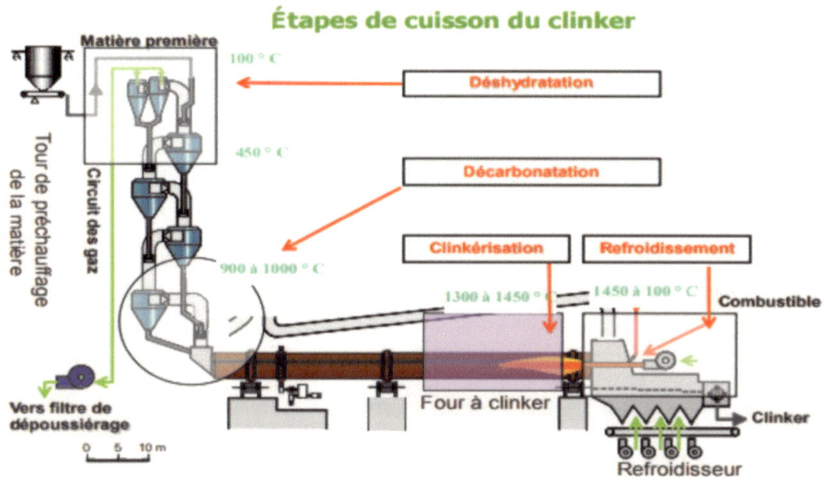

Figure 6.
Clinker firing stage in the cement plant.

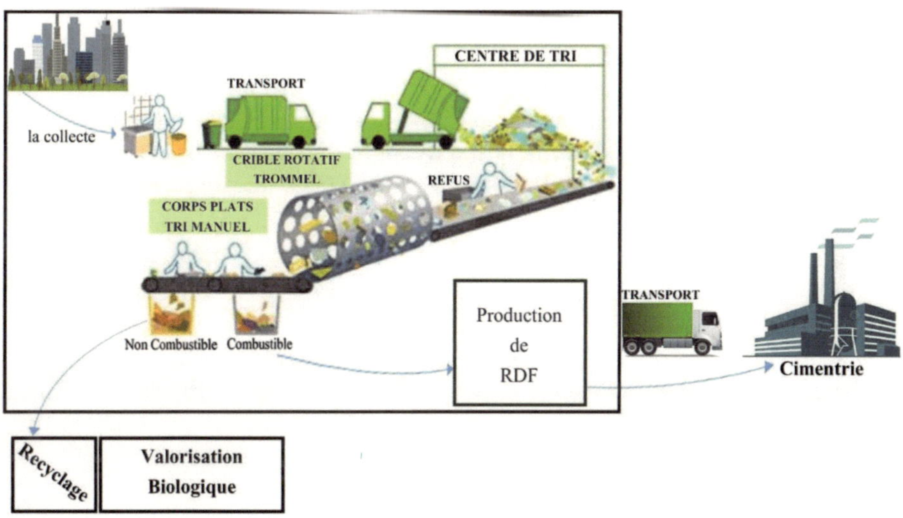

Figure 7.
RDF production scenario.

An economic model has been proposed taking into account the quantity of RDF produced, cost savings of fossil fuels, CO_2 emissions. Formula (1) is used to calculate the net savings of the cement plant.

$$\begin{aligned}\text{Net savings} = ((&\text{Savings on traditional fuels} + CO_2 \text{ emission cost reduction} \\ &-\text{RDF production cost reduction}) * (100 - \text{Energy loss}))/100\end{aligned} \tag{1}$$

4.1.4.1 The substitution rate

The substitution rate of RDF in cement plants can reach very high percentages up to 45% depending on the process. In the case of the present study, a substitution

Communitie	Number of communities	Population 2019 [33]	Rate of waste generation kg per capita per day [6]	Waste generation in tons/ year*	RDF production in Tons/ year**
Urban communities	2	174,176	0.76	48,316	1 4495
Rural communities	20	205,463	0.29	59,584	17,875
Total of RDF in the study area				32,370	

Calculated using the number of population and the waste generation ratio.
**Calculated using waste generation and percentage of RDF in waste (30%).*

Table 2.
Estimated RDF production in the Study Area.

rate of 15% was chosen based on the results of the study by Kara [8] and Hemidat et al. [9] who found that 15% is the most optimal substitution rate from a technical and environmental point of view [8, 9].

4.1.4.2 RDF requirement in cement plant

In order to calculate the amount of RDF required achieving 15% substitution percentage of pet coke, the energy content of RDF was taken into account based on the LCV value determined for the waste in the study area. In fact, a ton of pet coke does not have the same calorific value as a ton of RDF. The data used for the calculation of RDF required to substitute 15% of the pet coke are presented in **Table 3**.

4.1.4.3 Energy requirement

The amount of energy required to produce one kilogram of clinker is 730 kcal/ kg. Therefore the amount of energy to be extracted from RDF with 15% substitution is given in Eqs. (2) and (3).

$$\text{ERDF} = \frac{730 \times 15}{100} = 109.5\ \text{kcal} \tag{2}$$

$$\text{EPC} = \frac{730 \times 85}{100} = 620.5\ \text{kcal} \tag{3}$$

where ERDF is the energy required from RDF with a 15% substitution rate to produce one kilogram of clinker; EPC is the energy required from pet coke with a substitution rate of 85% to produce one kilogram of clinker.

Energy required to produce one kilogram of clinker [35]	730 kcal/kg
LCV of petroleum coke	7500 kcal/kg
LCV of RDF	4454 kcal/kg
Annual production of petroleum coke	1,000,000 tons

Table 3.
RDF requirement calculation data.

4.1.4.4 Requirement in mass quantity

The NCV of the RDF in the study area is 4453 kcal/kg, hence, the amount of RDF required to produce one kilogram of clinker in the case of 15% substitution is given by Eq. (4).

$$\text{Mass of RDF corresponding to 109.5 kcal} = 109{,}5\ \text{kcal} \times \frac{1}{\text{LCV RDF}} = 0.024\text{kg} \tag{4}$$

where LCV RDF is the lower calorific value of RDF (for the case of this study, it equals 4454 kcal/kg).

The quantity of pet coke required is given according to Eq. (5).

$$\text{Mass of pet coke corresponding to } 620.5\ \text{kcal} = 620.5\ \text{kcal} \times \frac{1}{\text{LCV PC}} = 0.083\ \text{kg} \tag{5}$$

where LCV PC is the lower calorific value of Pet coke (for the case of this study it is equal to 7500 kcal/kg).

The production of one ton of clinker requires the mixture of 0.024 ton of RDF and 0.083 ton of pet coke.

4.1.4.5 Fuel consumption as a function of time

The production capacity of the cement plant close to the study area is 1,600,000 tons of cement per year, the calculation to be made in this study will concern the economic cost of using RDF to produce 1 million tons of clinker per year. **Table 4** shows the daily and hourly production of clinker. The cement plant is shut down for a period of one month in order to maintain the combustion furnace.

On the basis of clinker production as a function of time, the tonnage of fuel used will be deducted according to Eq. (6).

$$\text{fuel consumption per hour} = \text{Production of} \frac{\text{clinker}}{\text{hour}} \times \text{The amount of RDF needed to produce one tonne of clinker} \tag{6}$$

$$\text{RDF consumption per hour} = 124.37 \times 0.024 = 2.99 \text{ tons per hour} \tag{7}$$

The same formula (6) is used to calculate pet coke consumption per hour:

$$\text{pet coke consumption per hour} = 124.37 \times 0.083 = 10.32 \text{ tons per hour} \tag{8}$$

4.1.4.6 CO_2 emissions

The amount of carbon dioxide (CO_2) saved has been estimated by assuming that 70% of one kilogram of petroleum coke is emitted as CO_2 [8]. It is then converted

Production (tons/year)	Production (tons/day)	Production (tons/hour)
1,000,000	2985	124.34

Table 4.
Clinker production per year, per day and per hour.

into CO_2 savings in the form of an emission of 1 kg of CO_2, which is estimated at USD 0.015 [36].

5. Results and discussion

As shown in the experimental study by Hemidat et al. [9] and Kara [8], the use of 15% RDF as a substitute for pet coke for the generation of thermal energy for clinker production does not cause any quality problems [8, 9]. The consumption of pet coke in kg/hour is 10,320 if the substitution rate is 15% and 2990 kg/hour of RDF which will save 1782 kg/hour of petroleum coke (**Table 5**).

Hence, the use of 15% RDF will save 1782 kg/h of pet coke, so the annual saving of pet coke is:

$$1.782\frac{\text{tons}}{\text{hour}} \times 24\frac{\text{hour}}{\text{day}} \times 335\frac{\text{days}}{\text{year}} = 14327.28\frac{\text{tons}}{\text{year}} \tag{9}$$

As a result, 15,610. 32 tons of pet coke will be saved annually if 15% RDF is used in the cement plant kiln.

Table 6 shows the results of the calculation of the CO_2 emission parameters as well as the net savings in USD per hour.

The price of petroleum coke is variable and depends on the price of oil. In this study a price of 150 USD/ton was taken as the annual average selling price of petroleum coke, so the annual saving in terms of petroleum coke if 15% RDF is used as a substitute is:

$$14\ 327.28\frac{\text{tons}}{\text{ans}} \times \frac{150\text{USD}}{\text{ton}} = 2,149,092\ \text{USD/year} \tag{10}$$

Since the consumption of RDF is 2.99 ton/h, then the annual consumption is:

$$\text{annual consumption of RDF} = \frac{2.99\text{tons}}{\text{h}} \times \frac{24\text{h}}{\text{day}} \times \frac{335\text{day}}{\text{year}} = 24\ 039.6\ \text{tons/year} \tag{11}$$

	Rate of RDF substitution %	Consumption of pet coke %	Consumption of pet coke (kg/h)	Consumption of RDF (kg/h)	Pet coke saving (kg/h)
Scenario 1	0	100	12,102	0	0
Scenario 2	15	85	10,320	2990	1782

Table 5.
Calculation results for the pet coke saving.

	Rate of RDF substitution %	Pet coke saving (kg/h)	Pet coke saving (USD/h)	CO_2 emissions saving (kg/h)	CO_2 emissions saving (USD/h)	Cost of RDF production (USD/h)	Loss of efficiency %	Net saving (USD/h)
Scenario 1	0	0	0	0	0	0	0	0
Scenario 2	15	1782	151.47	1247.7	18.72	247.68	3	37.19

Table 6.
The relation between emission and saving in the view of CO_2.

The market price of one ton of RDF is 24 USD/ton, hence, the annual purchase price of RDF is:

$$\frac{24\ 039.6\text{tons}}{\text{year}} \times 24\text{USD} = 576,950.4\ \text{USD}/\text{year} \tag{12}$$

The real financial economy is:

$$2,149,092\ \frac{\text{USD}}{\text{year}} - 576,950.4\frac{\text{USD}}{\text{Year}} = \frac{1,572,141.6\text{USD}}{\text{year}} \tag{13}$$

The results obtained show the real savings achieved through the use of RDF in the cement plant.

In addition, savings related to the substitution of petroleum coke by the more expensive RDF, indirect savings related to CO_2 emissions can be achieved.

Given that the price of a ton of pet coke is USD 150, with 15% substitution by RDF.

Therefore, the financial saving on pet coke is:

$$\frac{1\,782\text{kg}}{\text{h}} \times \frac{0.15\text{USD}}{\text{Kg}} = 267.3\ \text{USD}/\text{h} \tag{14}$$

The amount of CO_2 emissions to be saved is:

$$\frac{1\,782\text{kg}}{\text{h}} \times 0.7 = 1\,247.7\ \text{kg}/\text{h} \tag{15}$$

The saved cost related to CO_2 emissions is:

$$\frac{1\,247.7\ \text{kg}}{\text{h}} \times \frac{0.015\text{USD}}{\text{kg}} = 18.72\frac{\text{USD}}{\text{h}} \tag{16}$$

The cost of RDF is:

$$\frac{10\ 320\text{kg}}{\text{h}} \times \frac{0.024\text{USD}}{\text{kg}} = 247.68\ \text{USD}/\text{h} \tag{17}$$

The loss of efficiency is given as follows:

$$20\% \times \text{RDF\%conumtion} \times 100 \tag{18}$$

$$(0.2 \times 0.15) \times 100 = 3\%$$

The net saving per hour is:

$$\text{Net Savings} = ((\text{Savings on Conventional Fuels} + CO_2\ \text{Emission Cost Reduction} - \text{RDF Production Cost Reduction}) * (100 - \text{Loss of Energy}))/100 \tag{19}$$

$$\frac{[(267.3 + 18.72 - 247.68\ ) \times (100 - 3)]}{100} = 37.19\ \text{USD}/\text{h}$$

The energy recovery of RDF in the cement plant has shown the economic and environmental advantage of substituting fossil fuels (Petroleum Coke) by alternative fuels (RDF). This case study shows that the cement plant can save its pet coke consumption as well as CO_2 emissions with a saving of 37 USD/hour. Such a study on a cement plant in Turkey showed that it can save 19 USD/h [8]. In Jordan,

Hemdiat et al. found that the savings that a cement plant can make by substituting 15% RDF for petroleum coke can be as high as 389 USD/h [9]. The results found and the potential for the combustible fraction in Moroccan waste [6, 30] are encouraging in order to develop an RDF production chain in all the regions where there are cement plants in Morocco. In addition to the advantage of sustainable disposal of household waste, other types of waste such as medical waste, pandemic waste such as COVID-19, and sludge from wastewater treatment plants can be thermally treated in the kilns of cement plants [37, 38].

6. Conclusion

Energy recovery is considered to be a sustainable way of managing household waste. The study concerns the case of a developing country with several problems related to the waste management sector. In this chapter, the RDF recovery process in cement kilns has been studied for the case of a region in Morocco. The results of the evaluation have led to the conclusion that the substitution of petroleum coke with RDF with a percentage of 15% saves 389 USD/hour. In addition to these benefits, the co-incineration of RDF reduces the volume of waste, increases the life of the landfill and provides sustainable and renewable energy.

Acknowledgements

The authors are grateful to the cement plant CIMAT, the province of Khenifra and Team of Agro industrial and Environmental Processes of Sultan Moulay Slimane University.

Conflict of interest

The authors declare no conflict of interest.

Author details

Aziz Hasib[1*], Abdellah Ouigmane[1,2], Otmane Boudouch[1], Reda Elkacmi[1], Mustapha Bouzaid[1] and Mohamed Berkani[2]

1 Team of Agro-Industrial and Environmental Processes, University of Sultan of Moulay Slimane, Beni Mellal, Morocco

2 Team of Applied Spectro-Chemometry and Environment, University of Sultan of Moulay Slimane, Beni Mellal, Morocco

*Address all correspondence to: azhasib@yahoo.fr

IntechOpen

© 2020 The Author(s). Licensee IntechOpen. This chapter is distributed under the terms of the Creative Commons Attribution License (http://creativecommons.org/licenses/by/3.0), which permits unrestricted use, distribution, and reproduction in any medium, provided the original work is properly cited.

References

[1] Youb O, Youb A, Bouabdessalam H. Municipal waste management in the Algerian high plateaus. Energy Procedia. 2014;**50**:662-669. DOI: 10.1016/j.egypro.2014.06.081

[2] Tahraoui DN, Matejka G, Chambon S, Touil D. Composition of municipal solid waste (MSW) generated by the city of Chelf (Algeria). Energy Procedia. 2012;**18**:762-771. DOI: 10.1016/j.egypro.2012.05.092

[3] Shen S, Chen Y, Zhan L, Xie H, Bouazza A, He F. Methane hotspot localization and visualization at a large-scale Xi'an landfill in China: effective tool for landfill gas management. Journal of Environmental. Management. 2018;**225**:232-241

[4] Hussein M, Yoneda K, Zaki ZM, Othman NA, Amir A. Leachate characterizations and pollution indices of active and closed unlined landfills in Malaysia. Environ. Nanotechnologie Monitoring Management. 2019;**12**:1-9

[5] Ouda OKM, Cekirge HM, Raza SA, Rehan M, Al-Waked R, Korres NE. Waste to energy potential: A case study of Saudi Arabia. Renewable and sustainable Energy Review. 2016;**61**: 328-340

[6] Ouigmane A, Boudouch O, Hasib A, Berkani M. Management of Municipal Solid Waste in Morocco: The Size Effect in the Distribution of Combustible Components and Evaluation of the Fuel Fractions. Handbook of Environmental Material Management. 2018. DOI: 10.1007/978-3-319-58538-3_82-1

[7] Psomopoulos CS, Bourka A, Themelis NJ. Waste-to-energy: a review of the status and benefits in USA. Waste Management. 2009;**29**:1718-1724

[8] Kara M. Environmental and economic advantages associated with the use of RDF in cement kilns. Resources Conservation and Recycling. 2012;**68**:21-28

[9] Hemidat S, Saidan M, Al-Zu'bi S, Irshidat M, Nassour A, Nelles M. Potential Utilization of RDF as an Alternative Fuel to be Used in Cement Industry in Jordan. Sustainability. 2019; **11**:5819. DOI: 10.3390/su11205819

[10] Sabino DG, Agnese C, Luca T, Michele N. Energy, environmental and operation aspects of a SRF-fired fluidized bed waste-to-energy plant. Waste Management. 2018;**73**: 271-286

[11] Samolada MC, Zabaniotou AA. Energetic valorization of SRF in dedicated plants and cement kilns and guidelines for application in Greece and Cyprus. Resources Conservation and Recycling. 2014;**83**:34-43

[12] Garcés D, Díaz E, Sastre H, Ordóñez S, Gon José M, González LF. Evaluation of the potential of different high calorific waste fractions for the preparation of solid recovered fuels. Waste Management. 2016;**47**:164-173

[13] Sever A, Atimtay A, Sanin FD. Comparison of fuel value and combustion characteristics of two different RDF samples. Waste Management. 2016;**47**:217-224

[14] Natalia EA, Antonio G, Francisco J, Colomer M. Characterization of SRF from MBT plants: Influence of the input waste and of the processing technologies. Fuel Processing Technology. 2016;**153**:19-27

[15] Ting W, Yuening L, Jing Z, Jingbo Z, Yan L, Luna S, et al. Evaluation of the potential of pelletized biomass from different municipal solid wastes for use as solid fuel. Waste Management. 2017; **74**:260-266

[16] Punin W, Maneewan S, Punlek C. The feasibility of converting solid waste into refuse-derived fuel 5 via mechanical biological treatment process. Journal of Material Cycles and Waste Management. 2014;**16**:753-762. DOI: 10.1007/s10163-013-0215-9

[17] Rada EC, Ragazzi MA. Selective collection as a pretreatment for indirect solid recovered fuel generation. Waste Management. 2014;**34**:291-297

[18] Lei Z, Apostolos G, Wan-Yee L, Sheng-Xuan L, Ke Y. Characterization of Singapore RDF resources and analysis of their heating value. Sustainable Environment research. 2016;**26**:51-54

[19] Pieper C, Liedmanna B, Wirtza S, Scherera V, Bodendiekb N, Schaefer S. Interaction of the combustion of refuse derived fuel with the clinker bed in rotary cement kilns: A numerical study. Fuel. 2020;**266**:117048

[20] Kok G, Siu HL, Gjalt-Jorn YP, Robert ACR. Changing energy-related behavior: an intervention mapping approach. Journal of Energy Policy. 2011;**39**:5280-5286

[21] Mohr SH, Wang J, Ellem G, Ward J, Giurco D. Projection of world fossil fuels by country. Fuel. 2015;**141**:120-135. DOI: 10.1016/j.fuel.2014.10.030

[22] USGS, Cement Statistics and information 2018 [Internet]. Availabe from: https://minerals.usgs.gov/minerals/pubs/commodity/cement/index.html

[23] Subic A, Shabani B, Hedayati M, Crossin E. Performance analysis of the capability assessment tool for sustainable manufacturing. Journal of Sustainability. 2013;**5**:3543-3561

[24] Aplak HS, Sogut MZ. Game theory approach in decisional process of energy management for industrial sector. Journal of Energy Conversation and Management. 2013;**74**:70-80

[25] IEA (International Energy Agency), Cement Tracking Clean Energy Progress. 2020 [Internet]. Available from : https://www.iea.org/tcep/industry/cement/

[26] DGCL Direction Générale des Collectivités Locales, Loi organique relative aux communes. Dahir n°1–15-85 du 20 ramadan 1436 (7juillet 2015) portant promulgation de la loi organique n°113–14 relative aux communes, 2015.

[27] Ministère de l'environnement, 3ème rapport sur l'état de l'environnement du Maroc, 2015.

[28] SWEEP-NET, Rapport sur la gestion des déchets solides au MAROC The regional solid waste exchange of information and expertise network in Mashreq and Maghreb countries April 2014, 2014.

[29] Naimi Y, Saghir M, Cherqaoui A, Chatre B. Energetic recovery of biomass in the region of Rabat, Morocco. International Journal of Hydrogen Energy. 2016;**42**(2):1396-1402

[30] Ouigmane A, Boudouch O, Hasib A, Berkani M, Aadraoui M, Dhairi E. The size effect in the distribution of combustible components in the municipal solid waste produced in the summertime. Case of the city of Beni Mellal Morocco. Journal of Material and. Environmental Sciences. 2017;**8**: 2729-2737

[31] Banque mondiale, Royaume du Maroc, Le Coût de La dégradation de L'environnement au Maroc. Rapport No. 105633-MA, 2015.

[32] APC (Association professionnelle des cimentiers), Secteur du ciment au Maroc. 2020 [Internet]. Available from: www.apc.ma

[33] HCP, Haut-commissariat au plan, Population légale de la région par province et commune région de Béni

Mellal-Khénifra, 2014 [Internet]. Available from www.hcp.ma

[34] EN 15400, Solid recovered fuels, Determination of calorific value, 2011.

[35] CIMAT, Emission d'un emprunt obligataire non cote amortissable sur 7 ans. Note d'information; 2017.

[36] Lechtenberg, D. MVW Lechtenberg. 2020 [Internet]. Available from: http://www.lechtenberg-partner.de

[37] Aadraoui M, Elbaghdadi M, Rais J, Barakat A, Ennaji W, Karroum LA, et al. Characteristics of sewage sludge produced from wastewater treatment plant in the Moroccan city Khouribga. Desalination and Water Treatment. 2018;**112**:179-185

[38] Ouhsine O, Ouigmane A, Layati EL, Aba B, Isaifan RJ, Berkani M. Impact of COVID-19 on the qualitative and quantitative aspect of household solid waste. Global Journal of Environmental Science and Management. 2020;**6**:41-52

Chapter 7

Effectiveness of Anaerobic Technologies in the Treatment of Landfill Leachate

Imran Ahmad, Norhayati Abdullah, Shreeshivadasan Chelliapan, Ali Yuzir, Iwamoto Koji, Anas Al-Dailami and Thilagavathi Arumugham

Abstract

Improper Solid Waste Management leads to the generation of landfill leachate at the landfills. To reduce the negative impacts of highly toxic and recalcitrant leachate on the environment, several techniques have been used. A lot of research is conducted to find suitable methods for the treatment of landfill leachate such as biological processes, chemical oxidation processes, coagulation, flocculation, chemical precipitation, and membrane procedures. The biological process is still being used widely for the treatment of leachate. The current system of leachate treatment consists of various unit processes which require larger area, energy and cost. In addition, the current aerobic treatment is not able to treat entirely the pollutants which require further treatment of the leachate. Anaerobic wastewater treatment has gained considerable attention among researchers and sanitary engineers primarily due to its economic advantages over conventional aerobic methods. The major advantages of anaerobic wastewater treatment in comparison to aerobic methods are: (a) the lack of aeration, which decreases costs and energy requirements; and (b) simple maintenance and control, which eliminates the need for skilled operators and manufacturers. Several anaerobic processes have been used for leachate treatment such as up-flow anaerobic sludge blanket (UASB) reactor, anaerobic filter, hybrid bed reactor, anaerobic sequencing batch reactor and Anaerobic baffled reactor. The following chapter provides an insight to the solid waste management at the landfills, generation of leachate and details of some of the highly efficient anaerobic treatment systems that are used for the overall treatment of landfill leachate.

Keywords: landfills, leachate, anaerobic reactors, biological, removal

1. Introduction

Currently, Municipal Solid Waste (MSW) generation is increasing day by day with the rapid growth of population, industrial developments to match the changing life standards of the people followed by uncontrolled urbanization are triggering the generation of municipal solid waste. It is estimated that currently about 2 billion tonnes per year of MSW is generated globally, which accounts to an average of about 0.74 kg/cap/day. It is predicted to reach a value of 3.4 billion tonnes in the year 2050.

The tragic situation even worsens when from the waste which is collected by municipalities (~67% of the total waste) about 70% is disposed in landfills and dumpsites, 19% gets recycled, about 11% goes for energy recovery [1]. Since most of the underdeveloped and developing countries are still far behind the efficient solid waste management system, therefore the study reveals that about 46% of the world population is unable to avail basic waste management facilities [2]. Researchers are suggesting the concept of circular economy where the preference of solid waste management is modified to the order of reduce, reuse, recycle, recovery (4R) and disposal of waste [3]. When the waste is disposed and carried forward to anaerobic digestion then biogas and the digestate is produced, this digestate is very rich in nutrients therefore it can be used as fertilizers creating the possibility of a fifth R that is rejuvenate.

The practice of landfilling is the organized disposal of MSW at a designated site called as landfill. But in terms of by-products landfill is extremely threatening to environment. Sanitary landfill is the most common MSW disposal method due to the simple disposal procedure, low cost, and landscape-restoring effect on holes from mineral workings. The primary objective of the landfill site design is to provide effective control measures to prevent negative effects on surface water, groundwater, soil and air [4]. Nevertheless, inappropriate management of the landfills and especially landfill leachate as it is declared as a hazardous substance leads to ecological and social problems, such as air, soil, surface water and groundwater pollution, flooding, noise from the garbage collection vehicles, and scavenging activities next to the landfills [5, 6]. Landfills can broadly be classified as open dumping landfills, semi-controlled landfills and sanitary landfills [7]. The details are clearly shown in **Figure 1** [8]. Open dump landfilling is mostly practiced in almost all the developing countries where the solid waste is dumped arbitrarily in open and low-lying areas causing serious environmental and health hazards. Semi controlled landfills are having basic facilities like sorting, segregation, shredding and compaction of solid waste followed by soil covering. While sanitary landfills are engineered and technologically advanced landfills. In addition to all the facilities of semi controlled landfills they have proper leachate collection and recirculation system, appropriate lining system and gas collection system [9].

When rainwater and the moisture is mixed and gets percolated with the waste it forms highly polluted, toxic, colored, and odorous liquid called as landfill leachate (LFL). LFL is highly concentrated liquid containing organic and inorganic chemicals, heavy metals, nitrogen, ammonia, humic acids, fulvic acids and xenobiotics [10, 11]. The characteristics and composition of landfill leachate is varying, depending upon its age (young, intermediate, and old) and this governs primarily the selection of the treatment technology (**Table 1**). Till date, most of the research on the treatment of landfill leachate is focused on using physical, chemical, and biological processes. Young landfill leachate contains significant amount of biodegradable organic fraction and therefore conventional biological techniques can be employed while intermediate and old landfill leachate contains high amount of recalcitrant compounds and low BOD/COD ratio thereby requiring combined or integrated technologies [12]. Leachate treatment include anaerobic biological treatment technologies i.e. anaerobic bioreactors; aerobic biological treatment methods i.e. aerobic ponds/lagoons, activated sludge; physico-chemical treatment including coagulation, flocculation, air stripping, chemical precipitation, filtration and adsorption [13].

The selection of the optimum treatment technology depends upon the characteristics of landfill leachate and its composition [14]. Landfill leachate treatment generally involves multistage or integrated technologies for better removal efficiency, as any single technology cannot obtain desired results for the effluent of LFL to be discharged into water bodies [15]. The previous studies suggest that biological

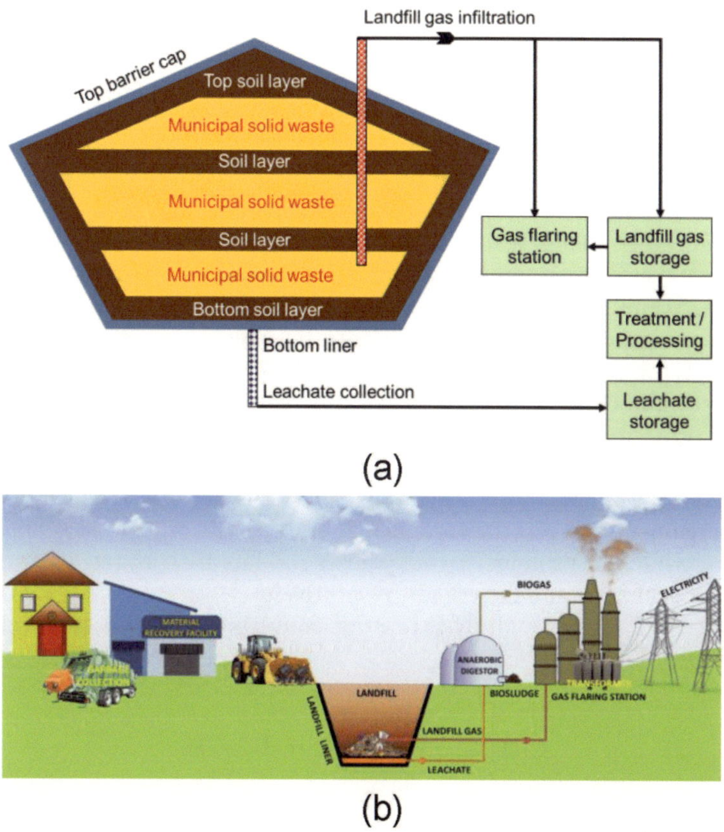

Figure 1.
Details of a sanitary landfill (a) processes (b) structural {adapted from [8]}.

Parameters	Young	Intermediate	Old
Age(years)	<5	5–10	>10
pH	<6.5	6.5–7.5	>7.5
COD (mg/l)	>10,000	4000–10,000	<4000
BOD_5/COD	>0.3	0.1–0.3	<0.1
Biodegradability	High	medium	low
NH_3-N (mg/l)	<400	—	>400
Organic composition	VFA (80%)	VFA (5–30%), humic and fulvic acid	Humic and fulvic acid
Heavy metals	Low-medium	low	low

Table 1.
The composition of leachate based on age [15, 19].

treatment can be utilized to treat the biodegradable matter present in waste, ammonia is removed by ion exchange, coagulation/flocculation is used for colloids, adsorption is adopted for the metals and organics while advanced oxidation process for the organic compounds [16, 17]. Anaerobic digestion of municipal solid waste is very advantageous because we can obtain biogas which contributes to about 35% of the bioenergy obtained from different biomass sources [18].

2. Anaerobic treatment

Anaerobic treatment technology is an attractive and demanding pathway because it serves the purposes of pollutant removal and energy recovery. Anaerobic treatment can be achieved efficiently for the complex industrial wastewater which may contain toxic substances [20]. Anaerobic treatment of landfill leachate can become a viable option as it has following advantages: (i) less space is required (ii) low energy requirement (no aeration is required) (iii) no or little sludge production (iv) Methane production and recovery thus helping to reduce the emission of green-house gas (CH4 potential is 25 times more than that of CO_2, [21]. Anaerobic digestion of waste includes biological action of different types of microorganisms acting together to breakdown the biomass typically in the absence of oxygen [22]. Anaerobic digestion is a process carried out by microorganisms that can live in an oxygen-deprived environment. The disintegration of organic substance happens in four stages: hydrolysis, acidogenesis, acetogenesis and methanogenesis are shown in detail in **Figure 2** [23, 24].

The first stage of anaerobic digestion is called as hydrolysis in which the anaerobic microorganisms convert the organic matter into basic organic substances like monomers, while, the proteins, carbohydrates and fats are converted to amino acids, monosaccharide and fatty acids, respectively.

Eq. (1) explains how a hydrolysis reaction converts organic waste into a simple sugar (glucose) [25].

$$C_6H_{10}O_4 + 2H_2O \rightarrow C_6H_{12}O_6 + 2H_2 \tag{1}$$

During the second stage of anaerobic digestion the acidogenic bacteria convert the products of the hydrolytic reaction into alcohols, short chain VA, ketones, hydrogen, and carbon dioxide. The products obtained in the acidogenesis stage are propionic acid (CH_3CH_2COOH), butyric acid ($CH_3CH_2CH_2COOH$), acetic acid (CH_3COOH), formic acid ($HCOOH$), lactic acid ($C_3H_6O_3$), ethanol (C_2H_5OH) and methanol (CH_3OH). From these products, the hydrogen, carbon dioxide and acetic acid will omit the acetogenesis stage and be utilized by the methanogenic bacteria in the methanogenesis stage (**Figure 2**). Eqs. (2)-(4) [25] represent three typical acidogenesis reactions where glucose is converted to ethanol, propionate and acetic acid, respectively.

$$C_6H_{12}O_6 \leftrightarrow 2CH_3CH_2OH + 2CO_2 \tag{2}$$

$$C_6H_{12}O_6 + 2H_2 \leftrightarrow 2CH_3CH_2COOH + 2H_2O \tag{3}$$

$$C_6H_{12}O_6 \rightarrow 3CH_3COOH \tag{4}$$

Acetogenesis is the stage in which all the acidogenesis products (butyric acid propionic acid and alcohols) are converted into carbon dioxide, hydrogen and acetic acid with the help of acetogenic bacteria (**Figure 2**). Eq. (5) shows the conversion of propionate to acetate. Glucose and ethanol are also converted to acetate during the third stage of anaerobic fermentation (Eqs. (6) and (7)) [25].

$$CH_3CH_2COO^- + 3H_2O \leftrightarrow CH_3COO^- + H^+ + HCO_3^- + 3H_2. \tag{5}$$

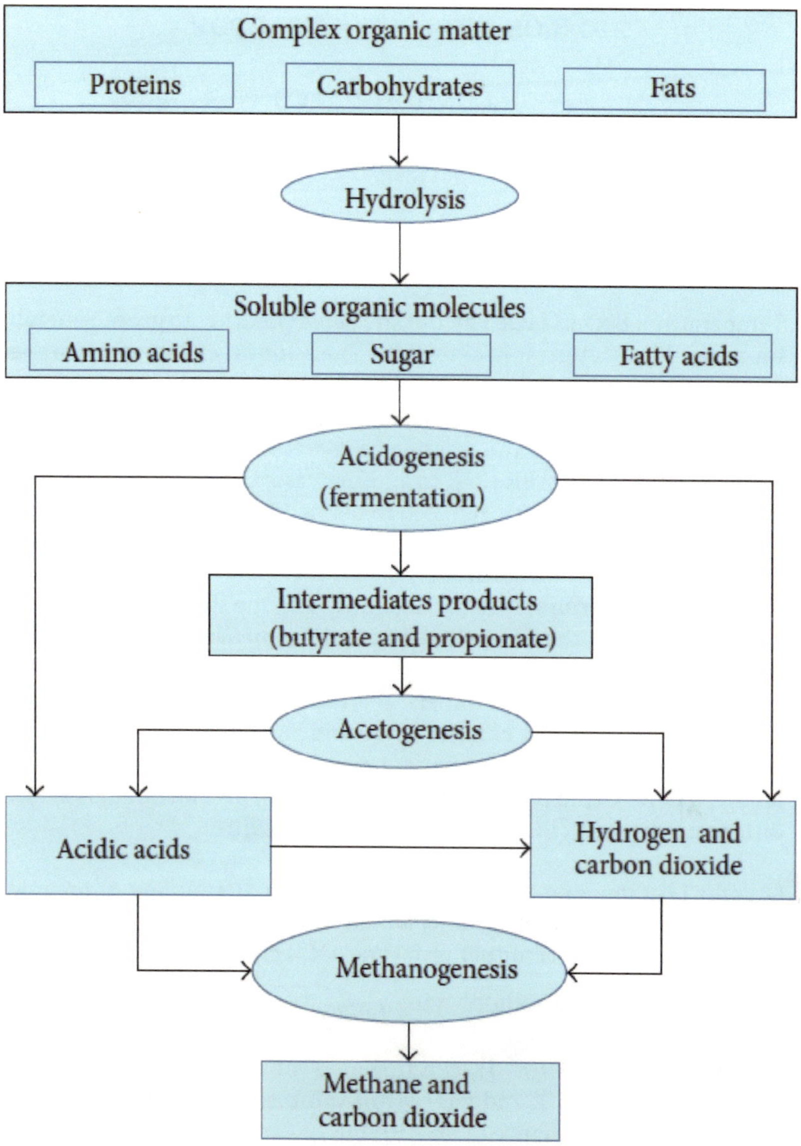

Figure 2.
Degradation steps of anaerobic digestion process [23, 24].

$$C_6H_{12}O_6 + 2H_2O \leftrightarrow 2CH_3COOH + 2CO_2 + 4H_2 \quad (6)$$

$$CH_3CH_2OH + 2H_2O \leftrightarrow CH_3COO^- + 2H_2 + H^+ \quad (7)$$

The last accomplishing stage of the anaerobic digestion is termed as methanogenesis. During methanogenesis the microbes convert the acetic acid and hydrogen to methane gas and carbon dioxide [25]. The anaerobic microorganisms that help to perform this conversion are called as methanogens. Waste is considered completely reduced in anaerobic treatment when methane gas and carbon dioxide are produced.

$$CO_2 + 4H_2 \rightarrow CH_4 + 2H_2O \quad (8)$$

$$2C_2H_5OH + CO_2 \rightarrow CH_4 + 2CH_3COOH \tag{9}$$

$$CH_3COOH \rightarrow CH_4 + CO_2 \tag{10}$$

2.1 Factors Affecting the Anaerobic treatment of landfill leachate

Anaerobic digestion of the pollutants present in landfill leachate depends on several factors such as temperature, pH, OLR and HRT, they are discussed below:

i. Temperature: Bacteria need an optimum temperature to grow, generally for anaerobic reactors, it is 25 to 35°C. The removal efficiencies dropped if the temperatures are below the optimum range [26]. The temperature was found to influence the SS removal, and high VFA concentration prevailed at low temp, showing that the reaction rates were influenced by the decrease in temperature in an ABR [27]. In another case, the reaction rate decreased when the temperature was reduced to below 15°C in an ABR system [28].

ii. pH: pH is an important controlling factor for operation of the ABR. The pH in the ABR is determined by the alkalinity and the VFA concentration. As mentioned above, there is compartmentalization in the ABR, and the favorable pH of each compartment differs. Due to fermentative bacteria, the VFAs accumulate in the initial chambers, but the pH increases down the reactor due to a decrease in VFA concentration and an increase in alkalinity [26]. The souring caused by excessive accumulation of the VFAs can lead to the process failure. Therefore, to prevent these fluctuations, pH can be adjusted using different substances like NaOH and $NaHCO_3$ [29].

iii. Organic Loading Rate (OLR): The OLR refers to the amount of organic material per unit reactor volume, which is subjected to the anaerobic digestion process in the reactor per unit time. OLR can be expressed as $OLR = \frac{Q \times COD}{V}$, upon simplifying $OLR = \frac{COD}{HRT}$ where OLR is organic loading rate (kg COD/m^3·d), Q is flow rate (m^3/d), COD is chemical oxygen demand (kg COD/m^3), and V is reactor volume (m^3). OLR does not directly influence the performance of an ABR but has an impact on the removal efficiencies. ABR treating a complex wastewater was operated at different OLRs ranging from 0.6 to 2 kg COD/m^3/day, for about 600 days without wasting sludge at temperatures of 20 to 38°C.The average COD removal decreased with a decrease in OLR. At max OLR i.e. at minimum HRT, the COD removal exceeded 88% [30]. It can be concluded that the OLR is an indicator of the nutritional condition of microorganisms.

Therefore, when low-concentration wastewater is being treated, lower HRT and higher OLR are preferred to ensure the availability of nutrients to the microorganisms. When high-concentration wastewater is being treated, lower OLR is suggested to enable complete biodegradation of the substrate and prevent sludge floating caused by higher yields of biogas [26].

iv. Hydraulic Retention Time (HRT): Hydraulic retention time is the volume of the aeration tank divided by the influent flow rate can be shown by the expression $HRT\ [d] = \frac{\text{Volume of reactor}[m3]}{\text{Influent flow rate}[m3/d]} = \frac{V}{Q}$ where HRT is in days or hours, V is volume of reactor in m^3 and Q is influent discharge in m^3/d [31]. HRT is the macro-conceptual time of the stay of organic material in the reactor the inverse of which is called as dilution rate and if the dilution rate is greater than the growth rate of microorganisms the microbes will be washed out. Otherwise the accumulation of microbes will take place [24]. The decrease in efficiencies at very lower HRTs could be because the bacteria did not get enough time to consume the substrate. Hydraulic shock loads can also result in process souring and failure due to the accumulation of VFAs, as they could not be degraded effectively by the heterotrophic bacteria and methanogens. HRTs also can influence the dead space volume, at lower HRTs, hydraulic dead space increases, and at higher HRT, biological dead space increases [26].

3. Anaerobic technologies treating landfill leachate

Anaerobic technologies are widely utilized for the treatment of wastewater, more precisely for the treatment of landfill leachate as they have following merits over aerobic technologies; Remarkably less sludge production, energy production in the form of methane, and efficient removal of pollutants [32]. Some of the treatment technologies/reactors are mentioned in **Table 2**.

Anaerobic reactor	Process parameters	Leachate type	COD removal (%)	References
Anaerobic contact reactor	COD = 16,250 mg/l	Young	37.5%	[33]
Anaerobic membrane bioreactor	COD = 7000 mg/l	Young	90%	[34]
UASB reactor	COD = 6000 mg/l	Intermediate	77%	[35]
Anaerobic filters	COD = 15,200 mg/l HRT = 4.5 days	Young	40%	[36]
Fluidised bed reactor	COD = 2000 mg/l HRT = 0.6 days	Young	80%	[37]

Table 2.
Some of the anaerobic treatments of leachate.

3.1 Anaerobic contact reactor

Anaerobic contact reactors are widely used for anaerobic treatment process. ACR consists of a main reactor and a sedimentation tank from where the settled sludge is brought back into the parent reactor. The ACR reaches steady state due to proper mixing and can even work for short HRTs getting higher removal efficiencies. The drawback usually encountered is the gas formation in the settling tank which causes reactor upset [38]. The drawback of this reactor is the development of gas in the settling tank, which upsets the solid settlement process. Şentürk et al. [39] studied an anaerobic contact reactor treating potato-chips wastewaters (COD = 5500 mg/l, OLR = 0.6 to 8 kg $COD/m^3/d$). The performance of ACR was evaluated based on COD removal, VFA production and the composition of biogas. The removal of COD was 86–97% and the methane content of the biogas production was about 68–89% accounting an yield of 0.42 m^3 CH_4/kg COD removed. El-Gohary and Kamel [33] recently found that an anaerobic contact reactor was able to remove 37.5 and 40.5% COD and BOD, respectively, from young leachate.

3.2 Anaerobic membrane bioreactor

The membrane bioreactor works on the application external membrane filter before/after the anaerobic reactor. This helps to capture the solids preventing the solids washout and getting them returned to the reactor sludge. Membrane bioreactor (MBR) technology became viable and popular as compared to activated sludge systems because of the following additional merits; MLSS concentration is high, low cost of treatment, less sludge production and quality of effluent is high [12]. The limitation of the system is the high probability of organic fouling in the membrane. Bohdziewicz and Kwarciak [40] found that using an anaerobic membrane bioreactor as much as 90% COD removal was possible for landfill leachate treatment. In another study by Zayen et al. [41], 90% COD removal was obtained using this type of reactor. In a separate study, an anaerobic membrane bioreactor achieved 26% COD removal at a low HRT of 0.4 days during the anaerobic treatment of leachate [34]. However, Trzcinski and Stuckey [42] demonstrated that the same reactor achieved 60% COD removal during the treatment of young leachate. Nuansawan et al. [43] found that treatment of young leachate using an anaerobic membrane bioreactor attained 81 and 92.1% removal of COD and BOD, respectively.

3.3 Up-flow anaerobic sludge blanket (UASB)

In an UASB reactor the sludge blanket provided at the bottom of the reactor serves the purpose of a filter and medium helping the anaerobic microbes to grow and utilize the organic matter. Influent wastewater is introduced by an inlet at the bottom and goes in an up-flow manner with the help of a pump. When the wastewater passes the anaerobic sludge blanket it is being treated by the microorganisms. This is the principle which governs the mechanism of UASB globally. Singh and Mittal [44] found that treatment of old leachate by UASB was only able to remove 35% of COD. Abood et al. [45] studied leachate treatment by UASB and found that the treatment could achieve COD, NH_3-N, and BOD_5 removal percentages of 69.27%, 92.18% and 23.81%, respectively. In a separate study by Tauseef et al. [46] found that leachate treatment by UASB was able to remove 80% COD and produce 70% methane. Montalvo et al. [47] found that treatment of leachate via UASB was capable of removing 92.4% nitrate, whereas a study conducted by Liu et al. [48] reported that leachate treatment by UASB could achieve removal of NH_3-N, TN and COD as high as 99.3%, 85.4% and 90.3%, respectively. In support of this, Moharram et al. [49] also found out that UASB could achieve 50 to 75% of COD removal. Lu et al. [50] stated that UASB could achieve COD removal rates between 77% and 91%. Alvarino et al. [51] stated that they could achieve 96.7% COD removal via UASB. Intanoo et al. [52] discovered that by using UASB, up to 60% COD removal could be attained, while according to Wu et al. [16] leachate treatment via UASB could achieve COD removal of 95%. Lu et al. [53] found that leachate treatment by UASB could attain COD removal rates of 93%.

3.4 Anaerobic filters

An anaerobic filter consists of a filter media usually made up of packed material (non-degradable polymer) having high surface area to volume ratio. These filters facilitate microorganisms to get developed as a biofilm and forming an anaerobic channel mat. The problem in such type of reactors arises when the wastewater is rich in solids causing clogging. Wang et al. [54] revealed that by applying an anaerobic filter in leachate treatment more than 90% COD removal could be accomplished. A recent study by Zayen et al. [17] reported 40% COD removal from young leachate.

Nanayakkara et al. [55] studied the treatment of 10% diluted landfill leachate using downflow anaerobic filters. One of the columns was filled with a mixture of Washed Sea Sand (WSS), Dewatered Alum Sludge (DAS) and Firewood Charcoal (FWC) while in the other the same materials were used but in layers. The parameters studied and their removal efficiencies using both columns are given below.

Parameters	COD	BOD_5	TN	NH_3-N	TP	PO_4^{3-}-P	Pb	Cd	Cu	Mn
Mixed column	59%	87%	49%	26%	71%	78%	40%	48%	41%	52%
Layered column	73%	84%	61%	55%	76%	79%	54%	37%	54%	57%

3.5 Fluidised bed reactor

In a fluidised bed reactor, the biomass grows as a biolayer around particles made up of plastic, polymer or sand which are suspended and remain fluidized because of upward movement of water. Some of the advantages are higher treatment capacity, no clogging as in the case of anaerobic filters but the limitation is that sometimes particles aggregate too much with biomass and settles after becoming dense [38]. Tisa et al. [56] found that fluidised bed reactor could remove 80% COD from landfill leachate. The role of the fluidised bed reactor in removing metal ions was explored by Sahinkaya et al. [37] who found that it was able to remove 80 to 99.9% of metals. According to Eldyasti et al. [57], their fluidised bed reactor was capable of achieving COD, nitrogen, and phosphorus removal efficiencies of 85%, 80%, and 70%, respectively at a low carbon-to-nitrogen ratio of 3: 1 and nutrients loading rates of 2.15 kg COD/m^3/d, 0.70 kg N/m^3/d, and 0.014 kg P/m^3/d).

In another study by Sahinkaya et al. [37], treatment of young leachate using a fluidised bed reactor resulted in 80% of COD removal and 60% of sulphate removal.

3.6 Leach bed reactor

This reactor works on an opposite principle to a UASB reactor in that the flow of wastewater is in the opposite direction: downflow direction. However, it shares some similarities with the UASB in terms of the sludge blanket. The difference is that effluent will leach out of the sludge bed and will be re-circulated as influent back into the reactor until maximum treatment is achieved [38]. According to Xu et al. [58] a leach bed reactor is capable of removing up to more than 80% COD. In a recent study by Degueurce et al. [59], a leach bed reactor was able to remove 27% COD from a young leachate; whereas, according to Ko et al. [60], treatment of young leachate via leach bed reactor was able to remove 80% COD.

3.7 Hybrid bed filter

A hybrid bed filter with a filter volume of 2.75 L and HRT of 2.4 d consisted of the combination of an anaerobic filter at the top and an up-flow sludge blanket situated at the bottom resulted in the removal efficiency of 37.5 to 76% COD from landfill leachate [61]. Karabelnik et al. [62] showed that at steady state a hybrid bed filter achieved COD removal efficiencies of 83 to 88% under an OLR of 2.50 kgCOD/m^3/d. Deng et al. [63] found that under the similar operational condition the hybrid bed filter was capable of achieving COD removal of more than 90% from leachate. In another study by Dastyar et al. [64] a hybrid bed filter was able to remove 45% COD from young leachate.

3.8 Anaerobic baffled reactor (ABR)

This reactor comprises of a progression of UASB reactors in series. The wastewater will stream over and under every baffle, which acts to isolate every chamber or compartment, thus counteracting solids washout and thus helping to retain the solids in the reactor. The successful compartmentalisation of the reactor guarantees phase division inside the compartments of acidogenic and methanogenic stages [38]. According to Rongrong et al. [65], an ABR demonstrated COD and Polyvinyl alcohol (in leachate) removal efficiencies around 42.0% and 18.0%, respectively. In a recent study by Yu et al. [66], leachate treatment by an ABR resulted in 80% of total nitrogen removal. Overview of landfill leachate treatment using different configurations of ABR is shown in **Table 3**.

Performance of an ABR treating landfill leachate was evaluated by Amin et al. [67], The influent COD of landfill leachate was 2700 mg/l and the pH during the treatment varied from 6.1 to 8.2 the maximum COD and nitrate removal obtained were 86 and 96.6%, respectively at an HRT of 48 h. Burbano-Figueroa et al. [68] studied the effect of OLR and sulphate loading rate (SLR) on landfill leachate treatment by a lab-scale ABR. The COD of landfill leachate was 3966–5090 mg/L with no traces of sulphate. Iron-sulphate was fed at a SLR of 0.05 g SO_4^{2-}/L/d during the reactor start-up. The range of organic loading rate was 0.30 up to 6.84 g COD/L/d, while SLR of 0.06–0.13 g SO_4^{2-} /L/d was adopted for SO_4^{2-} in the influent. The maximum value of COD removal obtained at an OLR of 3.58 g COD/L/d and SLR of 0.09 g SO_4^{2-}/L/d with a (COD/SO_4^{2-} = 40) was 66%. Sulphate is added for the consumption of molecular hydrogen and the organic content is degraded during methanogenesis.

ABR system of four compartments (volume = 64 L and HRT = 4 days) was used by Mohtashami et al. [69] to treat the landfill leachate and obtained the COD removal efficiencies of 82.38, 85.19, 82.53, 82.22, and 80.12% for OLR of 1.2, 2, 3, 5, and 7.75 kgCOD/m^3/d, respectively. The performance of an ABR was evaluated by Wang and Shen [70] as a hydrolysis-acidogenesis unit in treating the wastewater (landfill leachate mixed with municipal sewage) in different volumetric ratios. The study revealed that ABR substantially improved the biological treatability of the mixed wastewater by increasing its BOD_5/COD ratio to 0.4–0.6 from 0.15–0.3. The effects of the ratios of NH_4^+-N/COD and COD/TP in mixed

Anaerobic process/reactor	Studied pollutants	Performance	Reference
ABR (5compartments)	COD, TKN, Nitrate and Total dissolved salts	86%, 92.4%, 96.6% and 64%, respectively	[67]
ABR (5compartments)	COD	66%	[68]
ABR (4compartments)	COD	80% COD	[69]
ABR (4compartments)	BOD_5/COD ratio	BOD_5/COD ratio improved to 0.4–0.6 from the initial values of 0.15–0.3	[70]
MABR (4 Compartments)	COD, color and Heavy metals (As, Cr, Fe)	COD Removal-82% Color Removal-78% As Removal-88% Cr Removal-89% Fe Removal-88%	[71]

Table 3.
Different configuration of ABR in the treatment of landfill leachate.

wastewater on the operational performance were also studied, from which it was found that a reasonable NH_4^+-N/COD ratio should be lower than 0.02, and the phosphorus supplement was needed when the volumetric ratio was higher than 4: 6 for stable operation of ABR.

3.9 Anaerobic ammonium oxidation (Anammox)

It is an auto trophic nitrogen removal method which uses ammonium and nitrite as electron donor and acceptor respectively to attain nitrogen removal. Anammox is specially recommended for mature type of leachate, which has non-biodegradable COD and high concentration of nitrogen [72]. Anammox process overcomes the requirement of organic carbon for nitrification in activated sludge process, reduces the amount of energy required for aeration and there is less production of excess sludge and CO_2 emission [73]. A continuous flow process having nitrification and anammox has been studied to treat mature type of landfill leachate. The efficiency for removal of TN and COD were found to be 94 and 62% respectively [74].

3.10 Comparison of anaerobic reactors

Anaerobic reactors are comparable by the common features they share, such as HRT, COD removal and OLR (**Table 4**). Supposedly, the best reactor should be able to obtain high OLR, have short HRT and should have high COD removal. Of all the reactors discussed above OLR range from 1 to 30 kg COD/m^3/d. The reactors have an HRT ranging from 1 to 360 hours and COD removal of all anaerobic reactors ranges from 60 to 90%. From **Table 4** the fluidised bed reactor is the best reactor having an OLR of 2 to 50 kg COD m^{-3} d^{-1}, an HRT of 1 to 4 hours and a COD removal of 80 to 90%. Batch scale anaerobic digestion treating landfill leachate in Nepal (Sisdole landfill) obtained removal of COD as 50% at a retention time of 10 days while it was increased to about 85% using anaerobic sequential batch reactor (SBR) [75]. Due to obstacles in the operation of the fluidised bed reactor, UASB steals the spot of being the best type of reactor with OLR of 2 to 30 kg COD/m^3/d, an HRT of 2 to 72 hours and COD removal of 80 to 95%. This is also after considering issues of convenience in operating these types of reactors. That does not mean other types of reactors are not as good as each situation depends on the type of wastewater and the motivation to treat that specific type of wastewater.

Reactor type	OLR (kgCOD/m^3/d)	HRT (hr)	COD removal (%)
Conventional anaerobic reactor	1–5	240–360	60–80
Anaerobic contact reactor	1–6	24–120	70–95
Anaerobic sequencing batch reactor	1–10	6–24	75–90
Anaerobic filter	2–15	10–85	80–95
Fluidised bed	2–50	1–4	80–90
UASB	2–30	2–72	80–95
Anaerobic baffled reactor	3–35	9–32	75–95
Two phases anaerobic digestion	5–30	20–150	70–85

Table 4.
Comparison of various anaerobic reactors [53].

4. Combined technologies for landfill leachate treatment

Since the characteristics of landfill leachate is varying and the nature is recalcitrant, therefore no single technology is said to be sufficient for the overall treatment. To overcome this issue the technologies are applied as an integrated system in which various physicochemical and biological techniques with their different combinations are implemented for the removal of pollutants from landfill leachate. **Table 5** consists of some of the combined technologies used in the treatment of landfill leachate.

Claudia et al. [76] coupled the processes of photo electrooxidation (PEO) and activated carbon (AC) to treat highly concentrated stabilized leachate from a landfill and obtained the removal of 67.2%, 58.3% and 48.4% for COD, ammoniacal nitrogen and total Kjeldahl nitrogen respectively.

Mojiri et al. [77] performed the treatment of landfill leachate using the application of dual techniques by using electro-ozonation followed by sequencing batch reactor (SBR) process augmented with a composite adsorbent (P-BAZLSC) and obtained high efficiency in the removal of COD, color and nickel. In the electro-ozonation treatment the optimum ozone dosage and reaction time were kept as 120 mg/l and 96.9 min, respectively. The removal obtained was 64.8%, 90.4%, and 52.9% for COD, color and nickel, respectively. Sequentially the leachate was transferred to PB-SBR system. PB-SBR improvised the removal efficiencies from 64.8% to 88.2%, from 90.4% to 96.1%, and from 52.9% to 73.4% for COD, color, and nickel respectively.

The anaerobic treatment of landfill leachate having high concentration of (341.6 ± 21.3 mg/L) was combined by coagulation flocculation (CF) process in which the coagulant and flocculant used are ferric chloride and cationic polymer respectively. The removal efficiencies obtained at an optimum dose of 4.4 g/L of coagulant and 9.9 ml/L of flocculants: 80 ± 8.7, 69 ± 4.8, 94 ± 1.3 and 89 ± 6% for COD, turbidity, color and phenolic compounds respectively [78].

The treatment of landfill leachate was investigated using electrocoagulation process, the anode and cathode in the electrocoagulation system was both of iron. The conditions which were optimized to get the desired results were pH: 7.73, inter-electrode distance: 1.16 cm, and electrolyte concentration (NaCl): 2.00 g/l (key factors playing significant role). The process obtained the removal efficiency for

Type of treatment	COD/Pollutants	Performance	Reference
Photo-electro oxidation with activated carbon	1113 mg/L	69%	[76]
Electro-ozonation and a composite adsorbent augmented SBR	COD 3018 mg/L Color	88.2% 96.1%	[77]
Anaerobic combined with coagulation and flocculation (ferric chloride and cationic Polymer)	COD 11520 mg/L Color	80% 94%	[78]
Electro coagulation (iron as electrodes)	COD 7230 mg/L Color	45.1% 82.7%	[79]
Two stage anoxic/oxic combined membrane bioreactor	4000–20,000 mg/L	80.6%	[80]
Up-flow anaerobic sludge and semi fixed filter (UASB + AF)	68,500 mg/L	81%	[81]

Table 5.
Combined technologies for landfill leachate treatment.

COD and color as 45.1% and 82.7% respectively [79]. A two-stage anoxic/oxic (A/O) combined membrane bioreactor (MBR) developed by Liu et al. [80], was operated for 113 days to treat landfill leachate. The removal for different parameters obtained were COD = 80.6%, ammonia (NH_4^+ -N) = 99.04% and total nitrogen (TN) = 74.87%.

Hua et al. [81] developed an up flow anaerobic sludge semi-fixed filter for the treatment of landfill leachate by using soft polyurethane belt packing as the supporting carrier. The removal of COD increased with the gradual increase of OLR while the removal of sulphate decreased. However, the study showed that when the reactor was operated at the designed value of 9 kgCOD/m^3/d the removal of sulphate and COD were found to be 90 and 81% respectively. The results indicate that the semi fixed carrier can form an effective biofilm and the UASSF system can work efficiently in the treatment of landfill leachate.

5. Conclusion

Municipal solid waste disposal is a critical global issue which needs to be addressed to check the environmental hazards associated with improper disposal. Sanitary landfilling is the widely adopted method of disposal throughout the globe, but it is linked with the severe consequences of the generation of landfill leachate, which should be treated before disposal because of its toxic and recalcitrant nature. The chapter provides the brief overview of the landfills, landfill leachate and different treatment technologies suggested by the previous studies. Extensive details are incorporated about the anaerobic technologies treating landfill leachate followed by the hybrid or combined technologies. Hopefully, the chapter will give an understanding about different anaerobic bioreactors efficiently treating the landfill leachate.

Acknowledgements

The authors are thankful to Malaysia-Japan International Institute of technology (MJIIT) for providing the support to conduct the study and also grateful to the staff of Jeram sanitary landfill for providing the access into the Jeram Sanitary landfill to understand the basic components and treatment processes.

Conflict of interest

The authors find no conflict of interest.

Author details

Imran Ahmad[1*], Norhayati Abdullah[2], Shreeshivadasan Chelliapan[3], Ali Yuzir[4], Iwamoto Koji[1], Anas Al-Dailami[5] and Thilagavathi Arumugham[5]

1 Algae Biomass Research Centre, Malaysia-Japan International Institute of Technology (MJIIT), Universiti Teknologi Malaysia, Jalan Sultan Yahya Petra, Kuala Lumpur, Malaysia

2 UTM International, Level 8, Menara Razak, Universiti Teknologi Malaysia, Jalan Sultan Yahya Petra, Kuala Lumpur, Malaysia

3 Razak Faculty of Technology and Informatics, Universiti Teknologi Malaysia, Jalan Sultan Yahya Petra, Kuala Lumpur, Malaysia

4 Disaster Preparedness and Prevention Centre (DPPC), Malaysia-Japan International Institute of Technology (MJIIT), Universiti Teknologi Malaysia, Jalan Sultan Yahya Petra, Kuala Lumpur, Malaysia

5 Malaysia-Japan International Institute of Technology (MJIIT), Universiti Teknologi Malaysia, Jalan Sultan Yahya Petra, Kuala Lumpur, Malaysia

*Address all correspondence to: mustafwibinqamar@gmail.com

IntechOpen

© 2020 The Author(s). Licensee IntechOpen. This chapter is distributed under the terms of the Creative Commons Attribution License (http://creativecommons.org/licenses/by/3.0), which permits unrestricted use, distribution, and reproduction in any medium, provided the original work is properly cited.

References

[1] Bureau , U., US and world population clock. 2018.

[2] Atlas, W., Waste management for everyone. *Recuperado el*, 2018.**5**.

[3] Abuabdou, S.M., W. Ahmad, N.C. Aun, and M.J. Bashir, A review of anaerobic membrane bioreactors (AnMBR) for the treatment of highly contaminated landfill leachate and biogas production: effectiveness, limitations and future perspectives. *Journal of Cleaner Production*, 2020. **255**: p. 120215.

[4] Postacchini, L., F.E. Ciarapica, and M. Bevilacqua, Environmental assessment of a landfill leachate treatment plant: Impacts and research for more sustainable chemical alternatives. *Journal of Cleaner Production*, 2018. **183**: p. 1021-1033.

[5] Sun, H., Y. Peng, and X. Shi, Advanced treatment of landfill leachate using anaerobic–aerobic process: Organic removal by simultaneous denitritation and methanogenesis and nitrogen removal via nitrite. *Bioresource technology*, 2015. **177**: p. 337-345.

[6] Mishra, S., D. Tiwary, A. Ohri, and A.K. Agnihotri, Impact of Municipal Solid Waste Landfill leachate on groundwater quality in Varanasi, India. *Groundwater for Sustainable Development*, 2019. **9**: p. 100230.

[7] Narayana, T., Municipal solid waste management in India: From waste disposal to recovery of resources? *Waste management*, 2009. **29**(3): p. 1163-1166.

[8] Nanda, S. and F. Berruti, Municipal solid waste management and landfilling technologies: a review. *Environmental Chemistry Letters*, 2020: p. 1-24.

[9] Jayasinghe, P., J. Hettiaratchi, A. Mehrotra, and S. Kumar, Reaction mechanisms and rate constants of waste degradation in landfill bioreactor systems with enzymatic-enhancement. *Bioresource technology*, 2014. **162**: p. 279-282.

[10] Xu, Y., C. Chen, X. Li, J. Lin, Y. Liao, and Z. Jin, Recovery of humic substances from leachate nanofiltration concentrate by a two-stage process of tight ultrafiltration membrane. *Journal of Cleaner Production*, 2017. **161**: p. 84-94.

[11] Pasalari, H., M. Farzadkia, M. Gholami, and M.M. Emamjomeh, Management of landfill leachate in Iran: valorization, characteristics, and environmental approaches. *Environmental Chemistry Letters*, 2019. **17**(1): p. 335-348.

[12] Cirik, K. and S. Gocer, Performance of anaerobic membrane bioreactor treating landfill leachate. *JOURNAL OF ENVIRONMENTAL HEALTH SCIENCE AND ENGINEERING*, 2020.

[13] Raghab, S.M., A.M. Abd El Meguid, and H.A. Hegazi, Treatment of leachate from municipal solid waste landfill. *HBRC journal*, 2013. **9**(2): p. 187-192.

[14] Bashir, M.J., J.H. Lim, S.S.A. Amr, L.P. Wong, and Y.L. Sim, Post treatment of palm oil mill effluent using electro-coagulation-peroxidation (ECP) technique. *Journal of Cleaner Production*, 2019. **208**: p. 716-727.

[15] HA, A. and B. MJK, ASSESSMENT OF VARIOUS TROPICAL MUNICIPAL LANDFILL LEACHATE CHARACTERISTICS AND TREATMENT OPPORTUNITIES. 2015.

[16] Tee, P.F., M.O. Abdullah, I.A.W. Tan, N.K.A. Rashid, M.A.M. Amin, C. Nolasco-Hipolito, and K. Bujang, Review on hybrid energy systems for wastewater treatment and bio-energy production. *Renewable and Sustainable Energy Reviews*, 2016. **54**: p. 235-246.

[17] Lin, C.K., M.J. Bashir, S.S. Abu Amr, and L.C. Sim, Post-treatment of palm oil mill effluent (POME) using combined persulphate with hydrogen peroxide (S2O82−/H2O2) oxidation. *Water Science and Technology*, 2016. **74**(11): p. 2675-2682.

[18] Rasapoor, M., B. Young, R. Brar, A. Sarmah, W.-Q. Zhuang, and S. Baroutian, Recognizing the challenges of anaerobic digestion: Critical steps toward improving biogas generation. *Fuel*, 2020. **261**: p. 116497.

[19] Renou, S., Givauda, n GJ; Poulain, S.; Dirassouyan, F.; Moulin. *Landfill leachate treatment: Review and opportunity., Journal of Hazardous Materials*, 2008. **150**: p. 468-493.

[20] Wijetunga, S., X.-F. Li, and C. Jian, Effect of organic load on decolourization of textile wastewater containing acid dyes in upflow anaerobic sludge blanket reactor. *Journal of Hazardous Materials*, 2010. **177**(1-3): p. 792-798.

[21] Nanda, S., S.N. Reddy, S.K. Mitra, and J.A. Kozinski, The progressive routes for carbon capture and sequestration. *Energy Science & Engineering*, 2016. **4**(2): p. 99-122.

[22] Mittal, G.S., Treatment of wastewater from abattoirs before land application—a review. *Bioresource technology*, 2006. **97**(9): p. 1119-1135.

[23] Prakash , Vimala Sockan , and Jayakaran P., MATHEMATICAL MODEL DEVELOPMENT FOR BOD REMOVAL EFFICIENCY IN TANNERY WASTE TREATMENT. *British Journal of Environmental Sciences*, 2015. **3**(1): p. 12.

[24] Abdelgadir, A., X. Chen, J. Liu, X. Xie, J. Zhang, K. Zhang, H. Wang, and N. Liu, Characteristics, process parameters, and inner components of anaerobic bioreactors. *BioMed Research International*, 2014. **2014**.

[25] Abdallah, R., H. Djelal, A. Amrane, W. Sayed, F. Fourcade, T. Labasque, F. Geneste, S. Taha, and D. Floner, Dark fermentative hydrogen production by anaerobic sludge growing on glucose and ammonium resulting from nitrate electroreduction. *International Journal of Hydrogen Energy*, 2016. **41**(12): p. 5445-5455.

[26] Zhu, G., R. Zou, A.K. Jha, X. Huang, L. Liu, and C. Liu, Recent developments and future perspectives of anaerobic baffled bioreactor for wastewater treatment and energy recovery. *Critical reviews in environmental science and technology*, 2015. **45**(12): p. 1243-1276.

[27] Feng, H., L. Hu, Q. Mahmood, C. Fang, C. Qiu, and D. Shen, Effects of temperature and feed strength on a carrier anaerobic baffled reactor treating dilute wastewater. *Desalination*, 2009. **239**(1-3): p. 111-121.

[28] Nasr, F.A., H.S. Doma, and H.F. Nassar, Treatment of domestic wastewater using an anaerobic baffled reactor followed by a duckweed pond for agricultural purposes. *The Environmentalist*, 2009. **29**(3): p. 270-279.

[29] Amirfakhri, J., M. Vossoughi, and M. Soltanieh, Assessment of desulfurization of natural gas by chemoautotrophic bacteria in an anaerobic baffled reactor (ABR). *Chemical Engineering and Processing: Process Intensification*, 2006. **45**(3): p. 232-237.

[30] Krishna, G.G., P. Kumar, and P. Kumar, Complex wastewater treatment using an anaerobic baffled reactor. *Environmental progress*, 2007. **26**(4): p. 391-398.

[31] Kato, M.T., J.A. Field, P. Versteeg, and G. Lettinga, Feasibility of expanded granular sludge bed reactors for the anaerobic treatment of low-strength soluble wastewaters. *Biotechnology and bioengineering*, 1994. **44**(4): p. 469-479.

[32] Luo, H., Y. Zeng, Y. Cheng, D. He, and X. Pan, Recent advances in municipal landfill leachate: A review focusing on its characteristics, treatment, and toxicity assessment. *Science of The Total Environment*, 2020. **703**: p. 135468.

[33] El-Gohary, F.A. and G. Kamel, Characterization and biological treatment of pre-treated landfill leachate. *Ecological Engineering*, 2016. **94**: p. 268-274.

[34] Trzcinski, A.P. and D.C. Stuckey, Inorganic fouling of an anaerobic membrane bioreactor treating leachate from the organic fraction of municipal solid waste (OFMSW) and a polishing aerobic membrane bioreactor. *Bioresource Technology*, 2016. **204**: p. 17-25.

[35] Wu, Y., C. Wang, X. Liu, H. Ma, J. Wu, J. Zuo, and K. Wang, A new method of two-phase anaerobic digestion for fruit and vegetable waste treatment. *Bioresource Technology*, 2016. **211**: p. 16-23.

[36] Zayen, A., G. Schories, and S. Sayadi, Incorporation of an anaerobic digestion step in a multistage treatment system for sanitary landfill leachate. *Waste management*, 2016. **53**: p. 32-39.

[37] Sahinkaya, E., N. Dursun, B. Ozkaya, and A.H. Kaksonen, Use of landfill leachate as a carbon source in a sulfidogenic fluidized-bed reactor for the treatment of synthetic acid mine drainage. *Minerals Engineering*, 2013. **48**: p. 56-60.

[38] Renou, S., J.G. Givaudan, S. Poulain, F. Dirassouyan, and P. Moulin, Landfill leachate treatment: Review and opportunity. *Journal of Hazardous Materials*, 2008. **150**(3): p. 468-493.

[39] Şentürk, E., M. İnce, and G.O. Engin, Kinetic evaluation and performance of a mesophilic anaerobic contact reactor treating medium-strength food-processing wastewater. *Bioresource technology*, 2010. **101**(11): p. 3970-3977.

[40] Bohdziewicz, J. and A. Kwarciak, The application of hybrid system UASB reactor-RO in landfill leachate treatment. *Desalination*, 2008. **222**(1-3): p. 128-134.

[41] Zayen, A., S. Mnif, F. Aloui, F. Fki, S. Loukil, M. Bouaziz, and S. Sayadi, Anaerobic membrane bioreactor for the treatment of leachates from Jebel Chakir discharge in Tunisia. *Journal of hazardous materials*, 2010. **177**(1-3): p. 918-923.

[42] Trzcinski, A.P. and D.C. Stuckey, Effect of sparging rate on permeate quality in a submerged anaerobic membrane bioreactor (SAMBR) treating leachate from the organic fraction of municipal solid waste (OFMSW). *Journal of Environmental Management*, 2016. **168**: p. 67-73.

[43] Nuansawan, N., J. Boonnorat, W. Chiemchaisri, and C. Chiemchaisri, Effect of hydraulic retention time and sludge recirculation on greenhouse gas emission and related microbial communities in two-stage membrane bioreactor treating solid waste leachate. *Bioresource technology*, 2016. **210**: p. 35-42.

[44] Singh and A.K. Mittal, Toxicity and treatability of leachate: application of UASB reactor for leachate treatment from Okhla landfill, New Delhi. *Water Sci Technol*, 2012. **65**(10): p. 1887-94.

[45] Abood, A.R., J. Bao, and Z.N. Abudi, Biological nutrient removal by internal circulation upflow sludge blanket reactor after landfill leachate pretreatment. *Journal of Environmental Sciences*, 2013. **25**(10): p. 2130-2137.

[46] Tauseef, S., T. Abbasi, and S. Abbasi, Energy recovery from

wastewaters with high-rate anaerobic digesters. *Renewable and Sustainable Energy Reviews*, 2013. **19**: p. 704-741.

[47] Montalvo, S., L. Guerrero, M. Robles, C. Mery, C. Huiliñir, and R. Borja, Start-up and performance of UASB reactors using zeolite for improvement of nitrate removal process. *Ecological engineering*, 2014. **70**: p. 437-445.

[48] Liu, M., Q. Yang, Y. Peng, T. Liu, H. Xiao, and S. Wang, Treatment performance and N2O emission in the UASB-A/O shortcut biological nitrogen removal system for landfill leachate at different salinity. *Journal of Industrial and Engineering Chemistry*, 2015. **32**: p. 63-71.

[49] MOHARRAM, M.A.A., *A2/O PROCESS PERFORMANCE IN DOMESTIC WASTEWATER TREATMENT REPLACING THE ANAEROBIC SELECTOR BY UASB*. 2015.

[50] Lu, X., G. Zhen, J. Ni, T. Hojo, K. Kubota, and Y.-Y. Li, Effect of influent COD/SO42– ratios on biodegradation behaviors of starch wastewater in an upflow anaerobic sludge blanket (UASB) reactor. *Bioresource technology*, 2016. **214**: p. 175-183.

[51] Alvarino, T., S. Suárez, M. Garrido, J. Lema, and F. Omil, A UASB reactor coupled to a hybrid aerobic MBR as innovative plant configuration to enhance the removal of organic micropollutants. *Chemosphere*, 2016. **144**: p. 452-458.

[52] Intanoo, P., P. Chaimongkol, and S. Chavadej, Hydrogen and methane production from cassava wastewater using two-stage upflow anaerobic sludge blanket reactors (UASB) with an emphasis on maximum hydrogen production. *International Journal of Hydrogen Energy*, 2016. **41**(14): p. 6107-6114.

[53] Lu, T., B. George, H. Zhao, and W. Liu, A case study of coupling upflow anaerobic sludge blanket (UASB) and ANITA™ Mox process to treat high-strength landfill leachate. *Water Science and Technology*, 2016. **73**(3): p. 662-668.

[54] Wang, X., J. Han, Z. Chen, L. Jian, X. Gu, and C.-J. Lin, Combined processes of two-stage Fenton-biological anaerobic filter–biological aerated filter for advanced treatment of landfill leachate. *Waste management*, 2012. **32**(12): p. 2401-2405.

[55] Nanayakkara, B., W. Dayanthi, H. Herath, K. Tharanga, and K. Kawamoto, Anaerobic Filter Treatment of Landfill-Leachate Using Low-Cost Filter Materials. *ENGINEER*, 2020. **53**(01): p. 29-39.

[56] Tisa, F., A.A.A. Raman, and W.M.A.W. Daud, Applicability of fluidized bed reactor in recalcitrant compound degradation through advanced oxidation processes: a review. *Journal of environmental management*, 2014. **146**: p. 260-275.

[57] Eldyasti, A., N. Chowdhury, G. Nakhla, and J. Zhu, Biological nutrient removal from leachate using a pilot liquid–solid circulating fluidized bed bioreactor (LSCFB). *Journal of Hazardous Materials*, 2010. **181**(1-3): p. 289-297.

[58] Xu, S.Y., H.P. Lam, O.P. Karthikeyan, and J.W. Wong, Optimization of food waste hydrolysis in leach bed coupled with methanogenic reactor: effect of pH and bulking agent. *Bioresource technology*, 2011. **102**(4): p. 3702-3708.

[59] Degueurce, A., N. Tomas, S. Le Roux, J. Martinez, and P. Peu, Biotic and abiotic roles of leachate recirculation in batch mode solid-state anaerobic digestion of cattle manure. *Bioresource Technology*, 2016. **200**: p. 388-395.

[60] Ko, J.H., F. Yang, and Q. Xu, The impact of compaction and leachate

recirculation on waste degradation in simulated landfills. *Bioresource Technology*, 2016. **211**: p. 72-79.

[61] Timur, H. and I. Özturk, Anaerobic treatment of leachate using sequencing batch reactor and hybrid bed filter. *Water Science and Technology*, 1997. **36**(6-7): p. 501-508.

[62] Karabelnik, K., M. Kõiv, K. Kasak, P.D. Jenssen, and Ü. Mander, High-strength greywater treatment in compact hybrid filter systems with alternative substrates. *Ecological Engineering*, 2012. **49**: p. 84-92.

[63] Deng, L., W. Guo, H.H. Ngo, X. Zhang, X.C. Wang, Q. Zhang, and R. Chen, New functional biocarriers for enhancing the performance of a hybrid moving bed biofilm reactor–membrane bioreactor system. *Bioresource technology*, 2016. **208**: p. 87-93.

[64] Dastyar, W., T. Amani, and S. Elyasi, Investigation of affecting parameters on treating high-strength compost leachate in a hybrid EGSB and fixed-bed reactor followed by electrocoagulation–flotation process. *Process Safety and Environmental Protection*, 2015. **95**: p. 1-11.

[65] Rongrong, L., L. Xujie, T. Qing, Y. Bo, and C. Jihua, The performance evaluation of hybrid anaerobic baffled reactor for treatment of PVA-containing desizing wastewater. *Desalination*, 2011. **271**(1-3): p. 287-294.

[66] Yu, J.-J., H. Chen, Q. Guo, Z.-Z. Zhang, L.-X. Guo, and R.-C. Jin, Response of performance of an anammox anaerobic baffled reactor (ABR) to changes in feeding regime. *Ecological Engineering*, 2015. **83**: p. 19-27.

[67] Arvin, A., M. Peyravi, M. Jahanshahi, and H. Salmani, Hydrodynamic evaluation of an anaerobic baffled reactor for landfill leachate treatment. *Desalination and Water Treatment*, 2016. **57**(42): p. 19596-19608.

[68] Burbano-Figueroa, O., M. Jaramillo, M. Moreno-Moran, and P. Fernández-Izquierdo, Effect of sulfate loading rate and organic loading rate on anaerobic baffled reactors used for treatment of sanitary landfill leachates. *Brazilian Journal of Chemical Engineering*, 2015. **32**(2): p. 385-395.

[69] Mohtashami, S.R., A. Karimie, and T. Bidokhti, Performance of anaerobic baffled reactor (ABR) in landfill leachate treatment. *Water and Wastewater*, 2008. **66**: p. 10-8.

[70] Wang, B. and Y. Shen, Performance of an anaerobic baffled reactor (ABR) as a hydrolysis-acidogenesis unit in treating landfill leachate mixed with municipal sewage. *Water science and technology*, 2000. **42**(12): p. 115-121.

[71] Ahmad, I., Chelliapan, S., Othman, N., Nasri, N.S., Krishnan, S., Treatment of landfill leachate using modified anaerobic baffled reactor. Desalination and Water Treatment, 2020. **183**:p. 268-275.

[72] Wu, L., Z. Li, C. Zhao, D. Liang, and Y. Peng, A novel partial-denitrification strategy for post-anammox to effectively remove nitrogen from landfill leachate. *Science of the Total Environment*, 2018. **633**: p. 745-751.

[73] Zhang, F., Y. Peng, L. Miao, Z. Wang, S. Wang, and B. Li, A novel simultaneous partial nitrification Anammox and denitrification (SNAD) with intermittent aeration for cost-effective nitrogen removal from mature landfill leachate. *Chemical Engineering Journal*, 2017. **313**: p. 619-628.

[74] Wang, Z., Y. Peng, L. Miao, T. Cao, F. Zhang, S. Wang, and J. Han, Continuous-flow combined process of nitritation and ANAMMOX

for treatment of landfill leachate. *Bioresource Technology*, 2016. **214**: p. 514-519.

[75] Adhikaria, B. and S. Koiralab, Anaerobic digestion process for the treatment of Sisdole Landfill leachate in Nepal. Journal of Southwest Jiaotong University , 2020. 55(4): p. 1-8

[76] Klauck, C.R., A. Giacobbo, C.G. Altenhofen, L.B. Silva, A. Meneguzzi, A.M. Bernardes, and M.A.S. Rodrigues, Toxicity elimination of landfill leachate by hybrid processing of advanced oxidation process and adsorption. *Environmental Technology & Innovation*, 2017. **8**: p. 246-255.

[77] Mojiri, A., L. Ziyang, W. Hui, Z. Ahmad, R.M. Tajuddin, S.S.A. Amr, T. Kindaichi, H.A. Aziz, and H. Farraji, Concentrated landfill leachate treatment with a combined system including electro-ozonation and composite adsorbent augmented sequencing batch reactor process. *Process Safety and Environmental Protection*, 2017. **111**: p. 253-262.

[78] Bakraouy, H., S. Souabi, K. Digua, O. Dkhissi, M. Sabar, and M. Fadil, Optimization of the treatment of an anaerobic pretreated landfill leachate by a coagulation–flocculation process using experimental design methodology. *Process Safety and Environmental Protection*, 2017. **109**: p. 621-630.

[79] Huda, N., A. Raman, M. Bello, and S. Ramesh, Electrocoagulation treatment of raw landfill leachate using iron-based electrodes: Effects of process parameters and optimization. *Journal of environmental management*, 2017. **204**: p. 75-81.

[80] Liu, J., H. Zhang, P. Zhang, Y. Wu, X. Gou, Y. Song, Z. Tian, and G. Zeng, Two-stage anoxic/oxic combined membrane bioreactor system for landfill leachate treatment: pollutant removal performances and microbial community. *Bioresource technology*, 2017. **243**: p. 738-746.

[81] Hua, J., S. Bai, Z. Li, and H. Zhou. *Treatment of landfill leachate using an up-flow anaerobic sludge semi-fixed filter*. in *Proceedings of 3rd International Conference on Water Resource and Environment (WRE 2017)*. 2017.

Chapter 8

Hydrometallurgical Recovery of Gold from Mining Wastes

Emilia Neag, Eniko Kovacs, Zamfira Dinca, Anamaria Iulia Török, Cerasel Varaticeanu and Erika Andrea Levei

Abstract

Gold is a highly required material for a wide range of personal and industrial applications. The high demand for gold, together with the shortage of natural resources and high pollution potential of wastes generated during mining and ore processing activities led to search for alternative sources of gold. A possible source is represented by mine wastes resulting from the processing of polymetallic or sulfidic ores. The reprocessing of wastes and old tailings with moderate to low content of gold offers not only a business opportunity, but also enhances the quality of the surrounding environment, changes the land use and offers a wide range of socio-economic benefits. Cyanidation, the most widespread Au leaching option, is progressively abandoned due to the high risk associated with its use and to the low public acceptance. Therefore, alternative methods such as thiocyanate, thiourea, thiosulphate and halide leaching gained more and more interest. This chapter presents the most important features of some Au leaching methods, emphasizing their advantages, limitations and potential applications.

Keywords: gold recovery, nonferrous mining wastes, leaching, technology, circular economy

1. Introduction

From ancient times, gold was associated with power and wealth, being used for the manufacture of tools and weapons, decorative objects and jewelries. Nowadays, gold is a highly required element in the field of electronics, nanotechnology, medicine, food, cosmetics, decorative or creative fashion, as well as in space technology [1–4].

Despite their economic importance, mining and ore processing have a low public acceptance and a high environmental pollution potential as they generate great amounts of wastes consisting in a mixture of solid waste materials (sand, fine grained ground-up rock with a size of 1–600 μm), water, chemicals and high concentrations of hazardous metals (Cu, Cd, Fe, Mn, Pb, Zn), metalloids (As, Se), together with precious metals (Au, Ag) [5–9].

The mining waste disposal and the long-term management of tailing storage facilities are critical issues of the mining process, as they can cause landscape damages and can lead to severe environmental contamination and destruction of living ecosystems [10, 11]. Worldwide, several tailing dam accidents with significant environmental damages and sometimes also with human lives loss were reported [11, 12]. One of the most important tailings dam failures occurred in 2000 in Baia Mare, Romania, due to an improper design and lack of effective management of the tailings impoundment, causing catastrophic damages to the environment [13, 14]. Another severe mining failure was reported in 1971 in the Certej River catchment, Romania, where a large volume of mine tailings flooded the valley and generated a significant pollution of the surrounding environment, together with 100 human lives loss [15]. An important pollution accident occurred in Spain in 1998, when a massive amount of acid water and mud containing toxic metals were released into the Agrio and Guadiamar River from the dam of the Aznalcollar tailings pond [16].

Mining wastes and by-products are valuable secondary resources since they contain important amounts of base, precious or strategic metals that can be recovered [17]. Beside their economic importance, the wastes valorization by reprocessing could improve the quality of the environment. The recycling, reuse and recovery of extractive wastes is also encouraged in the Extractive Waste Directive 2006/21/EC as it could lead to sustainable mining by resources conservation and reduced environmental impact [17, 18]. Therefore, new processing methods and technologies need to be developed and implemented. The most used method for Au leaching from wastes is based on cyanidation. However, in the context of raising social awareness and straightening environmental regulation, cyanide has become a socially and environmentally undesirable method for Au recovery. Therefore, the interest in finding other alternatives to cyanide, with low impact on the environment increased [19–22]. There are a considerable number of gold leaching methods which are currently tested or developed as pilot-scale studies, but only a few are available on commercial scale. The most tested leaching agents for gold are thiosulfate, thiourea, thiocyanate and halides [19–21]. An effective Au recovery process from mining wastes could provide new resources for various industrial fields [23]. This chapter presents an overview of the most used leaching methods for Au recovery with their advantages and limitations.

2. Gold leaching methods

2.1 Cyanide leaching

Cyanide is a cheap but highly toxic reagent that is very effective in leaching gold from low-grade minerals and mining wastes. Therefore, cyanidation is the most widely used method for the extraction of gold from mining wastes. Despite its advantages, is considered an unacceptable and highly hazardous approach. The health and safety concerns related to the use of cyanide as a leaching agent were raised after the occurrence of several technological accidents that severely damaged the environment [20, 24, 25]. Such incidents led to the development of a voluntary program in the gold mining industry entitled the "International Cyanide Management Code" with the objective to safely manage cyanide and safeguard human health and the environment [26, 27].

The cyanide leaching is based on the Au complexation with cyanide ions in the presence of oxygen in an alkaline solution according to Eq. (1) [22].

$$4Au + 8CN^{-} + O_2 + 2H_2O = 4\left[Au(CN)_2\right]^{-} + 4OH^{-} \tag{1}$$

Cyanide compounds are classified into three main types: free cyanides (hydrogen cyanide (HCN), ionic cyanide (CN^-)), weak acid dissociable (WAD) cyanide complexes (with Cd, Cu, Ni, and Zn) and strong cyanide complexes (with Co, Au, Ag, and Fe). The chemistry of these compounds offers perspectives on their actions regarding performance, safety and environment [28]. There are a couple of main ways through which cyanide can damage the environment: leakages, spills and evaporation from open leaching basins [21]. To reduce the negative impact on the environment, the naturally occurring cyanide dissociation mechanisms such as volatilization, complexation, precipitation, adsorption, biological transformation, and sulfidation can be artificially enhanced [27]. By complexation, most often with formation of iron cyanocomplexes, cyanide can be removed from wastes. However, considering that these complexes can dissociate photochemically into free cyanides, some concerns regarding the environmental risks were raised [27]. The adsorption of weak and strong cyanometallic complexes on goethite, manganese oxides, aluminum oxides, silica, and clays is another option for cyanide reduction [27]. Biological transformations assisted by bacteria, fungi or plant species may break down cyanide via oxidative, reductive, hydrolytic or assimilatory pathways to carbon and nitrogen species used for their growth [27]. The rate of cyanide attenuation in tailings is influenced by cyanide speciation, pH of the solution, temperature, redox conditions, exposure to sunlight and microbial activity [27].

2.2 Thiourea leaching

Thiourea ($SC(NH_2)_2$) dissolves gold by forming a complex in acidic solution according to Eq. (2) [20, 22, 29, 30]. In the leaching process, ferric sulfate is added as a catalyst to enhance the gold oxidation [20, 22].

$$Au^+ + 2SC(NH_2)_2 = Au\left(SC(NH_2)_2\right)_2^+ \tag{2}$$

Gold dissolution in thiourea is faster than in cyanide, but high volumes of thiourea solutions are needed in the dissolution process [22]. This shortcoming is avoided by using a mixture of thiourea, thiocyanate and ferric sulfate [21]. Thiourea presents low sensitivity to base metals present in mining wastes and tailings used as raw material for Au recovery [29]. Regardless of its low toxicity compared to cyanide, thiourea is classified as a potential carcinogen [20, 29].

Extensive research has been carried out on Au leaching using acid thiourea solution at laboratory scale. Moreover, thiourea leaching of Au was tested in pilot plants and industrial operations [28, 30]. The pH of the solution, leaching potential, ferric sulfate concentration, thiourea concentration and leaching time are critical parameters for the leaching efficiency [20]. The optimum conditions for thiourea leaching can be achieved by using an appropriate quantity of oxidant to ensure the oxidation of 50% of the thiourea to formamidine disulfide. An excessive amount of oxidant will lead to high thiourea consumptions. High consumptions combined with the use of reagents for pH adjustment and potential control will increase the cost of the leaching process [28].

2.3 Thiocyanate leaching

Thiocyanate (SCN^-) forms two stable and soluble complexes with gold, $Au(SCN)_2^-$ (aurothiocyanate) and $Au(SCN)_4^-$ (aurithiocyanate), out of which $Au(SCN)_4^-$ is the most stable (Eqs. (3) and (4)) [28, 31].

$$Au + 2SCN^- = Au(SCN)_2^- + e^- \quad (3)$$

$$Au + 4SCN^- = Au(SCN)_4^- + 3e^- \quad (4)$$

Thiocyanate has low toxicity, high stability, but also slow leaching rate. Thus, ferric ion as an oxidant is used to increase the leaching rate. Gold leaching using thiocyanate takes place in the presence of ferric ions, according to Eq. (5) [19].

$$Au + 4SCN^- + 3Fe^{3+} = Au(SCN)_4^- + 3Fe^{2+} \quad (5)$$

The thiocyanate/ferric sulfate system proved to be suitable for a wide range of ferric ion/thiocyanate molar ratios and slowed the rate of thiocyanate decomposition [32]. Generally, gold leaching using thiocyanate (0.01–0.05 M) occurs at a potential of 0.4–0.45 V, pH 1–3, in the presence of an oxidant like ferric ions (2–5 g/L) or peroxide. It has been shown that, under optimal conditions, a gold extraction yield of 95% can be achieved [21]. Thiocyanate concentrations in the range of 0.5 to 5 g/L and Fe (III) concentrations in the range of 6 to 12 g/L have been used in laboratory and small-scale pilot tests. The thiocyanate concentration must be maintained for the effective leaching of Au [28]. Thiocyanate leaching has not yet been commercialized due to its complex operating process [32]. As the leaching takes place at low pH, special reactors are required to resist in highly corrosive and oxidizing media [29]. Before its large-scale implementation, more research is needed to identify the optimum conditions of the process and to reduce the thiocyanate consumption.

2.4 Thiosulfate leaching

The thiosulphate leaching proved to be a very promising, environmental-friendly alternative to cyanide leaching for Au and Ag recovery [20]. Usually it is used under alkaline conditions to avoid thiosulfate decomposition in the presence of oxygen as oxidation agent (Eq. (6)) [20, 21, 28].

$$4Au + 8S_2O_3^{2-} + O_2 + 2H_2O = 4Au(S_2O_3)_2^{3-} + 4OH^- \quad (6)$$

Generally, the dissolution rate of Au in alkaline thiosulphate is slow, but it can be enhanced in the presence of ammonia and Cu^{2+} [20, 21]. The stability of thiosulfate and copper complexes depends on the pH of the solution [22]. The Au dissolution in ammoniacal-copper thiosulfate takes place according to Eq. (7) [28].

$$Au + 5S_2O_3^{2-} + Cu(NH_3)_4^{2+} = Au(S_2O_3)_2^{3-} + 4NH_3 + Cu(S_2O_3)_3^{5-} \quad (7)$$

The main advantages of thiosulphate leaching compared with other methods are the low toxicity, high reaction selectivity, ability to recirculate the leaching solutions, lower reagent cost and the possibility to recover the dissolved gold by adsorption and electrodeposition [8, 33]. The main disadvantage of alkaline thiosulphate leaching is the high reagent consumption and low extraction rates [21].

Recently, Ubaldini investigated the use of thiosulphate for Au extraction using mine tailings from Ribita and Criscior [8]. A gold extraction of 75% after leaching and a recovery of 90% Au after purification (adsorption–desorption–electrodeposition cycle) was obtained, while the overall process achieved a recovery of 65–67% Au [8]. The Au and Ag recovery from mineral tailings using glycine and sodium thiosulphate showed a leaching recovery of Au more than 80% after 48 h leaching tests with thiosulfate at a solid–liquid ratio of 1:1 [34].

Several studies have been carried out over the last decades to establish the commercial feasibility of Au leaching using thiosulphate. The high consumption of thiosulfate during Au leaching represents a disadvantage for scaling up the process as thiosulphate is easily oxidized by the copper ions added as catalyzer [33]. Moreover, the low affinity of activated carbon for the gold complex makes the recovery of Au more difficult [33].

Mahmoud and Awad studied the recovery of Au from thiosulfate solution on activated carbon in the presence of ammonium persulfate [35]. The obtained results showed that increasing the ammonium persulfate concentrations to 0.01 M, an efficiency of 85% for gold adsorption after only 10 min was obtained, and 95% of Au was recovered after 90 min [36]. The recovery of Au from the thiosulphate leachate using strong base anion resins compared with weak base anion resins presents several advantages such as higher adsorption capacities of gold complex and independence of the adsorption performances on the pH of the solution. However, their selectivity for $[Au(S_2O_3)_2]^{3-}$ against $[Cu(S_2O_3)_3]^{5-}$ is low and complex processes are required for the complete separation of gold and copper from the anion resin [33].

2.5 Halide leaching

2.5.1 Chlorination

Before the large-scale use of cyanide leaching, chlorination was widely applied for gold recovery [20, 21]. Gold dissolution occurs in two stages according to Eqs. (8) and (9) [28].

$$Au + Cl^- = AuCl + e^- \quad (8)$$

$$AuCl_2^- + 2Cl^- = AuCl_4^- + 2e^- \quad (9)$$

Compared to alkaline cyanide leaching, chlorination offers a high dissolution rate, but requests acidic media, high temperatures and high concentrations of chloride [21]. In the case of minerals containing silver and lead the metal recovery is low. Moreover, during the leaching process highly toxic and corrosive chlorine gases are released [21]. The reagent consumption is high when low concentrations of sulfides are present in the wastes, leading to the reduction of the gold complex to metallic gold [20].

Recently, Ahtiainen and Lundstrom studied cyanide-free gold leaching in mild chloride media obtaining a gold extraction of 72% at a redox potential <520 mV vs. Ag/AgCl [37].

The combination of chlorination with roasting for the Au extraction showed that 91.6% of Au was recovered using 4% $CaCl_2$, while heating at 1323 K for 2 h [38]. Li studied the gold extraction from tailings using sulfuric acid as a pretreatment before calcium hypochlorite leaching [39]. The obtained results showed that the leaching rate of Au was 81% using 8% calcium hypochlorite, 333 K chlorination temperature and 2 h chlorination time [39]. The use of chlorine for gold extraction remains difficult to use due to the high reagent consumption, its corrosive effect, high cost of the overall process and challenges experienced in Au recovering process [28].

2.5.2 Bromine

Gold dissolution in bromide (Eq. (10)) is influenced by the concentration of bromide and Au, the pH and the electrochemical potential of the anodic and cathodic processes [21, 40].

$$Au + 4Br^{-} = AuBr_4^{-} + 3e^{-} \tag{10}$$

Bromide leaching has the advantages of short extraction time, high dissolution rates, high selectivity and adaptation to a wide range of pH values. However, bromide is not suitable to be used as a large-scale industrial process as it is difficult to handle and has high reagent costs [20–22, 40].

Over the last years, gold dissolution was investigated using different oxidants like ferric ion, hydrogen peroxide and hypochlorite. The results showed a slow dissolution of gold using hydrogen peroxide and ferric ion [40]. The efficiency of bromine produced in-situ using NaBr, NaOCl and HCl to dissolve auriferous gold ore from the Castromil deposit (Portugal) was proven to be comparable with that of cyanide leaching and twice higher than of thiosulfate [40].

2.5.3 Iodine

Triiodide ion formed by iodine (I_2) and iodide ions (I^-) acts as an oxidant complexing gold (Eq. (11)) [21, 29].

$$Au + 4I^{-} = AuI_4^{-} + 3e^{-} \tag{11}$$

Iodine gold leaching can be a promising alternative to cyanide leaching because of its low volatility and hazardousness [22]. The process presents high leaching rates and the formed gold iodide complexes are more stable in aqueous solutions than the complexes with other halogens [20]. However, iodine was not used at industrial scale due to its high cost [22]. The electrolytic deposition could be an efficient method to reduce the costs through electrolytic recovery of gold and regeneration of iodine [29]. Recently, electrodeposition of gold from iodine leaching solution using response surface methodology was used to study the interactions between variables and their effect on gold deposition rate. The proposed method showed a high deposition rate (94.02%), but a low coulombic efficiency (2.53%) [41].

Presently, the application of halide systems is limited due to the difficulties encountered in maintaining the gold complex in the solution [20].

2.6 Aqua regia leaching

Aqua regia is a mixture of concentrated nitric acid (HNO_3) and hydrochloric acid (HCl). The dissolution of gold with aqua regia is a simple, fast and effective process, but the amount of NO_x released in the atmosphere can be a significant source of air pollution [42]. The HNO_3 favors the formation of trivalent gold ions, which further react with chloride to form tetrachloroaurate anions, according to Eq. (12) [21, 43].

$$Au + HNO_3 + 4HCl = AuCl^-_4 + H^+ + NO + 2H_2O \tag{12}$$

The aqua regia leaching is mostly used for alloys with high gold content [36]. In case of higher Ag content, it is necessary to reduce the amount of Ag to prevent the incomplete dissolution of gold by blending doré materials with feedstocks containing low amounts of Ag or by pretreatment with HNO_3 for Ag removal before dissolution. Aqua regia is known as an effective leaching agent due to its high dissolution rate, but is extremely corrosive [21]. During the leaching process, toxic NO_x gases are released. The NO_x emissions depend on the acid concentrations, temperature and air flow rates of the dissolution process [42]. The effectiveness of the dissolution process in aqua regia is influenced by the material granulation which can offer a large surface area to enable the reaction kinetics. In addition, the solution can be heated during dissolution to allow a rapid reaction.

2.7 Microbial leaching

Recovery of value-added metals from various wastes using microbial species has attracted much interest in recent years due to the long-term decline of ore grades and concentrates. Microorganisms play an important role especially in the gold recovery process from mining wastes and tailings. Some specialized bacteria, fungi, yeasts, algae or actinomycetes are increasingly being used to facilitate the extraction of gold from low-grade auriferous ore [44]. These microorganisms can enhance the oxidation of metallic minerals and may be used as flotation agents or as biosorbents in the gold recovery process [24, 45].

In recent years, two different types of biomining processes have attracted researchers' interest as alternatives to conventional methods: bioleaching and biological oxidation, as they proved to be cost-efficient, sustainable and non-hazardous [46–48].

Bioleaching is a solubilization process in which bacteria help to dissolve gold from ores or wastes, while in the biooxidation process, the acidophilic microorganisms release gold from minerals during sulfide oxidation [49]. Biooxidation of gold can be applied as heap or dump leaching and stirred tank leaching. The static biooxidation techniques are based on the principle of circulating water and air through waste heaps to activate the growth of microorganisms that amplify the oxidation [50]. Cyanogenic microorganisms as *Chromobacterium violaceum, Pseudomonas fluorescens* and *Pseudomonas plecoglossicida* were able to mobilize gold when grown in the presence of various metal-containing solids. Compared to chemical oxidation, biological oxidation offers the advantages of low production costs, low temperatures, low pressures, partial sulfide oxidation, decreased leachate consumption and no atmospheric pollution [51]. In polymetallic sulfidic ores several acidophilic, chemolithotrophic iron and sulfur oxidizing bacteria are present. Mesophilic iron and sulfur oxidizing bacteria as *Acidithiobacillus ferroxidans*, sulfur-oxidizing *Acidithiobacillus thioxidans*, iron-oxidizing *Leptospirillum ferriphilum* and *Leptospirillum ferrooxidans*, moderately thermophilic bacteria, such as sulfur-oxidizing *Acidithiobacillus caldus* and sulfur and iron oxidizing *Sulfobacillus* spp. has been reported to assist in the oxidation of sulfides [44, 52].

Various microorganisms were tested for gold biomining [51]. A recent study has reported the Au recovery from polymetallic sulfide minerals using biooxidation followed by acid washing and citrate leaching [53]. Thus, the biooxidation stage removed the refractory ores, increasing the gold extraction from 17.3 to 86.4% [53]. In the biooxidation process, sulfides are oxidized by mixed mesophilic culture mainly consisting of *Acidithiobacillus ferrooxidans.* A combined procedure for Au, Ag and Pb recovery from sulfide minerals was proposed by Lorenzo-Tallafigo [54].

Biosorption by microbial biomass is another promising, cost efficient and eco-friendly method for the gold recovery from wastes [23, 54]. Biosorption is a passive sorption and/or complexation method of gold in the cell wall of diverse algae, fungi and bacteria biomass [54, 55]. Stationary or dead microbial biomass bind and concentrate gold ions from pregnant leachates [56]. In biosorption processes a series of green and brown algae (*Chlorella vulgaris, Fucus vesiculosus, Sargassum natans),* fungi (*Aspergillus niger*, *Mucor rouxii*, *Rhizopus arrihus*, *Aspergillus oryzae*, *Chaetomium globosum*, *Gibberella fujikuroi*, *Mucor hiemalis*, *Penicillium chrysogenum*, *Purpureocillium lilacinum*), yeast (*Candida krusei*, *Candida robusta*, *Candida utilis*, *Cryptococcus albidus*, *Cryptococcus laurentii*, *Debaryomyces hansenii*, *Endomycopsis fibuligera*, *Hansenula anomala*, *Hansenula saturnas*, *Kluyveromyces* spp., *Saccharomyces cerevisiae*, *Sporobolomyces salmonicolor*, *Torulopsisaeria*) or bacteria (*Streptomyces phaeochromogenes* HUT6013, *Acinetobacter calcoaceticus, Erwinia herbicola*, *Pseudomonas aeruginosa*, *Pseudomonas maltophilia*) are used for gold recovery [24]. Some microbial species (*Bacillus subtilis*, *Escherichia coli*, *Streptomyces albus, Candida utilis*, *Aspergillus niger*) can contribute to the passive sorption of gold from solution or have the capacity to accumulate gold in an EPS capsule (*Hyphomonas adhaerens* MHS-3) [51]. A gold recovery rate of 85% has been reported by Kenney when non-metabolizing bacteria cells of *Bacillus subtilis* and *Pseudomonas putida* were used [57].

Recent studies revealed effective results for Au recovery with other biomining methods as bioprecipitation, biomineralization, bioflotation, bioflocculation, biosorption and bioaccumulation [58–60]. All these methods are based on gold harvesting microorganisms, which are either isolated from the gold enriched areas and domesticated or bioengineered strains with exceptional gold retrieval efficiency [48].

Due to the fact that various microbial communities have different structure, functions and dynamics in the gold metabolization, their use in bio-hydrometallurgical processes still remain a challenge. Even if many thermophilic or acidophilic bacteria, archaea or other types of microorganisms have been isolated, characterized, and even used for extracting precious metals, new strains isolated from different sources of wastes are needed [47]. At the same time, it is necessary to find combinations of chemicals compatible with efficient microbial agents to recover high levels of gold [61].

In the mining industry, naturally-occurring microorganisms which can be exploited through different strategies for the extraction and recovery of gold have a great potential [62]. The use of microorganisms for the recovery of precious metals from waste is economical and can avoid environmental pollution [44]. Furthermore, microbe driven technologies based on processes like biofiltration using specialized biofilters can assure a specific recovery of the gold ions [63]. Future gold recovery processing systems based on microorganisms will revolutionize the gold production.

3. Conclusions

Mining wastes represent a valuable resource for various elements, among which precious metals like gold. These wastes present both challenges and opportunities, as it require long term management to reduce the environmental risks, but could act as important resources for base and precious metals. In order to secure the high global demand for gold, new, low-cost, highly efficient but also environmentally friendly methods need to be developed. Although there is a lot of research in the field of developing less-toxic alternatives to cyanide and several leaching agents proved their efficiency, till now, there is no viable industrial scale alternative to cyanide. Another important challenge is the recovery of Au from mine waste leachates containing several soluble metals in various concentrations.

Acknowledgements

This research was funded by a grant of the Romanian National Authority for Scientific Research and Innovation, CCCDI-UEFISCDI, project number 52/2018, COFUND-ERANET-ERAMIN-MINTECO-2, within PNCDI III.

Conflict of interest

The authors declare no conflict of interest.

Author details

Emilia Neag[1], Eniko Kovacs[1,2], Zamfira Dinca[1], Anamaria Iulia Török[1], Cerasel Varaticeanu[1] and Erika Andrea Levei[1]*

1 INCDO-INOE 2000, Research Institute for Analytical Instrumentation, Cluj-Napoca, Romania

2 University of Agricultural Sciences and Veterinary Medicine, Cluj-Napoca, Romania

*Address all correspondence to: erika.levei@icia.ro

IntechOpen

© 2020 The Author(s). Licensee IntechOpen. This chapter is distributed under the terms of the Creative Commons Attribution License (http://creativecommons.org/licenses/by/3.0), which permits unrestricted use, distribution, and reproduction in any medium, provided the original work is properly cited.

References

[1] Ahmad B, Hafeez N, Bashir S, Rauf A, Mujeeb Ur R. Phytofabricated gold nanoparticles and their biomedical applications. Biomedicine & Pharmacotherapy. 2017;**89**:414-425. DOI: 10.1016/j.biopha.2017.02.058

[2] Berners-Price SJ. Gold-Based Therapeutic Agents: A New Perspective. Bioinorganic Medicinal Chemistry2011. 197-222 p. DOI: 10.1002/9783527633104.ch7

[3] Hwu S, Garzuel M, Forro C, Ihle SJ, Reichmuth AM, Kurdzesau F, et al. An analytical method to control the surface density and stability of DNA-gold nanoparticles for an optimized biosensor. Colloids and Surfaces. B, Biointerfaces. 2020;**187**:110650. DOI: 10.1016/j.colsurfb.2019.110650

[4] Langley RC. Gold coatings for temperature control in space exploration. Gold Bulletin. 1971;**4**(4):62-66. DOI: 10.1007/bf03215144

[5] Edraki M, Baumgartl T, Manlapig E, Bradshaw D, Franks DM, Moran CJ. Designing mine tailings for better environmental, social and economic outcomes: A review of alternative approaches. Journal of Cleaner Production. 2014;**84**:411-420. DOI: 10.1016/j.jclepro.2014.04.079

[6] Park I, Tabelin CB, Jeon S, Li X, Seno K, Ito M, et al. A review of recent strategies for acid mine drainage prevention and mine tailings recycling. Chemosphere. 2019;**219**:588-606. DOI: 10.1016/j.chemosphere.2018.11.053

[7] Wang L, Ji B, Hu Y, Liu R, Sun W. A review on in situ phytoremediation of mine tailings. Chemosphere. 2017;**184**:594-600. DOI: 10.1016/j.chemosphere.2017.06.025

[8] Ubaldini S, Guglietta D, Vegliò F, Giuliano V. Valorization of mining waste by application of innovative Thiosulphate leaching for Gold recovery. Metals. 2019;**9**(3). DOI: 10.3390/met9030274

[9] Levei E, Frentiu T, Ponta M, Tanaselia C, Borodi G. Characterization and assessment of potential environmental risk of tailings stored in seven impoundments in the Aries river basin, Western Romania. Chemistry Central Journal. 2013;**7**(1):5. DOI: 10.1186/1752-153X-7-5

[10] Rintala L, Leikola M, Sauer C, Aromaa J, Roth-Berghofer T, Forsén O, et al. Designing gold extraction processes: Performance study of a case-based reasoning system. Minerals Engineering. 2017;**109**:42-53. DOI: 10.1016/j.mineng.2017.02.013

[11] Adiansyah JS, Rosano M, Vink S, Keir G. A framework for a sustainable approach to mine tailings management: Disposal strategies. Journal of Cleaner Production. 2015;**108**:1050-1062. DOI: 10.1016/j.jclepro.2015.07.139

[12] Owen JR, Kemp D, Lèbre É, Svobodova K, Pérez Murillo G. Catastrophic tailings dam failures and disaster risk disclosure. International Journal of Disaster Risk Reduction. 2020;**42**. DOI: 10.1016/j.ijdrr.2019.101361

[13] Lyu Z, Chai J, Xu Z, Qin Y, Cao J. A comprehensive review on reasons for tailings dam failures based on case history. Advances in Civil Engineering. 2019;**2019**:1-18. DOI: 10.1155/2019/4159306

[14] Macklin MG, Brewer PA, Balteanu D, Coulthard TJ, Driga B, Howard AJ, et al. The long term fate and environmental significance of contaminant metals released by the January and March 2000 mining tailings dam failures in Maramureş County,

upper Tisa Basin, Romania. Applied Geochemistry. 2003;**18**(2):241-257. DOI: 10.1016/s0883-2927(02)00123-3

[15] Sima M, Dold B, Frei L, Senila M, Balteanu D, Zobrist J. Sulfide oxidation and acid mine drainage formation within two active tailings impoundments in the Golden quadrangle of the Apuseni Mountains, Romania. Journal of Hazardous Materials. 2011;**189**(3):624-639. DOI: 10.1016/j.jhazmat.2011.01.069

[16] Grimalt JO, Ferrer M, Macpherson E. The mine tailing accident in Aznalcollar. Science of The Total Environment. 1999;**242**(1-3):3-11. DOI: 10.1016/s0048-9697(99)00372-1

[17] Kinnunen PHM, Kaksonen AH. Towards circular economy in mining: Opportunities and bottlenecks for tailings valorization. Journal of Cleaner Production. 2019;**228**:153-160. DOI: 10.1016/j.jclepro.2019.04.171

[18] Directive 2006/21/EC of the European Parliament and of the Council of 15 March 2006 on the management of waste from extractive industries and amending Directive 2004/35/EC. 2004.

[19] Aylmore MG. Alternative Lixiviants to cyanide for leaching Gold ores. Gold Ore Processing. 2016:447-484. DOI: 10.1016/b978-0-444-63658-4.00027-x

[20] Hilson G, Monhemius AJ. Alternatives to cyanide in the gold mining industry: What prospects for the future? Journal of Cleaner Production. 2006;**14**(12-13):1158-1167. DOI: 10.1016/j.jclepro.2004.09.005

[21] Gökelma M, Birich A, Stopic S, Friedrich B. A review on alternative Gold recovery Re-agents to cyanide. Journal of Materials Science and Chemical Engineering. 2016;**04**(08): 8-17. DOI: 10.4236/msce.2016.48002

[22] Birich A, Stopic S, Friedrich B. Kinetic investigation and dissolution behavior of cyanide alternative Gold leaching reagents. Scientific Reports. 2019;**9**(1). DOI: 10.1038/s41598-019-43383-4

[23] Calderon ARM, Alorro RD, Tadesse B, Yoo K, Tabelin CB. Repurposing of nickeliferous pyrrhotite from mine tailings as magnetic adsorbent for the recovery of gold from chloride solution. Resources, Conservation and Recycling. 2020;**161**. DOI: 10.1016/j.resconrec.2020.104971

[24] Syed S. Recovery of gold from secondary sources—A review. Hydrometallurgy. 2012;**115-116**:30-51. DOI: 10.1016/j.hydromet.2011.12.012

[25] Rico M, Benito G, Salgueiro AR, Díez-Herrero A, Pereira HG. Reported tailings dam failures. Journal of Hazardous Materials. 2008;**152**(2):846-852. DOI: 10.1016/j.jhazmat.2007.07.050

[26] International Cyanide Management Code for the Gold Mining Industry. Available from: https://www.cyanidecode.org/

[27] Johnson CA. The fate of cyanide in leach wastes at gold mines: An environmental perspective. Applied Geochemistry. 2015;**57**:194-205. DOI: 10.1016/j.apgeochem.2014.05.023

[28] Marsden JO, House CI. The Chemistry of Gold Extraction. 2nd ed. Gold Bulletin. Littleton, Colorado: Society for Mining, Metallurgy, and Exploration (SME); 2006

[29] Liang CJ, Li JY. Recovery of gold in iodine-iodide system – A review. Separation Science and Technology. 2018;**54**(6):1055-1066. DOI: 10.1080/01496395.2018.1523931

[30] Li J, Miller JD. A review of Gold leaching in acid Thiourea solutions. Mineral Processing and Extractive

Metallurgy Review. 2006;**27**(3):177-214. DOI: 10.1080/08827500500339315

[31] Li J, Safarzadeh MS, Moats MS, Miller JD, LeVier KM, Dietrich M, et al. Thiocyanate hydrometallurgy for the recovery of gold. Part I: Chemical and thermodynamic considerations. Hydrometallurgy. 2012;**113-114**:1-9. DOI: 10.1016/j.hydromet.2011.11.005

[32] Li J, Safarzadeh MS, Moats MS, Miller JD, LeVier KM, Dietrich M, et al. Thiocyanate hydrometallurgy for the recovery of gold. Hydrometallurgy. 2012;**113-114**:10-18. DOI: 10.1016/j.hydromet.2011.11.007

[33] Xu B, Kong W, Li Q, Yang Y, Jiang T, Liu X. A review of thiosulfate leaching of Gold: Focus on thiosulfate consumption and Gold recovery from pregnant solution. Metals. 2017;**7**(6). DOI: 10.3390/met7060222

[34] Munive GT, Encinas MA, Salazar Campoy MM, Álvarez VE, Vazquez VM, Choque DC. Leaching Gold and silver with an alternative system: Glycine and thiosulfate from mineral tailings. Journal of Metals. 2019;**72**(2):918-924. DOI: 10.1007/s11837-019-03652-z

[35] Mahmoud M, Awad HM. Improved recovery of gold and silver from thiosulfate solution on activated carbon in presence of ammonium persulfate. Physicochem Probl Miner Process. 2019;55:5:1271-85. DOI: https://doi.org/10.5277/ppmp19051

[36] Habashi F. Gold – An Historical Introduction. Gold Ore Processing2016. 1-20 p. DOI: 10.1016/b978-0-444-63658-4.00001-3

[37] Ahtiainen R, Lundström M. Cyanide-free gold leaching in exceptionally mild chloride solutions. Journal of Cleaner Production. 2019;**234**:9-17. DOI: 10.1016/j.jclepro.2019.06.197

[38] Li H, Ma A, Srinivasakannan C, Zhang L, Li S, Yin S. Investigation on the recovery of gold and silver from cyanide tailings using chlorination roasting process. Journal of Alloys and Compounds. 2018;**763**:241-249. DOI: 10.1016/j.jallcom.2018.05.298

[39] Li H, Yin S, Li S, Zhang L, Peng J, Yang K. Investigation on the recovery of gold from pretreated cyanide tailings using chlorination leaching process. Separation Science and Technology. 2019:1-9. DOI: 10.1080/01496395.2019.1708108

[40] Sousa R, Futuro A, Fiúza A, Vila MC, Dinis ML. Bromine leaching as an alternative method for gold dissolution. Minerals Engineering. 2018;**118**:16-23. DOI: 10.1016/j.mineng.2017.12.019

[41] Meng Q, Li G, Kang H, Yan X, Wang H, Xu D. A study of the electrodeposition of Gold process in iodine leaching solution. Metals. 2019;**10**(1). DOI: 10.3390/met10010050

[42] Mooiman MB, Simpson L. Refining of Gold- and Silver-Bearing Doré. Gold Ore Processing2016. 595-615 p. DOI: 10.1016/b978-0-444-63658-4.00034-7

[43] Rao MD, Singh KK, Morrison CA, Love JB. Challenges and opportunities in the recovery of gold from electronic waste. RSC Advances. 2020;**10**(8):4300-4309. DOI: 10.1039/c9ra07607g

[44] Fashola M, Ngole-Jeme V, Babalola O. Heavy metal pollution from Gold mines: Environmental effects and bacterial strategies for resistance. International Journal of Environmental Research and Public Health. 2016;**13**(11). DOI: 10.3390/ijerph13111047

[45] Aitimbetov T, White DM, Seth I. Biological gold recovery from gold–cyanide solutions. International Journal of Mineral Processing.

2005;**76**(1-2):33-42. DOI: 10.1016/j.minpro.2004.09.003

[46] Johnson DB. Development and application of biotechnologies in the metal mining industry. Environmental Science and Pollution Research. 2013;**20**(11):7768-7776. DOI: 10.1007/s11356-013-1482-7

[47] Pollmann K, Kutschke S, Matys S, Kostudis S, Hopfe S, Raff J. Novel biotechnological approaches for the recovery of metals from primary and secondary resources. Minerals. 2016;**6**(2). DOI: 10.3390/min6020054

[48] Rana S, Mishra P, Za W, Thakur S, Pant D, Singh L. Microbe-mediated sustainable bio-recovery of gold from low-grade precious solid waste: A microbiological overview. Journal of Environmental Sciences. 2020;**89**:47-64. DOI: 10.1016/j.jes.2019.09.023

[49] Johnson DB. Biomining—Biotechnologies for extracting and recovering metals from ores and waste materials. Current Opinion in Biotechnology. 2014;**30**:24-31. DOI: 10.1016/j.copbio.2014.04.008

[50] Morin D, Lips A, Pinches T, Huisman J, Frias C, Norberg A, et al. BioMinE – Integrated project for the development of biotechnology for metal-bearing materials in Europe. Hydrometallurgy. 2006;**83**(1-4):69-76. DOI: 10.1016/j.hydromet.2006.03.047

[51] Kaksonen AH, Mudunuru BM, Hackl R. The role of microorganisms in gold processing and recovery—A review. Hydrometallurgy. 2014;**142**:70-83. DOI: 10.1016/j.hydromet.2013.11.008

[52] Chingwaru W. Potential of biotechnology for metals extraction in Zimbabwe: A review. Journal of the Southern African Institute of Mining and Metallurgy. 2017;**117**(4):381-386. DOI: 10.17159/2411-9717/2017/v117n4a10

[53] Lorenzo-Tallafigo J, Iglesias-González N, Mazuelos A, Romero R, Carranza F. An alternative approach to recover lead, silver and gold from black gossan (polymetallic ore). Study of biological oxidation and lead recovery stages. Journal of Cleaner Production. 2019;**207**:510-521. DOI: 10.1016/j.jclepro.2018.10.041

[54] Mata YN, Torres E, Blázquez ML, Ballester A, González F, Muñoz JA. Gold(III) biosorption and bioreduction with the brown alga Fucus vesiculosus. Journal of Hazardous Materials. 2009;**166**(2-3):612-618. DOI: 10.1016/j.jhazmat.2008.11.064

[55] Mao J, Won SW, Vijayaraghavan K, Yun Y-S. Surface modification of Corynebacterium glutamicum for enhanced reactive red 4 biosorption. Bioresource Technology. 2009;**100**(3):1463-1466. DOI: 10.1016/j.biortech.2008.07.053

[56] Dobson RS, Burgess JE. Biological treatment of precious metal refinery wastewater: A review. Minerals Engineering. 2007;**20**(6):519-532. DOI: 10.1016/j.mineng.2006.10.011

[57] Kenney JPL, Song Z, Bunker BA, Fein JB. An experimental study of Au removal from solution by non-metabolizing bacterial cells and their exudates. Geochimica et Cosmochimica Acta. 2012;**87**:51-60. DOI: 10.1016/j.gca.2012.03.023

[58] Achinas S, Achinas V, Euverink GJW. A technological overview of biogas production from biowaste. Engineering. 2017;**3**(3):299-307. DOI: 10.1016/j.eng.2017.03.002

[59] Fairbrother L, Etschmann B, Brugger J, Shapter J, Southam G, Reith F. Biomineralization of Gold in biofilms ofCupriavidus metallidurans. Environmental Science & Technology. 2013;**47**(6):2628-2635. DOI: 10.1021/es302381d

[60] Nancharaiah YV, Mohan SV, Lens PNL. Biological and bioelectrochemical recovery of critical and scarce metals. Trends in Biotechnology. 2016;**34**(2):137-155. DOI: 10.1016/j.tibtech.2015.11.003

[61] Singh R, Pant D. Polyvinyl chloride degradation by hybrid (chemical and biological) modification. Polymer Degradation and Stability. 2016;**123**:80-87. DOI: 10.1016/j.polymdegradstab.2015.11.012

[62] Olson GJ, Brierley JA, Brierley CL. Bioleaching review part B. progress in bioleaching: applications of microbial processes by the minerals industries. Appl Microbiol Biotechnol. 2003;**63**(3):249-257. DOI: 10.1007/s00253-003-1404-6

[63] Yang C, Qian H, Li X, Cheng Y, He H, Zeng G, et al. Simultaneous removal of multicomponent VOCs in biofilters. Trends in Biotechnology. 2018;**36**(7):673-685. DOI: 10.1016/j.tibtech.2018.02.004

Section 4

Sustainable Products from Solid Wastes

Chapter 9

Bioelectricity from Organic Solid Waste

M. Azizul Moqsud

Abstract

Resource recovery and recycling of organic waste is a great challenge in the world. The unmanaged organic waste causes a great damage to the environment and the public health both in the developing countries and industrial parts of the world. In this research, an innovative method was adopted to generate bioelectricity from the organic waste by using the Microbial Fuel Cell (MFC). Various types of organic wastes such as livestock waste, food waste, fruit waste were used as the substrates of the microbial fuel cell. All the experiments were carried out in the same sized one chamber microbial fuel cell and the similar electrode materials. It was observed that all the organic wastes can be used to generate bioelectricity through microbial fuel cell. The generated electricity can be used in several environmental monitoring sensors and can be used as an alternate power source in the developing countries. The by-products of the bioelectricity generation can be used as soil conditioner in the organic depleted soil and agricultural fields.

Keywords: organic waste, bioelectricity, voltage generation, soil conditioner

1. Introduction

1.1 Organic waste state

Organic waste is generated in our everyday life. The amount of organic waste is increasing all over the world. By comparing other types of waste materials such as plastic waste, paper waste or metal waste, organic waste is the least cared waste in the world. The recycling rate of organic waste is not prominent both in developing countries and the developed countries. In Japan, the organic waste is burnt in the incineration plants [1]. However, to burn the organic waste is not good as the calorific value of the organic waste was not so high. The higher content of moisture of the organic waste can reduce the calorific value. The unmanaged organic waste has created several environmental pollutions and health hazards, especially in the developing countries. The traditional method of organic waste management such as composting is often not suitable and caused problems in the urban areas [2]. The landfill of organic waste is again causing a huge burden to the waste collection systems and the transportation and final disposal system in the hot and humid countries. So, to find some innovative method to recycle and resource recovery from organic waste is very crucial in recent time.

1.2 Microbial fuel cell to generate electricity

Microbial fuel cell is a biochemical device in where the bacteria can decompose the organic contents and generate the electricity [2–6]. In the previous research,

IntechOpen

it was observed that this MFC method can be used to clean the wastewater, bio-remediated the sulfide contaminated sediment, and consequently bioelectricity generation [7–9]. The benefit of this method is that it can generate bioelectricity while cleaning the environment. Moqsud et al. showed that MFC can also generate electricity from the organic waste in a compost type MFC [1]. Since then, other researchers are trying to use this novel technology to generate bioelectricity and recycling the organic waste as a resource recovery options from the organic waste. The modified version of MFC with the employment of plants are called the plant microbial fuel cell (PMFC). It was observed that in PMFC, by using the compost from the organic waste, the bioelectricity can be generated more [3].

1.3 World energy status

Due to the population increase in the world, the demand of clean energy is increasing day by day. It needs to find the new source of electricity as most of the fossil fuels are decreasing. The global warming challenge make this problem more critical. To find a new source of green energy is the major challenge in the world in this current state of the world. In this background, microbial fuel cell can be a potential candidate for the future green energy in the world. The accidents of nuclear power plant are devastating in many cases. So, it is also needed to generate bioelectricity from the safe source for the sustainable future generations.

The main objective of this research is that to evaluate the efficiency of the MFC by using the different types of organic wastes. Another objective is to check the feasibility of organic content as a soil conditioner from the by-products of bioelectricity generation.

2. Materials and methods

2.1 What is bioelectricity?

Bioelectricity is the electricity which can be generated from the biological sources and with the help of living materials [2]. Many times, the microorganism such as bacteria are the main working factors to generate electricity while biodegradable the organic waste both in the aerobic and anaerobic bacteria. The electro-active bacteria are most responsible for the electricity generation.

2.2 Organic waste composting

Organic waste poses exceptional challenges during waste collection, particularly in hot and humid climates, where timely collection and disposal are critical. In some cities as much as 79% of municipal waste is organic [4]. Thus, organic waste management needs priority attention. The composting process which is the most common method for organic waste management, involves microorganisms feeding on organic material and consuming oxygen. The composting process generates heat, drives off moisture, and reduces bulky organic waste into a beneficial soil-like material containing nutrients, humus, and microorganisms in just a few months. Material in an unmanaged pile of organic debris will eventually break down but the process will take a long time and may result in odor or other nuisance problems due to poor aeration. Composting efforts may be easier to start if organic waste from food industry entities is used rather than household organic waste, because the quality of the organic inputs can be more closely controlled.

2.3 Biogas generation from organic waste

Many researchers are trying to produce the biogas from different organic waste. The bacteria can decompose the organic waste and consequently generate the bio gas which are mainly methane and the carbon di oxide. The management of organic waste is a critical problem and biogas generation can be a solution of it, however, there are some socio-economic problems associated with the biogas production from the organic waste. The design of biogas plant in the urban area is a very difficult task due to the land requirements. Again, the use of biogas in the kitchen for cooking has not become popular among the users in the developing countries due to the misconception of the bad odour and aesthetic point of view [7, 8].

2.4 Laboratory experiments for microbial fuel cell

One chamber MFC has been used for different types of organic wastes to generate bioelectricity. **Figure 1** illustrates the schematic diagram of the MFC which has been used in the laboratory experiment. Anode was embedded into the biomass while cathode was placed on the surface. The anode was set approximately 5 cm below the surface of the biomass, while the cathode was placed immediately above the biomass surface, but under the water.

The biomass used in the MFC were livestock waste such as cow dung, chicken droppings, rice waste, food waste and fruit waste. The basic properties of moisture content and organic content are listed in **Table 1**. It was noticed that the organic content of the different organic waste is not so much varied among them. It was also observed that the pH value of the initial condition of the different organic waste are within the range of 6.1–7.2 which was relatively suitable for the microorganisms working in the microbial fuel cell.

The design of the MFC was kept constant while changing the substrates inside the MFC as shown in **Figure 1**. The cylindrical shaped MFC chamber is 15 x 10 cm. The cross-section of the cell was 10 x10 cm. The electrode materials which were used in the MFC was carbon fiber, carbon felt for all the cases. The electrode amount was kept constant for all type of organic substances. The effective area of electrodes (anode and cathode) was kept the same as the cell areas (100 cm^2).

The organic wastes such as cow dung was collected from the Department of Agriculture, Yamaguchi University at Yoshida campus, Japan while the chicken droppings, rice bran leaf were collected from Japan Agricultural Office, Ube city branch. The food waste and fruit waste were collected from the student's cafeteria of Yamaguchi University, Japan. In microbial fuel cell (MFC), bacteria used as biocatalyst to convert biodegradable organic substrates harmless by-products with the simultaneous production of electrical energy. The blended sample was poured into the container and placed the electrode and make the MFC. The external circuit was created by using the insulated copper wire connecting with an external resistor.

The voltage which generated across the resistor and capacitor was monitored every day at 1 pm by a multimeter. Polarization curve and power density–current curves were investigated by using different resistors and internal resistances and power densities were calculated as described elsewhere [8, 9]. Electrode output was measured in volts (V) against time. The current I in amperes (A) and power (P) was calculated using Ohm's law.

Statistical analysis was carried out and significant was taken when the p value was less than 0.05.

Experiments were conducted under a constant room temperature of 25^0C [4].

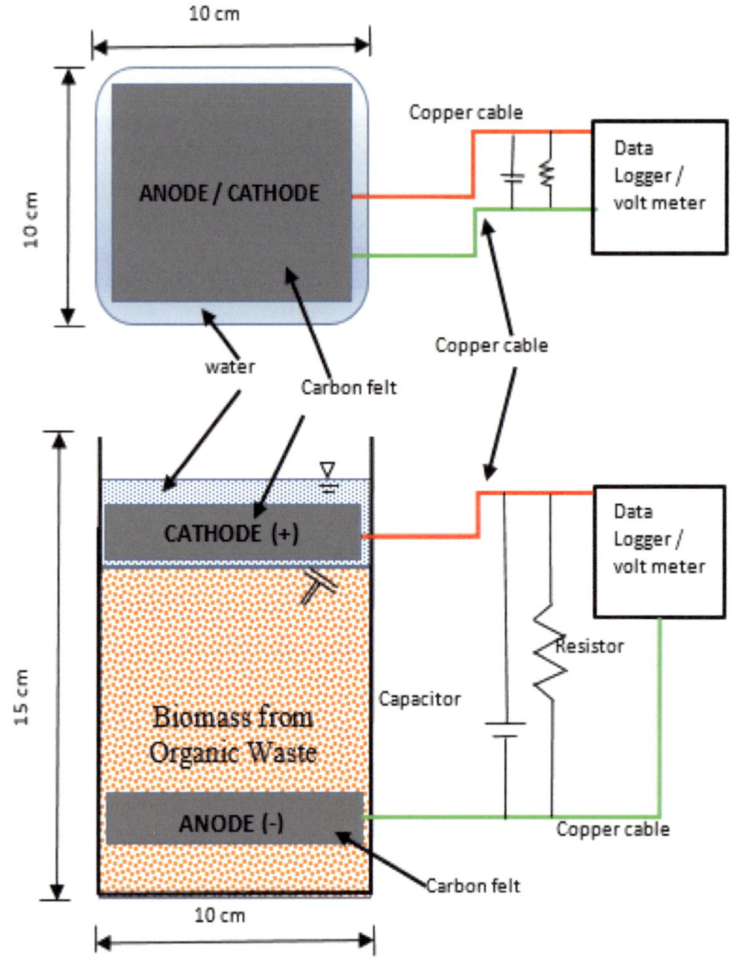

The

Figure 1.
Schematic diagram of the MFC used in the laboratory.

Sample used in the experiment	Moisture Content (%)	Loss on ignition (%)	pH
Fruit waste	70	80.33	6.9
Cow dung	79	87.24	6.1
Chicken dropping	65	82.55	6.3
Food waste	77	85	6.9
Rice bran	23	80	7.1
Leaf waste	20	87	7.2

Table 1.
Some basic properties of organic waste.

3. Results and discussion

Figure 2 illustrates the variation of voltage generation with time when using the feedstock waste as an organic waste in the MFC. It was found that when the cow dung and chicken dropping were used then the voltage generation was increasing sharply during the initial time. After one week the peak voltage reach at 450 mV and

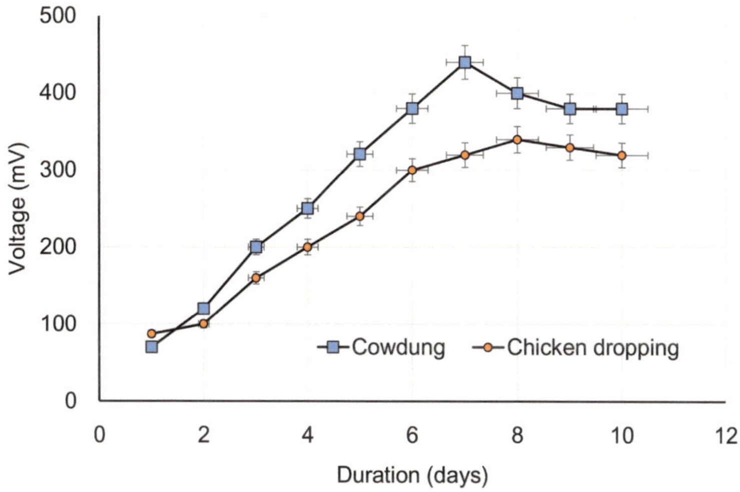

Figure 2.
Variation of voltage generation with duration by using live stock waste.

340 mV for the cow dung and the chicken droppings, respectively. It was also found that the cow dung generated more voltage than the chicken dropping. The organic content of cow dung was higher than the chicken dropping. This could be a reason why the voltage is higher while using the cow dung. Nevertheless, both feedstock waste can be used for the bioelectricity generation in the microbial fuel cell. The management of the feedstock waste was a great challenge for many years all over the world. The biogas generation is one option for recycling this waste however to setup a biogas plant is another big challenge in the urban area and the area where is densely populated. The use of cow dung and the chicken dropping in MFC as a substrate can be a great help for the future resource recovery in the future. The future research will be needed to control the smell from the MFC to make it more practicable for the household applications. The cost is significantly small in this system while comparing the biogas system. The feedstock waste can cause many environmental problems in the developing countries. The mismanagement of this waste is causing various environmental pollution such as water pollution and the soil pollution. In the future, if this feedstock can be used as the organic substance of the MFC system and generate bioelectricity, then it will be a source a resource. Many developing countries need to generate electricity for their development even in small amount.

Figure 3 shows the variation of the voltage with duration while using food waste and the fruit waste in the single chamber microbial fuel cell. It was found that when fruit waste was used then the MFC system can generate more electricity by comparing with the food waste. The fruit waste which were collected from the student's cafeteria contained a lot of fruit sections which were rich in sugar and carbohydrates. This sugar and the carbohydrates are the main source of energy for the electroactive bacteria. On the other hand, the food waste which are mainly comprised of the vegetable leftover and the other food remaining were not rich in sugar content and the carbohydrate content. This reason has influenced the result of the voltage generation while using the food waste and the fruit waste. The peak voltage reach at 380 mV and 300 mV when used as biomass in MFC in the fruit waste and food waste, respectively. While the voltage generation is lower when the food waste was used, it was also generated significant amount of voltage. This result reveals that the food waste which are currently disposed and burnt in the incineration plants in Japan can be recycled to generate bioelectricity in the MFC system.

Figure 4 illustrates that voltage generation with duration while using rice bran and the leaf waste. It was found that the bioelectricity can be generated from the rice bran

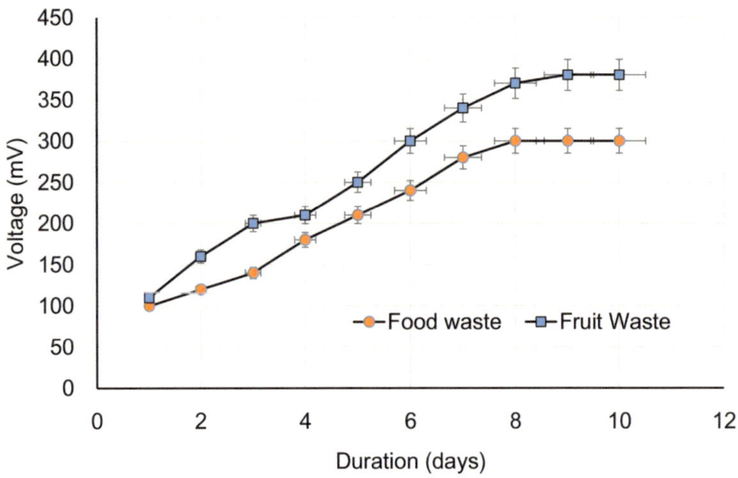

Figure 3.
Variation of voltage generation with duration by using food waste and fruit waste.

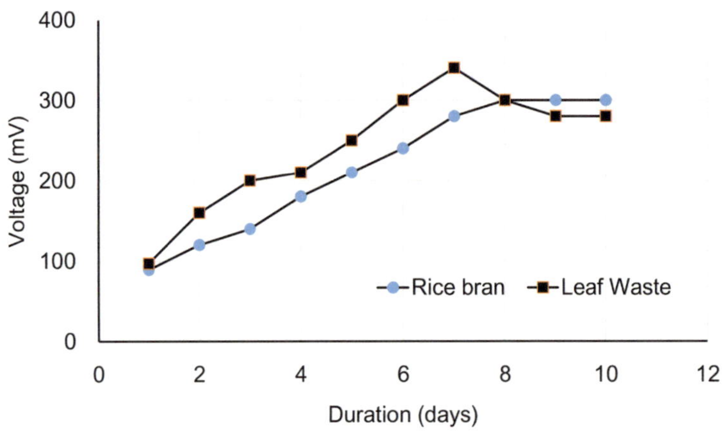

Figure 4.
Variation of voltage generation with duration by using rice bran and leaf waste.

and the leaf waste. The rice bran is produced in most of the time it was not reused or recycled in Japan. So, the use of this is very important for the bioelectricity generation in the MFC system. The garden waste often includes the dead leaves. Many times, this garden waste was not recycled and burnt with the other burnable waste. In this research this leaf can be used as the potential biomass in the MFC system. The carbon nitrogen ratio is very important for the microbial growth and the other activities for the best performance of MFC. However, this study showed that the voltage generation can be well even the garden waste was used in the MFC system. The peak voltage reached at 320 mV and 300 mV when using the rice bran and leaf waste, respectively. The interesting thig is that for the case of rice bran, the voltage generation was becoming constant after 8 days. The probable reason for that, the amount of food is depleted for the bacteria and the further biodegradation was not possible. The voltage generation by using the leaf mold decreased gradually after it reached the peak. The probable reason of this type of trend could be the substrates and the microbial degradation inside the biomass. As all the other factors are constant such as temperature, moisture content and sunlight, so it can be said that the organic content of the substances from the organic waste has the main influence to the voltage generation in this study. Nevertheless, the reason of this trend is, the organic waste from rice production and the garden waste can be used as a biomass in the MFC system for bioelectricity generation. In this research, the additional bacteria or food for the bacteria were not used to make the system uniform and compare it carefully. As a result, the electricity generation is the affected by the organic waste compositions mainly.

There are several types of organic waste all over the world. The management of this organic waste is always a great challenge for the people. So, the researchers are conducting their research to find out the innovative solutions to get rid of this problem. It is true that the MFC system needs to be more studied before it is practically used. The weather factors and the activities of the bacteria will be the major challenge in the future for the sustainable application in the real world. It is necessary to check the various factors which will be affecting in the field application of this system without any delay.

Resource recovery from organic waste is a long time due for the human society. The depletion of fossil fuels, global warming and climate change has increased the demand to find a new way to get rid of energy problems. The waste to energy is a popular term among the researchers all over the world. In these circumstances, the bioelectricity generation form the various organic waste is the very important part of advancement in this field.

One of the objectives of this experiment is to use the by-products from generating bioelectricity with MFCs of kitchen garbage and bamboo waste as soil conditioner or organic fertilizer in the agricultural fields. Hence, it is important to examine the values of different nutrients as presented in **Figure 5** [10]. Decomposition of organic matter is brought about by micro-organisms that use the carbon as a source of energy and nitrogen for building cell structure. From the results of both MFCs, nitrogen (N), phosphorus (P) and potassium (K) in the soil after bioelectricity generation were found to be in the range of 1.5–1.7%, 0.6–0.8% and 1.3–1.7% respectively, which is similar to the value of compost yielded by others [11]. It was observed that the values of nutrients, namely nitrogen, phosphorus, and potassium, were very similar to the soil reported in other countries [11]. As a result, the decomposed sample can be used as potential fertilizer or soil conditioner, offering a resolution to the problem of organic matter depletion in soil across the globe. Solid waste creation is a global dilemma due to development and industrialization. About 1.3 billion metric tons of municipal solid waste (MSW) is generated annually in the world and this quantity is expected to increase about 2.2 billion tons by 2025 [12–17]. The important thing is that the organic waste is all zero cost materials. It must be reused to get some resource for the future sustainable society.

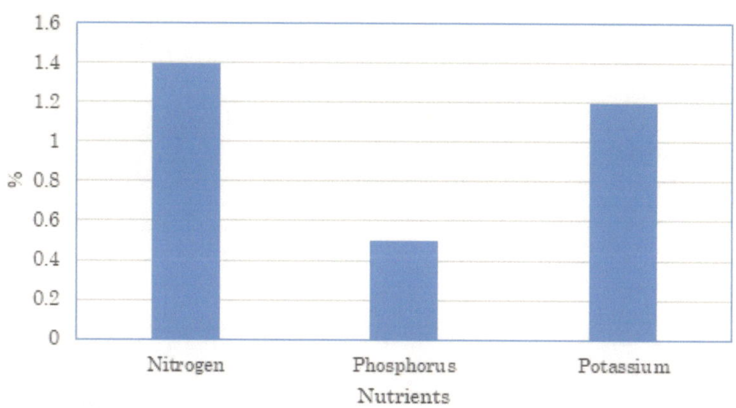

Figure 5.
Nutrient content of the by-products of bioelectricity generation.

4. Conclusion

Organic waste management is very critical in most of the developing countries in hot and humid conditions. It can pollute the environment including the surface water pollution and air pollution. These studies illustrate that the planet's tiniest inhabitants can address two of biggest environmental challenges our society faces today: generating clean renewable energy and handling vast quantities of organic waste. Through these studies, it is proven that MFCs are practical technology for the aforementioned problems. The generated bioelectricity can power devices such as LED lamps, phones, and geo-environmental sensors. Various kinds of organic waste such as livestock waste, kitchen garbage, agricultural waste can be used as a source of biomass for bioelectricity generation through MFC. The nutrient contents of the by-products of the MFC are rich and in a suitable range of a compost. Furthermore, the by-products from the decomposition of organic waste accelerated with the use of MFC can be used as soil conditioner, increasing the soil's organic content, and as a fertilizer to aid plant growth. In fact, there will be no by-product of generating bioelectricity by using the organic waste. The applicability of this study's results extends to both developing and developed countries where solid waste management and or sourcing of energy is a great concern. However, the future challenges for this research including the sustainable supply of organic waste will be a major problem in the industrialized parts of the world. Nevertheless, it can solve the problem of the waste management problems in the developing countries. In the future, the biomass such as algae can be used in the MFCs to generate the bioelectricity. MFCs can contribute to the maintenance of a healthy and pollutants-free environment for the future generation.

Acknowledgements

The author acknowledges the kind help of Dr. Tun Ahmad Gazali during the laboratory experiments. The authors also thank the people who provided the organic waste from the various sources in Yamaguchi agricultural field and the students cafeteria.

Conflict of interest

The authors declare no conflict of interest.

Author details

M. Azizul Moqsud
Department of Civil and Environmental Engineering, Yamaguchi University, Japan

*Address all correspondence to: azizul@yamaguchi-u.ac.jp

IntechOpen

© 2021 The Author(s). Licensee IntechOpen. This chapter is distributed under the terms of the Creative Commons Attribution License (http://creativecommons.org/licenses/by/3.0), which permits unrestricted use, distribution, and reproduction in any medium, provided the original work is properly cited.

References

[1] Moqsud, M.A., Omine, K., Yasufuku, N., Hyodo, M., Nakata, Y. MFC for bioelectricity generation from organic waste. Waste Management., 2013; 33 (11) : 2465-2471.

[2] Moqsud, M. A, Omine, K., Yasufuku, N., Hyodo, M., Nakata, Y. , Bioelectricity from bamboo and kitchen garbage. Waste Management and Research. 2014; 32(2): 124-30.

[3] Moqsud, M.A., Yoshitake, J., Bushra, Q., Hyodo, M., Omine, K., Srik, D. Compost in plant microbial fuel cell for bioelectricity generation. Waste Management. 2015; 36: 63-69.

[4] Moqsud, M.A. Bioelectricity generation and remediation of sulfide contaminated tidal flat sediment. International Journal of sediment research 35: (2020), pp. 91-96.

[5] Logan B E and Regan JM., (2006). Electricity-Producing Bacterial Communities in Microbial Fuel Cells. Trends Microbiology. 14:512-518.

[6] Toczylowska, R., Pielech-Przybylska, K., Sekrechka, A., Dziekojskakubczak. U., . Stimulation of electricity production in microbial fuel cells via regulation of syntrophic consortium development. Applied Energy. (2020), 271, 1151184.

[7] Yan, X., Lee, H.-S., Li, N., Wang, X. J. R., . The micro-niche of exoelectrogens influences bioelectricity generation in bioelectrochemical systems. Renewable and sustainable energy reviews. (2020)134,110184.

[8] Cao, Y., Mu, H., Liu, W., Zhang, R., Guo, Z., Xian, M., Liu, H.,. Electricigens in the anode of microbial fuel cells: pure cultures versus mixed communities. Microbial cell factories. 2019,18:39.

[9] Hong S W, Chang I, Choi Y and Chung T.,. Experimental evaluation of influential factors for electricity harvesting from sediment using microbial fuel cell. Bioresource Technology. 2009; 100: 3029-3035.

[10] C. Santoro, X.A. Walter, F. Soavi, J. Greenman, I. IeropoulosSelf-stratified and self-powered micro-supercapacitor integrated into a microbial fuel cell operating in human urine. Electrochim. Acta, 2019; 307, pp. 241-252.

[11] F. Soavi, C. Santoro Super capacitive operational mode in microbial fuel cell. Current Opinion on Electrochemistry, 2020, 22, pp. 1-8.

[12] Antonopoulou, G. , I. Ntaikou, C. Pastore, L. di Bitonto, S. Bebelis, G. LyberatosAn overall perspective for the energetic valorization of household food waste using microbial fuel cell technology of its extract, coupled with anaerobic digestion of the solid residue. Appl. Energy, 2019,242, pp. 1064-1073.

[13] Antonopoulou, G., K. Stamatelatou, S. Bebelis, G. LyberatosElectricity generation from synthetic substrates and cheese whey using a two-chamber microbial fuel cell. Biochem. Eng. J., 50 (2010), pp. 10-15.

[14] Barik, S. , K.K. Paul. Potential reuse of kitchen food waste. J. Environ. Chem. Eng., 2017, 5, pp. 196-204.

[15] Bernstad, A., J. la Cour Jansen. Review of comparative LCAs of food waste management systems – current status and potential improvements. Waste Management., 2012, 32, pp. 2439-2455.

[16] P. Choudhury, U.S.P. Uday, N. Mahata, O. Nath Tiwari, R. Narayan Ray, T. Kanti Bandyopadhyay, B. Bhunia. Performance improvement of microbial fuel cells for waste water treatment along with value addition: a review on past achievements and recent

perspectives. Renew. Sustain. Energy Rev., 2017, 79, pp. 372-389.

[17] Daud, S.,M.H.A. Bakar, B.H. Kim, M.R. Somalu, A. Muchtar, J.M. Jahim, S.A.M. Ali. Low-cost novel clay earthenware as separator in microbial electrochemical technology for power output improvement. Bioproc. Biosyst. Eng., 2020, 43, pp. 1369-1379.

Chapter 10

Agricultural Solid Wastes: Causes, Effects, and Effective Management

Isaac Oluseun Adejumo and Olufemi Adebukola Adebiyi

Abstract

The role of the agricultural sector in human development and economic development cannot be overemphasized. Awareness for increased agricultural production is on the increase, arising from the need to feed the ever-increasing human population. Interestingly, almost all agricultural activities generate wastes, which are generated in large quantities in many countries. However, these wastes may constitute a serious threat to human health through environmental pollution and handling them may result in huge economic loss. Unfortunately, in many developing countries where large quantities of these wastes are generated, they are not properly managed because little is known about their potential risks and benefits if properly managed. There are studies that address some of the challenges of agricultural solid wastes as well as suggestions on how they can be properly managed. In this chapter, we intend to explore the major sources of agricultural solid wastes, their potential risks, and how they can be properly managed.

Keywords: agricultural solid waste, animal feed, composting, environmental safety, recycling

1. Introduction

Increasing growth in human population has necessitated increased agricultural production. Agricultural production in the last five decades has been said to increase more than three times. Other factors responsible for increased agricultural production include technological advancement toward green revolution and expansion of soil for agricultural production [1, 2]. It has been estimated that agricultural sector provides about 24 million tons of food globally [1] with accompanying health risks and threat on ecosystems [3]. We cannot do without agriculture because food is a necessity across the globe, but the impact of agriculture on the environment is also evident. For example, it has been documented that about 21% of greenhouse gas emission comes from agriculture. The negative influence of agriculture on the environment, aquatic lives and human health have necessitated improvement in agricultural production, involving effective and efficient ways of handling agricultural solid wastes [4].

The global leaders have been mandated to prioritize production of more food and energy for increasing human population which is estimated to exceed 10 billion by 2050 as well as to tackle the impacts already caused. However, this mandate is expected to be achieved with lower emissions of pollutants, zero solid waste and

IntechOpen

less fossil fuel [5, 6]. The future prediction for increased agricultural production involves food production for human population, industrial needs, and animal feed [7]. However, every step of agricultural production, processing and consumption generates quantities of agricultural solid wastes, depending on the type of agricultural produce or product, processing techniques and purpose of use.

The agricultural sector is one of the main sectors generating the largest quantities of agricultural solid wastes, which may be allowed to accumulate indiscriminately and constitute nuisance to global health and threat to food security or used as raw materials for bio-economy [8, 9]. The benefits of recycling of agricultural solid wastes include reduction of greenhouse gas emissions and use as fossil fuel as well as contributing significantly to the development of new green markets, creation of jobs, production of bio-energy and bio-conversion of agricultural solid wastes to animal feed [10, 11].

The emphasis on the management of agricultural solid wastes cannot be overemphasis. Agricultural solid wastes are generated from many sources. One of such sources are pesticides, including herbicides and insecticides. It has been estimated that the global food production would fall by an estimate of about 42% if the use of pesticide is completely stopped [12]. The influence of agricultural solid wastes on human health, animal health, and the environment is significant and all hands must be on deck to tackle the menace posed by mismanagement of agricultural solid wastes. Agricultural solid wastes are mismanaged largely owing to ignorance. Many of the farmers and household managers who generate these wastes do not know how to effectively manage them. Many of them do not know the health implications of what they toy with, while some who know are 'handicapped'. Year after year, large tons of agricultural solid wastes are being produced, with an annual increase of about 7.5% [13, 14]. In many parts in developing countries, agricultural solid wastes are indiscriminately dumped or burnt in public places, thereby resulting in the generation of air pollution, soil contamination, a harmful gas, smoke and dust and the residue may be channeled into a water source thereby polluting the water and aquatic environment [15–17].

2. Classification and causes/sources of agricultural solid wastes

Agricultural solid wastes are produced mainly from farming activities. However, it is not limited to the production but other activities associated with farming and food chain. Every stage and phase of the agricultural-food chain can generate significant agricultural solid wastes. The broad classification of agricultural solid wastes includes the following:

a. Animal production solid wastes;

b. Food and meat processing solid wastes;

c. Crop production solid wastes;

d. On-farm medical solid wastes;

e. Horticultural production solid wastes;

f. Industrial agricultural solid wastes;

g. Chemical wastes.

1. **Animal production solid wastes**—animal production solid wastes are solid wastes generated from the production of livestock for whatever purposes. Examples of such wastes include bedding/litter, animal carcasses, damaged feeders, and water-trough, etc.

2. **Food and meat processing solid wastes**—this class of agricultural solid wastes are produced from the processing of crop or animal products for human consumption, such as abattoir or slaughterhouses. Examples of food and meat processing agricultural solid wastes include hoofs, bones, feathers, banana peels, etc.

3. **Crop production solid wastes**—crop solid wastes are associated with agricultural solid wastes typically produced from agricultural activities involving crop production. Examples of such agricultural solid wastes are crop residues, husks, etc.

4. **On-farm medical solid wastes**—on-farm medical solid wastes refer to solid wastes that are generated from the use of drugs, insecticides or vaccines used on or animals. Examples of such wastes include vaccine wrappers or containers, disposable needles, syringes, etc.

5. **Horticultural production solid wastes**—this group of agricultural solid wastes refer to solid wastes generated from cultivation and maintenance of horticultural plants and landscape for beautification. Examples of such wastes are prunings and grass cuttings.

6. **Industrial agricultural solid wastes**—agricultural produce and livestock are not only cultivated and produced for dietary consumption. They are used for other uses and it is not unlikely that such activities result in agricultural solid wastes. Wood processing and cuttings readily come to mind as a source of agricultural solid wastes. Paper production using agricultural products as raw materials also generate some quantities of agricultural solid wastes.

7. **Chemical wastes**—chemical wastes in this context have to do with agricultural solid wastes generated from the use of pesticides, insecticides and herbicides on the farm or store, such as pesticide containers or bottles. Agricultural activities still depend on the use of pesticides, insecticides, and herbicides, being handled by many uneducated and untrained farmers in developing countries, resulting in abuse by these uneducated farmers [18, 19]. Some uneducated farmers mishandle pesticide containers, thereby resulting in unpredictable environmental hazards. It has been reported that about 2% of pesticides remain in the containers after use, which some ignorant and uneducated users may throw in the ponds or on the open field resulting in food poisoning, environmental and water pollution, causing death of many lives [20, 21].

Agricultural solid wastes are usually generated through agricultural activities involving preparation, production, storage, processing and consumption of agricultural produce, livestock and their products. Agricultural solid wastes are produced via:

i. Farming activities

ii. Poor road network

iii. Poor electricity or lack of rural electrification

iv. Inadequate drying technique and storage facilities

v. Food spoilage

vi. Kitchen-generated agricultural solid wastes

1. Farming activities—the main source of agricultural solid waste generation is agriculture. Beginning from land clearing till harvest, every phase of farming activities results in the generation of agricultural waste. From preparing the pen for the arrival of the animals to the farm, preparation of pasture/paddock till the animals are slaughtered and sold, solid wastes are generated.

2. Poor road network for transporting harvested produce from the farm to the market or storage is another avenue of generating large quantities of agricultural solid wastes. This happens largely as a result of the bad road network in some developing countries, which may result in a road accident or delay of agricultural produce from farms to markets. When road accident occurs, perishable agricultural produce result easily in wastage, and when delayed, the same result may occur. The spoilt produce is either thrown away on the road or separated to be discarded once the farmer gets to the market. **Figure 1** shows agricultural produce being transported in a city in Nigeria.

3. Poor electricity or lack of rural electrification—the epileptic power supply and lack of rural electrification in some parts of developing countries with significant agricultural activities are contributing in no small measure to the generation of agricultural solid wastes. Stable electricity could have facilitated the cold storage of the harvested produce and thereby reduce spoilage and consequently agricultural solid wastes.

4. Inadequate drying technique and storage facilities—spoilage of much agricultural produce could be prevented with adequate drying techniques. If farmers have access to adequate drying technique or moisture monitor, it would have gone a long way in militating against food spoilage and agricultural solid waste, thereby enhancing food security and reducing the impact of agricultural solid waste on human health and the environment. Many of the farmers depend largely on the unpredictable solar system to dry their produce before they are stored, as well as rely on the conventional method of moisture monitoring which is neither effective nor accurate. Inadequate monitoring of moisture content in grain before storage has been reported to result in aflatoxin infestation. Aflatoxin is produced by *Aspergillus flavus*. Aflatoxin infestation is both a cause and a product of food spoilage [23] and its contamination of food and livestock feed can lead to significant annual crop losses globally [24].

It has been estimated that about 10% of global crop harvest is destroyed by filamentous fungi through contamination of food and feed with mycotoxins. Aflatoxins have been reported to produce liver carcinogens, impair human health in

Figure 1.
Transportation of agricultural produce in Nigeria. Source: Vanguard Newspaper [22].

developing countries, and result in the huge economic losses, in the U.S. corn alone amounting to about $280 million annually. The economic losses could be as high as 1 billion dollars if other crop-infestation such as cotton, peanuts and tree nuts are included. Aflatoxins B1 and B2 which cause preharvest and postharvest crop infestation are produced by *Aspergillus flavus* [23].

1. Food spoilage is another important source or cause of agricultural solid wastes. It has been estimated that about 40% of food is wasted in the US alone annually. This waste has been estimated to cost about 162 billion dollars Natural Resources Defense Council [25]. Pest and insect infestation may also increase wastage owing to spoilage.

2. Kitchen-generated agricultural solid wastes: in most cases, the end result of agricultural activities is family consumption. Usually, the consumption of agricultural produce at the family level is not without the production of agricultural solid wastes. Some of these wastes are generated out of necessity. For example, orange peels and banana peels are discarded as agricultural solid wastes in many homes. However, agricultural solid wastes may also be generated unintentionally, arising from food spoilage. Kitchen-generated agricultural solid wastes become significant when restaurants are included as kitchens (commercial kitchens). Of all the kitchen wastes considered in cities in China, agricultural solid wastes (food wastes) constitute between 88 and 94% [26]. **Figure 2**, **Tables 1** and **2** respectively show home-generated agricultural solid wastes, the composition of kitchen wastes and nutritional characteristics of kitchen wastes in selected cities in China.

Figure 2.
Home-generated agricultural solid wastes.

Cities	Food waste	Paper	Metal	Bone	Wood	Fiber	Plastic
Guiyang	92.09	0.80	0.10	5.20	1.01	0.10	0.70
Shenyang	92.16	0.42	0.08	5.22	1.31	0.12	0.69
Chongqing	94.13	0.31	0.00	5.24	0.02	0.13	0.19
Wuhan	88.40	2.80	0.20	5.20	1.00	0.30	2.10

Source: Li et al. [26].

Table 1.
Composition of kitchen wastes in Chinese cities (unit: %).

Cities	Moisture[a]	Volatile solid[b]	Crude protein[b]	Ether extract[b]	Oil[a]	Salinity[a]
Beijing	74.34	80.21	25.86	24.77	3.12	0.36
Tianjin	70.99	85.64	24.30	25.96	2.63	0.70
Chongqing	85.07	92.66	14.45	17.02	1.96	0.24
Suzhou	84.43	82.98	21.80	29.30	3.28	0.70
Hangzhou	74.94	91.50	16.46	24.31	2.09	1.32

Source: Li et al. [26].
[a]*Wet basis.*
[b]*Dry basis.*

Table 2.
Nutritional characteristics of kitchen wastes in Chinese cities (unit: %).

3. Influence of agricultural solid waste on human health and environment

The influence of agricultural production on human, health, change in climate, animal healthy and the environment cannot be over-emphasized. For example, it has been suggested the greenhouse gas emissions need to be reduced drastically to avert the impeding threat on the planet, earth and its inhabitants to avert temperature rise by at least an average rise of 35.6°F [27]. Animal production has been indicted to produce about 37 and 65% of global methane and nitrous oxide emissions respectively [28], which are more potent than carbon dioxide. Indiscriminate burning of agricultural solid wastes produces climate-relevant emissions. Improper handling of agricultural solid wastes influence change in climate and change in climate in turn hampers food production. The effects of indiscriminate disposal of agricultural solid wastes cannot be overemphasized. Some of the effects are outlined below:

i. Flood

ii. Health and environmental implication

iii. Food security

1. Flood: One major cause of flood has been the blockage of waterways. Waterways are blocked primarily when human beings build on waterways or when the canals or waterways are blocked by solid wastes. In an agricultural environment, the indiscriminate dumping of agricultural solid wastes can result in blockage of waterways which when that happens will result in floods which may result in losses of lives and properties.

2. Health and environmental implication—arising from indiscriminate burning of generated wastes. Indiscriminate dumping and burning of agricultural solid waste have resulted in pollution, a threat to human lives as well as other environmental problems, calling for global attention, although these wastes can be recycled to improve soil fertility, being rich in nutrient required for sustainable agricultural production [13, 29, 30]. **Figure 3** shows the agricultural solid wastes being dumped in open space.

3. Food security and agricultural solid wastes: Continuous human population growth has been linked with increased agricultural activities which consequently results in increased generation of agricultural solid wastes. There are currently about 7.5 billion people around the globe and a significant portion of this population still do not have enough food to eat. **Figure 4** is a chart comparing the human population according to continents while **Table 3** shows the current human population parameters according to continents. The effects of food insecurity are enormous, ranging from poor health, slow progress in education and employment development [34]. One of the important 17 Global Sustainable Goals is to end hunger, achieve food security and improve nutrition and promote sustainable agriculture by 2030. Unfortunately, 10 years ahead of the deadline for this goal, there are still about 821 hungry people across the globe [34]. It has been argued that the main problem of food insecurity is not that we are not producing enough food, but agricultural solid wastes, mainly food wastage is responsible. Africa and Asia have been noted as the fast-growing population in the world, incidentally, these are the regions with most food insecure people

and inefficient waste management [33, 35]. It has been estimated that one-third of the food we produce annually is lost or wasted, costing about one trillion US dollars annually. Wastage occurs mostly in developing countries during the production and supply chain while it occurs mainly in developed countries on the plate [34]. Agricultural solid wastes can be recycled as nonconventional feed ingredients to enhance food security by enhancing animal protein production [36]. **Figures 5** and **6** respectively show food wastage chart in America and estimate of unconsumed food by an average American family.

Figure 3.
Dumping of agricultural solid wastes at the public. Sources: Akande and Olorunnisola [31] and Olayiwola et al. [32].

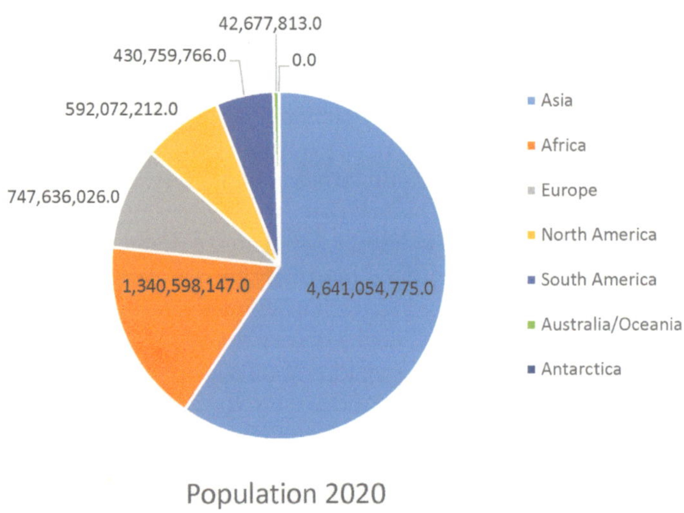

Figure 4.
Current population of the seven continents. Source: Worldometers [33].

Rank	Continent	Population	Area, km^2	Density, P/km^2	World population share, %
1	Asia	4,641,054,775	31,033,131	150	59.5
2	Africa	1,340,598,147	29,648,900	45	17.2
3	Europe	747,636,026	22,134,900	34	9.6
4	North America	592,072,212	21,330,000	28	7.6
5	South America	430,759,766	17,461,112	25	5.5
6	Australia/Oceania	42,677,813	8,486,460	5	0.6
7	Antarctica	0	13,720,000	0	0.0

Source: Worldometers [33].

Table 3.
List of continents ranked by current human population parameters.

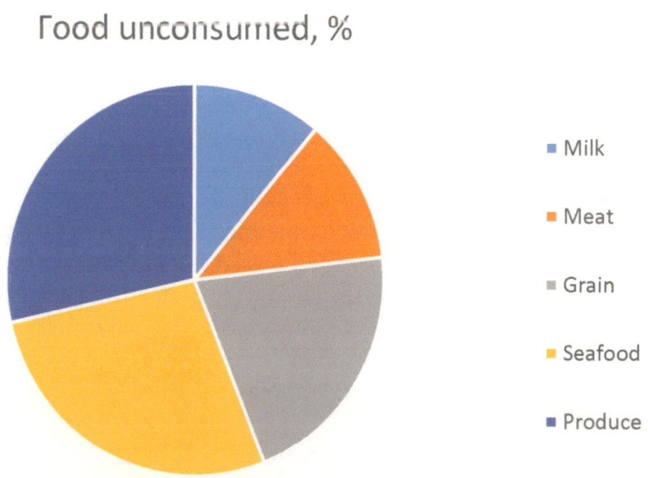

Figure 5.
Unconsumed food by an average American family. Source: Rescuing Leftover Cuisine [25].

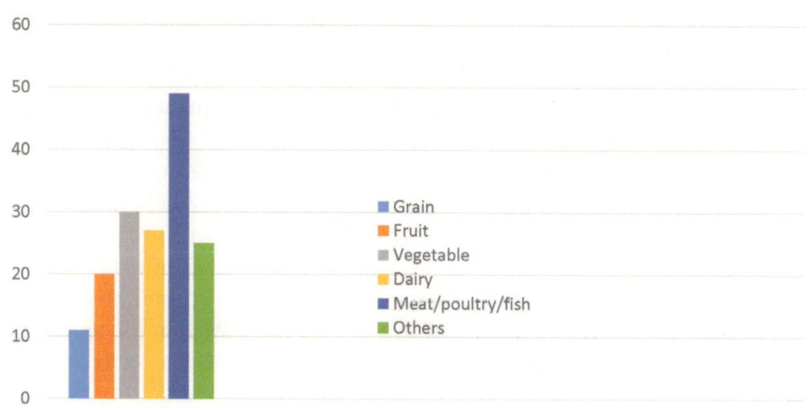

Figure 6.
Food wastage chart in America. Source: Rescuing Leftover Cuisine [25].

4. Effective management of agricultural solid wastes

There are options on how agricultural solid wastes could be handled. This chapter is necessary because of the need to focus people's attention on efficient ways of managing these wastes. Traditionally, shafts from palm oil processing could be used as fuel in fuel wood for cooking and heating. In the recent time, some of these wastes are put into better uses. Some of these agricultural solid wastes could be used as additives in cement mixes, water glass manufacturing, paper making, ethanol production, animal feed, electricity and biogas generation, heavy metal removal, mulching, organic fertilizers, and compost. An effective means of managing agricultural solid wastes is to recycle them to produce useful products. This can be achieved through:

i. Compositing/organic manure

ii. Substrates for edible fungi cultivation

iii. Nonconventional feed ingredient

iv. Traditional soap making

v. Alternative energy sources and bio-fuel production

vi. Production of silica

1. Compositing: Li et al. [26] recommended that kitchen wastes, largely agricultural solid waste from food wastage could be used as an animal feed via sterilization, fertilizer via composting and bioenergy via anaerobic digestion. These wastes are important candidates for compositing owing to their high organic matter content and nutrients, although their high salt, moisture content and oil may impair composting.

2. Substrates for mushroom cultivation: mushroom has been grown on different agricultural solid wastes as substrates [32, 37]. Steps involved in mushroom cultivation and its benefits are highlighted by Olayiwola et al. [32].

3. Nonconventional feed ingredient. Several attempts have been made to feed agricultural solid wastes to livestock as a means of recycling as well as a cheap source of feed for raising animal-source protein. A nonconventional feed ingredient, *mycomeat* has also been produced from agricultural solid wastes. The wastes served as substrate and a mixture of the substrates and the cultivated fungi (mushroom) was feed to broiler chicks, as a nonconventional feed ingredient, *mycomeat* [36–40] fed some agricultural solid wastes to albino rats and recommended processing of the wastes in order to obtain a better result. Adebiyi et al. [41] recommended the combination of 40% cassava peel +40% concentrate +20% watermelon wastes for feeding grower pigs. Poultry feathers could be used for several products instead of being indiscriminately discarded or burnt. Traditional, feathers are used for decoration, pillows and could be converted as nonconventional feed ingredients to feed livestock.

   Feathers are a group of agricultural solid wastes that are generated in large quantities annually as a by-product of poultry processing [42].

It may account for about 6% of the total live weight of a mature chicken. They are rich in a keratinous protein, which is a fibrous and insoluble protein [43]. Adejumo et al. [44] reported protein content of between 84 and 87% for feather meal, hence, effective use of feather meal as livestock feed ingredient may payoff than its use as other produce. Feathers can be used in erosion control, for diaper filling, as biodegradable composites, in the greenhouse industry, animal feeds, upholstery, artwork, paper alternatives, light-weight structural materials, water filtration fibers, fabric, aircraft, and automotive industries and thermal insulation [45, 46]. The major limitation to the use of feathers as a livestock feed ingredient is the insoluble keratinous protein, but recent studies are suggesting ways of overcoming the limitation [38, 44, 47]. It has been documented that about 80% of kitchen wastes, largely food wastage are fed to pigs in China, although direct feeding of kitchen waste has not been without restriction in China, arising from the concern of foot and mouth disease [48] Processing of agricultural solid wastes could enhance their value for feeding pigs [49, 50]. The effect of dried sweet orange (*Citrus sinensis*) peel has been tested on humoral immune response of broiler chickens [51] as well as maize replacement and its effect evaluated on growth performance and carcass qualities of broiler chickens [52], instead of allowing them to accumulate and constitute a nuisance as agricultural solid wastes.

4. Traditional soap making: traditional technology exists in Africa decades ago for turning some of the agricultural solid wastes into useful products. Cocoa pods which could turn agricultural solid wastes are usually either allowed to naturally decompose and enrich the soil or are used to make black soap, which may be used for washing dishes or bathing.

5. Alternative energy source and bio-fuel production: agricultural solid wastes can be converted to green energy through anaerobic digestion [9]. High protein and fat contents of these wastes may impair anaerobic digestion stability, as well as unavailability of efficient technology required for disposal of biogas residues [53]. However, pre-treatment techniques such as mechanical (sonication), chemical addition (acid or alkali), oxidative (ozone), biological (enzyme addition), thermal ad osmotic (freezing and sodium chloride treatment) may improve the physical and chemical properties of the wastes, thereby enhancing their solubilization of organic particles, sterilization effect as well as the promotion of their subsequent recycling (biogas production) [54, 55]. Despite many challenges confronting its production, bio-fuel and bio-energy attract many hopes as a sustainable renewable energy source, which tend to promote rural and regional development, reduction of CO_2 emission, creation of job opportunity as well as replacing the energy from nonrenewable fossil fuel with green energy [56–58]. Agricultural solid wastes (rich in cellulose, hemicellulose, starch, lipids and proteins) which are produced in large tons and burnt in open-field or allowed to accumulate in some developing countries may be channeled toward bio-fuel generation [59, 60]. Key players and political leaders, particularly in developing countries should team up with researchers to scale up the conversion of biomass to alternative energy sources or bio-fuel generation. This is expected not only to reduce the health menace

arising from open-field agricultural solid wastes burning or dumping but to improve energy production and reduce economic losses of waste disposal as well.

6. Production of silica: Production of silica: Silicon, the 2nd most abundant nonmetallic element in the earth crust with an atomic weight of 28 [61, 62] forms silica and silicates. It is rarely found in its elemental state owing to its affinity for oxygen [63]. It has been reported as a beneficial trace element, widely distributed in foods. Its health benefits include improvement of the structural integrity of nail, hair, skin, immunity, bone mineralization, bone calcification and reduces the occurrence of atherosclerosis [64–66]. In the presence of hydrochloric acid and other gastric fluids in the GIT, silicon compounds are degraded into bioavailable forms of silicic acid (ortho, meta, di, and tri-silicates) [67] and are diffused into different organs of the body [68, 69]. Silicon quantity decreases with age and tends to be more in plants than animal-sources, although dietary sources are low in silicon and may need to be supplemented in diets through other means [65, 70–72]. It does not bond with plasma proteins, hence, about 75% of plasma silicon is excreted within a few hours after ingestion [68, 73]. Agricultural solid wastes are potential sources of silica. Silica has been produced from agricultural solid wastes such as corn cob, rice husk, bagasse and rice straw using chemical, thermal, and microbial methods [74–79].

5. Conclusion

Food wastage is an important source of agricultural solid wastes. Hence, the prevention of food wastage at all levels before they are created will salvage some of these wastes and prevent unnecessary ill-health and environmental disadvantages as well as huge economic losses. This can be achieved through proper education and awareness of those involved with agricultural activities at all levels as well as being a little more generous by feeding hungry people with fresh food instead of keeping them till they are spoilt. There are hungry people everywhere in the world. Feeding animals saves food scraps and bioconversion of agricultural by-products, which may turn to agricultural solid wastes if their values are not enhanced and will go a long way in preventing such wastes as well. Composting and conversion of agricultural solid wastes to a renewable energy source is another effective way of managing agricultural solid wastes. It is high time attention is focused on turning these huge potential agricultural solid wastes to wealth, particularly in developing countries. To make our world safer for us to live, all hands must be on deck. Research activities should be geared toward commercial scaling of some productive findings made toward the efficient recycling of agricultural wastes.

Proper awareness should be made to everyone involved in agricultural activities whether at a middleman or woman, farmer, or consumer on the effects of indiscriminate disposal of agricultural solid wastes and benefits of efficient management of agricultural solid wastes. Political leaders, particularly in developing countries should be open-minded and formulate policies that ensure the efficient recycling of agricultural solid wastes and appropriate funds should be earmarked to achieving this. Attention should be focused on minimizing wastage by creating a more efficient sustainable agricultural supply chain through the development of sustainable durable markets and improving rural infrastructures such as electrification, roads, and storage [34].

It should also be noted that huge revenue could be generated from the conversion of agricultural solid wastes into useful products, as it has the potential of employing people if well-harnessed. Hence, its importance goes beyond the health implication but includes income generation for individual and governments which receive tax from companies and individual working in such establishments involved in the conversion of wastes to useful products. Also, it could contribute significantly to minimizing civil unrest plaguing some villages in developing countries. Some idle youths used to foment trouble could be scarce to find if they are gainfully employed, and that gainful employment could be companies or individuals who are efficiently engaging in turning agricultural solid wastes to wealth. Recycling of agricultural solid wastes into useful products could generate other sets of agricultural solid wastes, which may serve as raw materials for another useful products, thereby necessitating the continuous recycling of agricultural solid wastes until every potential waste is converted into wealth.

Conflict of interest

We have no conflicts of interest.

Author details

Isaac Oluseun Adejumo[1*] and Olufemi Adebukola Adebiyi[2]

1 Department of Animal Science, Federal University, Gashua, Nigeria

2 Department of Animal Science, University of Ibadan, Nigeria

*Address all correspondence to: smogisaac@gmail.com

IntechOpen

© 2020 The Author(s). Licensee IntechOpen. This chapter is distributed under the terms of the Creative Commons Attribution License (http://creativecommons.org/licenses/by/3.0), which permits unrestricted use, distribution, and reproduction in any medium, provided the original work is properly cited.

References

[1] Food and Agriculture Organization of the United Nations (FAO). Strategic work of FAO for sustainable food and agriculture. 2017. Available from: http://www.fao.org/3/a-i6488e.pdf [Accessed: 13 August 2020]

[2] Food and Agriculture Organization of the United Nations (FAO) & Organization for Economic Co-operation and Development (OECD). Background notes on sustainable, productive and resilient agro-food systems: Value chains, human capital, and the 2030 agenda. A Report to the G20 Agriculture Deputies. 2019. Available from: https://www.oecd-ilibrary.org/docserver/dca82200-en.pdf?expires=1563959111&id=id&accname=guest&checksum=5BD0A7A51327DB165936B4AE57A0E5CE [Accessed: 13 August 2020]

[3] Food and Agriculture Organization of the United Nations (FAO). The State of Food and Agriculture: Leveraging Food Systems for Inclusive Rural Transformation. 2017. Available from: http://www.fao.org/3/a-i7658e.pdf [Accessed: 13 August 2020]

[4] Food and Agriculture Organization of the United Nations (FAO). The State of Food and Agriculture. Climate Change, Agriculture and Food Security. 2016. Available from: from http://www.fao.org/3/a-i6030e.pdf [Accessed: 13 August 2020]

[5] European Commission Investing in Sustainable Development 2018. The EU at the Forefront in Implementing the Addis Ababa Action Agenda European Commission, Brussels, Belgium. Available from: 10.2841/874861 [Accessed: 13 August 2020]

[6] United Nations. Programme Performance Report 2018. UN Environment Programme. 2019a. Available from: https://wedocs.unep.org/bitstream/handle/20.500.11822/27734/PPR_2018_FINAL.pdf?sequence=1&isAllowed=y [Accessed: 13 August 2020]

[7] Food and Agriculture Organization of the United Nations (FAO). The future of food and agriculture: trends and challenges. 2017. Available from: http://www.fao.org/3/a-i6881e.pdf [Accessed: 13 August 2020]

[8] European Commission. EIP-AGRI Workshop Opportunities for Agriculture and Forestry in the Circular Economy. 2015. Workshop Report 28-29 October 2015. Brussels, Belgium. Available from: https://ec.europa.eu/eip/agriculture/sites/agri-eip/files/eip-agri_ws_circular_economy_final_report_2015_en.pdf [Accessed: 13 August 2020]

[9] Bracco S, Calicioglu O, Juan MGS, Flammini A. Assessing the contribution of bioeconomy to the total economy: A review of national frameworks. Sustainability. 2018;**10**:1698. DOI: 10.3390/su10061698

[10] McCormick K, Kautto N. The bioeconomy in Europe: an overview. Sustainability. 2013;5:2589-2608. DOI: 10.3390/su5062589

[11] Scarlat N, Dallemand JF, Monforti-Ferrario F, Nita V. The role of biomass and bioenergy in a future bioeconomy: Policies and facts. Environment and Development. 2015;**15**:3-34. DOI: 10.1016/j.envdev.2015.03.006

[12] Northerly. Top Causes of Agricultural Waste, and How Northerly Works to Combat Them. 2019. Available from: https://northerly.ag/causes-of-agricultural-waste/ [Accessed: 12 August 2020]

[13] Wang HY, Liu S, Zhai LM, Zhang JZ, Ren TZ, Fan BQ, et al.

Preparation and utilization of phosphate biofertilizers using agricultural waste. Journal of Integrative Agriculture. 2015;**14**:158-167

[14] Wang SR, Ru B, Dai GX, Sun WX, Qiu KZ, Zhou JS. Pyrolysis mechanism study of minimally damaged hemicellulose polymers isolated from agricultural waste straw samples. Bioresource Technology. 2015;**190**:211-218

[15] Varma VS, Yadav J, Das S, Kalamdhad AS. Potential of waste carbide sludge addition on earthworm growth and organic matter degradation during vermicomposting of agricultural wastes. Ecological Engineering. 2015;**83**:90-95

[16] Karak T, Sonar I, Nath JR, Paul RK, Das S, Boruah RK, et al. Struvite for composting of agricultural wastes with termite mound: Utilizing the unutilized. Bioresource Technology. 2015;**187**:49-59

[17] Wang B, Dong F, Chen M, Zhu J, Tan J, Xinmei F, et al. Advances in recycling and utilization of agricultural wastes in China: Based on environmental risk, crucial pathways, influencing factors, policy mechanism the tenth international conference on waste management and technology (ICWMT). Procedia Environmental Sciences. 2016;**31**:12-17

[18] Adejumo IO, Ologhobo AD, Babalola TO. Effect of pre-planting seed dressers on serum enzymes of laying chickens. American Chemical Science Journal. 2015;**9**(2):1-5. DOI: 10.9734/ACSJ/2015/19687

[19] Adejumo IO, Ologhobo AD, Adedeji IA, Ogunjimi SI. Status of exposure of bio-systems to restricted aluminium phosphide pesticide in Kano state, Nigeria. International Journal of Scientific Research in Knowledge. 2014;**2**(7):306-312

[20] Dien BV, Vong VD. Analysis of Pesticide Compound Residues in Some Water Sources in the Province of Gia Lai and DakLak. Vietnam: Vietnam Food Administrator; 2006

[21] Obi FO, Ugwuishiwu BO, Nwakaire JN. Agricultural waste concept, generation, utilization and management. Nigerian Journal of Technology. 2016;**35**(4):957-964

[22] Vanguard Newspaper. 2020. Available from: www.vanguardngr.com/2020/07/fg-signs-mou-to-curb-risks-in-transporting-agricultural-produce [Accessed: 03 August 2020]

[23] Klich MA. *Aspergillus flavus*: The major producer of aflatoxin. Molecular Plant Pathology. 2007;**1**(8):713-722. DOI: 10.1111/j.1364-3703.2007.00436.x

[24] Nierman WC, Yu J, Fedorova-Abrams ND, Losada L, Cleveland TE, Bhatnagar D, et al. Genome sequence of Aspergillus flavus NRRL 3357, a strain that causes aflatoxin contamination of food and feed. Genome Announcements. 2015;**3**(2):e00168-e00115. DOI: 10.1128/genomeA.00168-15

[25] Rescuing Leftover Cruisine. 2020. Available from: https://www.rescuingleftovercuisine.org/challenge [Accessed: 03 August 2020]

[26] Yangyang L, Jin Y, Li J, Chen Y, Gong Y, Li Y, et al. Current situation and development of kitchen waste treatment in China. In: The Tenth International Conference on Waste Management and Technology (ICWMT), Procedia Environmental Sciences. Vol. 31. 2016. pp. 40-49

[27] Jeremy W, Adrian W, Hughes John K, Mairi B, Richard M. Energy and the food system. Philosophical Transactions of the Royal Society B. 2010;**365**:2991-3006. DOI: 10.1098/rstb.2010.0172

[28] FAO. Livestock Long Shadow. 2006. Available from: http://www.fao.org/3/a-a0701e.pdf [Accessed: 13 August 2020]

[29] Liu Y, Dong JX, Liu GJ, Yang HN, Liu W, Wang L, et al. Co-digestion of tobacco waste with different agricultural biomass feedstocks and the inhibition of tobacco viruses by anaerobic digestion. Bioresource Technology. 2015;**189**:210-216

[30] Ibrahim RA. Tribological performance of polyester composites reinforced by agricultural wastes. Tribology International. 2015;**90**:463-466

[31] Akande OM, Olorunnisola AO. Potential of briquetting as a waste-management option for handling market-generated vegetable waste in Port Harcourt, Nigeria. Recycling. 2018;**3**(2):11. DOI: 10.3390/recycling3020011

[32] Akintola OA, Idowu OO, Lateef SA, Adebayo GA, Shokalu AO, Akinyoola OI. The Use of Waste Management Techniques to Enhance Household Income and Reduce Urban Water Pollution, Elements of Bioeconomy, Krzysztof Biernat. Rijeka: IntechOpen; 2019. DOI: 10.5772/intechopen.85580

[33] Worldometers. 2020. Available from: worldometers.info/geography/7-continents [Accessed: 03 August 2020]

[34] World Food Programme. 2020. Available from: https://www.wfp.org/zero-hunger [Accessed: 04 August 2020]

[35] FAO, IFAD and WHO. The State of Food Security and Nutrition in the World: Safeguarding Against Economic Slowdown and Downturns. Rome, Italy: World Food Programme; 2019. pp. 1-32

[36] Adejumo IO, Adetunji CO, Adeyemi OS. Influence of UV light exposure on mineral composition and biomass production of *mycomeat* produced from different agricultural substrates. The Journal of Agricultural Science. 2017;**62**(1):51-59. DOI: 10.2298/JAS1701051A

[37] Adetunji CO, Adejumo IO. Nutritional assessment of *mycomeat* produced from different agricultural substrates using wild and mutant strains from *Pleurotus sajor-caju* during solid state fermentation. Animal Feed Science and Technology. 2017;**224**:14-19 http://dx.doi.org/10.1016/j.anifeedsci.2016.12.004

[38] Oluwaseun AC, Oluseun AI. Efficacy of crude and immobilized immobilized enzymes from *Bacillus licheniformis* for production of biodegraded feather meal and their assessment on chickens. Environmental Technology and Innovation. 2018;**11**:116-124. DOI: 10.1016/j.eti.2018.05.002

[39] Oluseun AI, Adetunji CO, Nwonuma CO, Alejolowo OO, Maimako R. Evaluation of selected agricultural solid wastes on biochemical profile and liver histology of albino rats. Food & Feed Research. 2017;**44**(1):73-79. DOI: 10.5937/FFR1701073A

[40] Oluwaseun AC, Oluseun AI. Potency of agricultural wastes in mushroom (*Pleurotus sajor-caju*) biotechnology for feeding broiler chicks (*Arbor acre*). International Journal of Recycling of Organic Waste in Agriculture. 2018;**8**:37-45. DOI: 10.1007/ s40093-018-0226-6

[41] Adebiyi OA, Awotale HO, Adejumo IO, Osinowo OA, Muibi MA, Nwaodu OB. Performance, serum and haematological indices of pigs fed watermelon waste based-diet. Tropical Animal Production Investigation. 2019;**22**(1):10-16

[42] Fakhfakh-Zouari N, Hmidet N, Haddar AS, Kanoun S, Nasri M. A novel

serine metallokeratinase from a newly isolated *Bacillus pumilus* A1 grown on chicken feather meal: Biochemical and molecular characterization. Applied Biochemical Biotechnology. 2010;**162**:329-344

[43] Swetlana N, Jain PC. Feather degradation by strains of bacillus isolated from decomposing feathers. Brazilian Journal of Microbiology. 2010;**41**:196-200. DOI: 10.1590/S1517-83822010000100028

[44] Adejumo IO, Adetunji CO, Kunle O, Sonia ON. Chemical composition and amino acid profile of differently processed feather meal. The Journal of Agricultural Science. 2016;**61**(3):237-246. DOI: 10.2298/JAS1603237A

[45] Comis D. Chicken Feather Is the Eco-Friendly Plastics of the 21st Century. Washington, D.C., USA: Agricultural Research Service, USDA; 1998

[46] Schmidt WF. Innovative feather utilization strategies. In: Auburn AL, editor. Proceedings of the 1998 National Poultry Waste Management Symposium. Springdale, Arkansas: Auburn University Printing Services; 1998. pp. 276-282

[47] Oluseun AI, Oluwaseun AC. Production and evaluation of biodegraded feather meal using immobilized and crude enzyme from *Bacillus subtilis* on broiler chickens. Brazilian Journal of Biological Sciences. 2018;**5**(10):405-416. DOI: 10.21472/bjbs.051017

[48] Chen T, Jin Y, Qiu X, Chen X. A hybrid fuzzy evaluation method for safety assessment of food-waste feed based on entropy and the analytic hierarchy process methods. Expert Systems with Applications. 2014;**41**:7328-7337

[49] Adebukola AO, Michael S, Oluwanifemi AO, Oluseun AI. Effects of extruded rice bran based diets on the performance, intestinal microbiota and morphology of weaned pigs. Agricultura Tropica Et Subtropica. 2018;**51**(1):13-19. DOI: 10.2478/ats-2018-0002

[50] Adebiyi OA, Oboli UT, Adejumo IO, Osinowo OA, Chika CU. Palm oil industry waste as an animal feed and its influence on growth performance of grower pigs. Journal of Animal Science. 2019;**97**(Supple 3):386, 387. DOI: 10.1093/jas/skz258.769

[51] Pourhossein Z, Qotbi AAA, Seidavi A, Laudadio V, Mazzei D, Tufarelli V. Feeding of dried sweet orange (*Citrus sinensis*) peel on humoral immune response of broiler chickens. International Journal of Recycling of Organic Waste in Agriculture. 2019;**8**:361-367. DOI: 10.1007/s40093-019-0272-8

[52] Oluremi OIA, Ebe AI, Ngi J, Aku EO. Effect of naturally fermented sweet orange (*Citrus sinensis*) peel meal on its maize replacement value in broiler diet on performance and carcass indices. In: Proc. of 35th Ann. Conf. Nig. Soc. for Anim. Prod. 14-17 March. Nigeria: University of Ibadan; 2010. pp. 449-542

[53] Tsai WT, Lin CC, Yeh CW. An analysis of biodiesel fuel from waste edible oil in Taiwan. Renewable and Sustainable Energy Reviews. 2007;**11**:838-857

[54] Hiraoka M, Takeda N, Sakai S, Yasuda A. Highly efficient anaerobic digestion with thermal pretreatment. Water Science and Technology. 1984;**17**:529-539

[55] Climent M, Ferrer I, Baeza MD, Artola A, Vazquez F, Font X. Effects of thermal and mechanical pre-treatments of secondary sludge on biogas production under thermophilic conditions. Chemical Engineering Journal. 2007;**133**:335-342

[56] Elghali L, Clift R, Sinclair P, Panoutsou C, Bauen A. Developing a sustainability framework for the assessment of bioenergy systems. Energy Policy. 2007;**35**(12):6075-6083

[57] Wismeijer R, Kwant KW, Lammers EA, Novem S, Project Group. A framework for sustainable biomass. Schriftenreihezu Nachhaltigkeit und CSR. 2007;**1**

[58] Nguyen TL, Gheewala SH, Sagisaka M. Greenhouse gas savings potential of sugar cane bio-energy systems. Journal of Cleaner Production. 2010;**18**(5):412-418

[59] Daoutidis P, Marvin WA, Rangarajan S, Torres AI. Engineering biomass conversion processes: A systems perspective. AICHE Journal. 2013;**59**(1):3-18

[60] Engling G, He J, Betha R, Balasubramanian R. Assessing the regional impact of Indonesian biomass burning emissions based on organic molecular tracers and chemical mass balance modeling. Atmospheric Chemistry and Physics. 2014;**14**(15):8043-8054

[61] Exley C. Silicon in life: A bioinorganic solution to bioorganic essentiality. Journal of Inorganic Biochemistry. 1998;**69**:139-144

[62] Sjöberg S. Silica in aqueous environments. Journal of Non-Crystalline Solids. 1996;**196**:51-57

[63] Klein C. Rocks, minerals, and a dusty world. In: Guthrie GD Jr, Mossman BT, editors. Reviews in Mineralogy Vol. 28. Health Effects of Mineral Dust, Mineralogical Society of America. Washington DC: Bookcrafters Inc; 1993. p. 8

[64] Martin KR. The chemistry of silica and its potential health benefits. The Journal of Nutrition, Health & Aging. 2007;**11**:94-97

[65] Martin KR. Dietary silicon: Is biofortification essential? J Nutr and Food Sci Forecast. 2018;**1**:1006

[66] Nakanishi L, Bombonatti B, Muller LS, Villa RT, Velasco MV, Bedin V, et al. Oral supplementation of orthosilicic acid and its impact on hair quality. Medicina Cutánea Ibero-Latino-Americana. 2017;**45**:29-35

[67] Jugdaohsingh R, Anderson SH, Tucker KL, Elliott H, Kiel DP, Thompson RP, et al. Dietary silicon intake and absorption. The American Journal of Clinical Nutrition. 2002;**75**:887-893

[68] Popplewell JF, King SJ, Day JP, Ackrill P, Fifield LK, Cresswell RG, et al. Kinetics of uptake and elimination of silicic acid by a human subject: A novel application of 32Si and accelerator mass spectrometry. Journal of Inorganic Biochemistry. 1998;**69**:177-180

[69] Jugdaohsingh R. Silicon and bone health. The Journal of Nutrition, Health & Aging. 2007;**11**:99-110

[70] Chen F, Cole P, Wen L, Mi Z, Trapido EJ. Estimates of trace element intakes Chinese farmers. The Journal of Nutrition. 1994;**124**:196-201

[71] Anderson JJ. Plant-based diets and bone health: Nutritional implications. The American Journal of Clinical Nutrition. 1999;**70**:539S-542S

[72] D'Imperio M, Brunetti G, Gigante I, Serio F, Santamaria P, Cardinali A, et al. Integrated *in vitro* approaches to assess the bioaccessibility and bioavailability of silicon-biofortified leafy vegetables and preliminary effects on bone. In Vitro Cellular & Developmental Biology. Animal. 2017;**53**:217-224

[73] Sripanyakorn S, Jugdaohsingh R, Thompson RPH, Powell JJ. Dietary silicon and bone health. Nutrition Bulletin. 2005;**30**:222-230

[74] Kalapathy U, Proctor A, Shultz J. An improved method for production of silica from rice hull ash. Bioresource Technology;**85**(3):285-289

[75] Gu S, Zhou J, Luo Z, Wang Q, Ni M. A detailed study of the effects of pyrolysis temperature and feedstock particle size on the preparation of nanosilica from rice husk. Industrial Crops and Products. 2013;**50**:540-549

[76] Shim J, Velmurugan P, Oh BT. Extraction and physical characterization of amorphous silica made from corn cob ash at variable pH conditions via sol gel processing. Journal of Industrial and Engineering Chemistry. 2015;**30**:249-253

[77] Usman AM, Raji A, Waziri NH, Hassan MA. A study on silica and alumina potential of the savannah bagasse ash. IOSR Journal of Mechanical and Civil Engineering. 2014;**11**(3):48-52

[78] Vaibhav V, Vijayalakshmi U, Roopan SM. Agricultural waste as a source for the production of silica nanoparticles. Spectrochimica Acta Part A: Molecular and Biomolecular Spectroscopy. 2015;**139**:515-520

[79] Yuvakkumar R, Elango V, Rajendran V, Kannan N. High-purity nano silica powder from rice husk using a simple chemical method. Journal of Experimental Nanoscience. 2014;**9**(3):272-281